Refusing Treatment in Mental Health Institutions— Values in Conflict

Refusing Treatment in Mental Health Institutions— Values in Conflict

Proceedings of a Conference
Sponsored by the
American Society of Law & Medicine and
Medicine in the Public Interest, Inc.
November 1980

Published in Cooperation with the
American Society of Law & Medicine

Edited by
A. Edward Doudera, J.D.
Judith P. Swazey, Ph.D.

AUPHA Press
Ann Arbor, Michigan Washington, D.C.
1982

Copyright © 1982 by the Regents of the University of Michigan. Printed in the United States of America. All rights reserved. This book or parts thereof may not be reproduced in any form without written permission of the publisher.

Library of Congress Cataloging in Publication Data
Main entry under title:

Refusing treatment in mental health institutions.

  Bibliography: p.
  Includes index.
  1. Mental health laws—United States—Congresses.
2. Insanity—Jurisprudence—United States—Congresses.
3. Insane—Commitment and detention—United States—
Congresses. 4. Psychotherapy patients—United States—
Congresses. 5. Patient compliance—United States—
Congresses. I. Doudera, A. Edward, 1949–
II. Swazey, Judith P. III. American Society of Law
and Medicine. IV. Medicine in the Public Interest, inc.
KF3828.A75R43   344.73'044   82-1615
ISBN 0-914904-77-9   347.30444   AACR2

AUPHA Press is an imprint of Health Administration Press.

Health Administration Press
School of Public Health
The University of Michigan
Ann Arbor, Michigan 48109
  (313) 764-1380

Association of University Programs
  in Health Administration
One DuPont Circle
Washington, D.C.
  (202) 659-4354

Contents

Contributors viii
Introduction xiv

PART I: TREATMENT DECISIONS AND THE COURTS
  Chapter 1: Schizophrenia and Neuroleptic Drugs:
    A Biopsychosocial Perspective
      Barry Blackwell, M.D. 3

  Chapter 2: The Psychiatric Patient's Right to Refuse
    Medication: A Survey of the Legal Issues
      Richard J. Bonnie, LL.B. 19

  Chapter 3: Behind the Bench on *Rennie v. Klein*
      The Honorable Stanley S. Brotman 31

  Discussion   *Neil L. Chayet, J.D., Moderator* 42

PART II: LEGAL REACTIONS TO THE COURTS' DECISIONS

  Chapter 4: Patients' Rights: Too Much Courting,
    Not Enough Caring
      Eugene J. Comey, J.D. 49

  Chapter 5: Patients' Rights vs. Doctors' Rights:
    Which Should Take Precedence?
      Richard Cole, J.D. 56

  Discussion   *William J. Curran, J.D., LL.M., S.M.Hyg.,
    Moderator* 74

PART III: CLINICAL IMPLICATIONS OF THE COURTS' DECISIONS

  Chapter 6: Side Effects of a Right to Refuse Treatment
    Lawsuit: The Boston State Hospital Experience
      Michael J. Gill, M.D. 81

Chapter 7: Should There Be a Right to Refuse Treatment?
Scott H. Nelson, M.D., M.P.H. 88

Chapter 8: Clinical Approaches with Patients Who Refuse Medication
Thomas G. Gutheil, M.D. and Mark J. Mills, J.D., M.D. 95

Chapter 9: Legal Approaches to Treating the Treatment-Refusing Patient
Mark J. Mills, J.D., M.D. and Thomas G. Gutheil, M.D. 100

Discussion *Nathan T. Sidley, J.D., M.D., Moderator* 107

PART IV: COMMITMENT AND COMPETENCY: MEDICAL, LEGAL, AND JUDICIAL ISSUES

Chapter 10: Competence to Refuse Treatment
Robert Michels, M.D. 115

Chapter 11: The *Rennie* Philosophy and Treatment in the Private Sector
Irwin N. Perr, M.D., J.D. 120

Chapter 12: Assumptions Underlying Competency, Commitment, and Treatment Decisions
William J. Curran, J.D., LL.M., S.M.Hyg. 130

Chapter 13: Commitment and Other Matters: Some Comments from the Bench
The Honorable Alfred L. Podolski 135

Chapter 14: Implementing the Right to Refuse Psychotropic Medication: Can the Judiciary Respond?
Jonathan Brant, J.D. 143

Discussion *Leonard H. Glantz, J.D., Moderator* 148

PART V: TREATMENT DECISIONS: VALUES IN CONFLICT

Chapter 15: Refusing Treatment: The Patient's View
Judi Chamberlin 163

Chapter 16: The New Federal Role in Treatment Rights
Louis E. Kopolow, M.D. 169

Chapter 17: What We Do and Do Not Know About Treatment Refusals in Mental Institutions
Loren H. Roth, M.D., M.P.H. and Paul S. Appelbaum, M.D. 179

Discussion *Richard I. Shader, M.D., Moderator* 197

Selected Bibliography 206
Table of Cases 209
Index 211

Contributors

PAUL S. APPELBAUM is Assistant Professor of Psychiatry, Law and Psychiatry Program, Western Psychiatric Institute and Clinic, University of Pittsburgh School of Medicine. His research has focused on treatment refusal by psychiatric patients, competency to consent to treatment, legal and ethical issues in psychiatric research, and psychiatric decision making in legal contexts.

BARRY BLACKWELL is Professor and Chairman of the Department of Psychiatry at the Milwaukee Clinical Campus of the University of Wisconsin Medical School. He is also Director of the Behavioral Medicine Program at Mount Sinai Medical Center in Milwaukee. He received his M.B. and B.Chir. degrees from Guy's Hospital, London, and his M.D. from Cambridge University in 1966. Before joining the faculty of the University of Wisconsin Medical School, Dr. Blackwell's positions included Professor in the Departments of Psychiatry and Pharmacology at the Wright State University School of Medicine, Director of Psychiatric Research, Merrell–National Laboratories, and Professor of Psychiatry and Associate Professor of Pharmacology at the University of Cincinnati. He is a consultant to various organizations and agencies concerned with psychiatry and pharmacology, as well as the author of numerous publications on topics such as psychopharmacological drugs, psychosomatic medicine, and patient compliance.

RICHARD J. BONNIE is Professor of Law and Acting Director of the Institute of Law, Psychiatry and Public Policy at the University of Virginia. He received his LL.B. degree from the University of Virginia School of Law in 1969. Professor Bonnie's previous positions and public service activities have included serving as the Secretary of the National Advisory Council on Drug Abuse and as Associate Director of the National Commission on Marihuana and Drug Abuse. He is a member of the editorial advisory boards of the *Journal of Law and Human Behavior* and the *International Journal of Law and Psychiatry*, and the author of numerous books, monographs, and articles dealing with topics such as substance-abuse laws, criminal law, mental health law, and the interfaces between medicine, science, and law.

JONATHAN BRANT is Associate Professor of Law at the New England School of Law, where he teaches in the areas of law and medicine, law and psychiatry, constitutional law, and political and civil rights. After receiving his J.D. from Harvard University in 1971, Professor Brant's positions included staff attorney at the Boston University School of Law Center for Criminal Justice, Assistant General Counsel for the Massachusetts Executive Office of Human Services. As an Assistant Attorney General for the Commonwealth of Massachusetts, he served as a Senior Litigator for the Public Protection Bureau and was involved in cases such as *Custody of a Minor* (Chad Green) and *Superintendent of Belchertown State School v. Saikewicz*. Professor Brant is the author of articles in legal periodicals on topics such as criminal law, privacy, child abuse, and withholding treatment.

STANLEY S. BROTMAN is a judge of the United States District Court for the District of New Jersey, in which capacity he wrote the District Court's decision in *Rennie v. Klein*. He received his LL.B. degree from Harvard Law School in 1950, and was in private practice before becoming a federal judge in 1975. Among his many professional activities, Judge Brotman has served as a member of the Board of Bar Examiners of New Jersey, President of the New Jersey Bar Association, and as Chairman of the Editorial Board of the *New Jersey State Bar Journal*.

JUDI CHAMBERLIN is a member of the Mental Patients' Liberation Front in Boston, Massachusetts—a group that works to inform present and former mental patients about their rights, promotes and develops alternative "user-controlled" services, and informs the public about expatients' views on mental illness and its treatment, conditions in mental institutions, and patients' rights. She is chairperson of the National Committee on Patients' Rights and has served as a member of the Massachusetts Blue Ribbon Commission on the Future of Public Inpatient Mental Health Services. Ms. Chamberlin is also an active public speaker and a writer; her publications include *On Our Own: Patient-Controlled Alternatives to the Mental Health System*.

NEIL L. CHAYET is an attorney specializing in health law with the firm of Warner & Stackpole. He received his J.D. from Harvard Law School in 1963. Mr. Chayet is a lecturer in legal medicine at Harvard Medical School and a consultant in forensic psychiatry at Massachusetts General Hospital, a member of the Board of Directors, American Society of Law and

Medicine, Chairman of the Massachusetts Bar Association's Health Law Committee, and a legal correspondent for CBS Radio, with a daily presentation on "Looking at the Law." He is the author of *Legal Implications of Emergency Care* and articles and chapters on such medical-legal topics as abortion, drug abuse, mental illness, and informed consent.

RICHARD COLE is managing attorney at Greater Boston Legal Services. He received his J.D. from Boston University School of Law in 1974, and was an attorney with VISTA before joining Greater Boston Legal Services. One of his major areas of work is mental health law. He developed a Mental Health Law Clinic for inpatients at Boston State Hospital, served as chairman of the Hospital's Civil Rights Committee from 1974–1976, and was a counsel for the plaintiffs in *Rogers v. Okin*. Mr. Cole was also counsel for the patients at Boston State Hospital who intervened in *In the Matter of Guardianship of Richard Roe III*.

EUGENE J. COMEY is associated with the law firm of Rogovin, Stern, Huge & Lenzner in Washington D.C. He received his J.D. and M.B.A. degrees from the University of Chicago in 1975. Mr. Comey worked closely with Joel I. Klein, General Counsel to the American Psychiatric Association, on *Rennie v. Klein, Rogers v. Okin,* and *Jamison v. Farabee*.

WILLIAM J. CURRAN is Francis Glessner Lee Professor of Legal Medicine at Harvard Medical School and School of Public Health. He received his J.D. from Boston College Law School in 1950, and LL.M. from Harvard Law School in 1951, and an S.M.Hyg. from Harvard School of Public Health in 1958. In a previous academic appointment, Professor Curran was the first director of Boston University's Law-Medicine Research Institute. His current activities include serving as Administrative Director of Harvard's Interfaculty Program on Medical Ethics as a member of the Board of Directors of Medicine in the Public Interest. His numerous publications include *Modern Legal Medicine, Psychiatry, and Forensic Science*.

MICHAEL J. GILL is a senior psychiatrist at Boston State Hospital, Chief of the Hospital's Austin Unit, Clinical Director of Adult Services at Bay Cove Community Mental Health Center, and Clinical Professor of Psychiatry at Tufts Medical School. He received his M.D. from the Royal College of Surgeons in Dublin, Ireland, in 1957, and later trained at the Boston Psychoanalytic Institute. In addition to his clinical, teaching, and research work, Dr. Gill is in part-time private psychoanalytic practice.

Contributors

LEONARD H. GLANTZ is Assistant Professor of Health Law at Boston University Schools of Public Medicine and Public Health as well as Assistant Director of the School of Public Health. He received his A.B. and J.D. degrees from Boston University, and between 1973 and 1978 was a staff attorney at the Center for Law and Health Sciences at Boston University School of Law. In addition to writing numerous articles in the legal and medical literature, Professor Glantz is a coauthor of *Informed Consent to Human Experimentation* and *The Rights of Doctors, Nurses, and Allied Health Professionals*.

THOMAS G. GUTHEIL is Associate Professor of Psychiatry at Harvard Medical School, Visiting Lecturer at Harvard Law School, and Director of the Program in Psychiatry and the Law at the Massachusetts Mental Health Center. He received his M.D. from Harvard Medical School in 1967. Dr. Gutheil's publications include a number of articles on the Boston State Hospital case (*Rogers v. Okin*) and a forthcoming clinical handbook of psychiatry and law.

LOUIS E. KOPOLOW is Chief of the Patients' Rights and Advocacy Program, Mental Health Services Development, National Institute of Mental Health, and Clinical Assistant Professor in Psychiatry at Georgetown University School of Medicine. He received his M.D. from the University of Missouri School of Medicine in 1971 and has served as consultant to the American Psychiatric Association's Task Force to Develop Model Mental Health Legislation. His publications in the area of patients' rights and advocacy include *Consumers' Guide to Mental Health and Related Federal Programs*.

ROBERT MICHELS is Barklie McKee Henry Professor and Chairman of the Department of Psychiatry at Cornell University Medical College, and Psychiatrist-in-Chief of the New York Hospital's Payne Whitney Clinic and Westchester Division. He received his M.D. from Northwestern University Medical School in 1958, and his Certificate in Psychoanalytic Medicine from the Columbia University Psychoanalytic Center in 1967. Dr. Michels is a member of the American Psychiatric Association's Joint Commission on Public Affairs, Chairman of the Group for the Advancement of Psychiatry's Committee on Therapy, and a Fellow of the Institute for Society, Ethics, and the Life Sciences. His publications include a number of articles concerning ethical issues in psychiatry.

MARK J. MILLS is Commissioner of the Department of Mental Health, Commonwealth of Massachusetts and Assistant Professor (on leave),

Department of Psychiatry, Harvard Medical School. He received his J.D. from Harvard Law School in 1970 and his M.D. from Stanford Medical School in 1975. Dr. Mills is a member of the American Psychiatric Association's Commission on Judicial Action.

SCOTT H. NELSON is Deputy Secretary and Commissioner of Mental Health, Department of Public Welfare, Commonwealth of Pennsylvania. He received his M.D. from the Harvard Medical School in 1966 and his M.P.H. from the Harvard School of Public Health in 1970. Dr. Nelson was previously Director of the Behavioral Health Services Division for New Mexico's Health and Environment Department and Director of Planning and Evaluation for the Alcohol, Drug Abuse, and Mental Health Administration, Department of Health, Education, and Welfare. He has written numerous articles in both professional journals and government publications on a wide variety of mental health issues.

IRWIN N. PERR is Professor of Psychiatry and of Environment and Community Medicine and Director of Forensic Psychiatry at Rutgers Medical School, Piscataway, New Jersey, and an Adjunct Professor of Law at Rutgers Law School–Newark. He received his M.D. from Jefferson Medical College in 1950 and his J.D. from Cleveland State University School of Law. Dr. Perr is a member of many professional organizations, and was President of the American Academy of Psychiatry and the Law from 1977 to 1979. He is on the editorial board of several journals, including the *American Journal of Law & Medicine* and the *Journal of Forensic Sciences*, and has written extensively in the area of law and psychiatry.

ALFRED L. PODOLSKI is Chief Justice/Administrative Justice of the Probate and Family Court Department of the Trial Court of the Commonwealth of Massachusetts. He received his J.D. from Boston College Law School, and was an assistant attorney general and in private practice before being named a justice in 1971. Among his many legal and judicial activities, Chief Justice Podolski is a member of the Commonwealth's Standing Advisory Committee on the Rules of Civil Procedure, chairman of the Governor's Special Commission on Probate and Family Court Procedures, president-elect of the National College of Probate Judges, and chairman of the Courts and the Community Committee of the National Conference of Special Court Judges of the American Bar Association.

LOREN H. ROTH is Associate Professor of Psychiatry at the University of Pittsburgh School of Medicine, and Director of the Law and Psychiatry Program at the University's Western Psychiatric Institute and Clinic. He received his M.D. from Harvard Medical School in 1966, and his M.P.H. from the Harvard School of Public Health in 1972. As a member of the American Psychiatric Association's Commission on Judicial Action from 1974 to 1981, Dr. Roth was involved in developing *amicus* briefs for *Rennie v. Klein, Rogers v. Okin*, and other mental health cases. His publications include papers on such topics as informed consent, privacy and confidentiality, competency, and civil commitment.

RICHARD I. SHADER is Professor and Chairman of Psychiatry at Tufts University School of Medicine and Psychiatrist-in-Chief at the New England Medical Center Hospital. He received his M.D. from New York University School of Medicine in 1960. Dr. Shader is Editor-in-Chief of the *Journal of Clinical Psychopharmacology*, a member of the Board of Directors of the Medical Foundation, and a Director of the American Board of Psychiatry and Neurology, Inc. He has written extensively on psychopharmacology and other aspects of psychiatric therapeutics.

NATHAN T. SIDLEY is Director of the Court Clinic, Fourth District Court of Eastern Middlesex County, Massachusetts, Clinical Associate at Harvard Medical School, and Assistant Attending Psychiatrist at McLean Hospital in Belmont, Massachusetts. He received his M.D. from the University of Minnesota Medical School in 1953. Dr. Sidley served as President of the American Academy of Psychiatry and the Law in 1979–80 and is now an Associate Editor of the Academy's *Bulletin*. He has written many publications in the area on forensic psychiatry.

Introduction

In the rapidly expanding area of mental disability law, the right to refuse treatment has attracted considerable attention from psychiatrists and other mental health professionals, from lawyers, and from patients and ex-patients. The issue is not an easy one. As Loren Roth, one of this book's contributors, has noted, the right to refuse "raises a host of complex issues relating to the professional and personal values of mental health professionals and patients, the pragmatics of institutional care, the causation of human behavior (as understood both by law and by psychiatry), and other broad issues of social policy." Moreover, not everyone sees the issue in the same light, and considerable dialogue often is necessary even to get various concerned parties to talk to each other. For example, Loren Roth, a psychiatrist, has noted that "the fundamental question concerning the right to refuse is whether some mentally ill persons, because they exhibit mental impairment, should be treated differently than are other persons who may not be treated unless their consent is first obtained." But to William Curran, Professor of Legal Medicine at Harvard, the question is a manifestation of the clash between two opposing legal traditions. First, premised on notions of parens patriae and the police power, commitment laws are designed so that certain mentally ill persons will receive care and treatment. The second is the common law tradition that adults are presumed competent to make decisions concerning their medical care.

This text attempts to examine the issues involved in the right to refuse mental health treatment ideas through a series of chapters prepared by experts from the fields of law and psychiatry as well as by judges, former patients, and state mental health administrators. The papers and discussions are derived from a national conference, *Refusing Treatment in Mental Health Institutions: Values in Conflict*, sponsored by the American Society of Law & Medicine and Medicine in the Public Interest in November 1980.

The conference was generated by two federal court decisions that have had and will continue to have a substantial effect upon the entire mental health system: *Rennie v. Klein* and *Rogers v. Okin*. Both cases resulted in

Introduction

numerous hearings and orders by the federal district courts in New Jersey and Massachusetts, respectively, and attracted the intense interest of many psychiatrists, state mental health officials, and mental health attorneys. The United States Court of Appeals for the Third Circuit has now issued its opinion in *Rennie*, and upheld the legal basis of the district court's decision and substantially upheld the remedy ordered by Judge Brotman—a contributor to this book. *Rogers* has been decided by the United States Court of Appeals for the First Circuit, and is presently on appeal before the United States Supreme Court, where it was scheduled to be heard during Fall 1981. Similar cases are pending in California and elsewhere. Courts in Ohio, Colorado, and Oklahoma have now decided the question and have found in favor of the patient's right to refuse antipsychotic medication.

While it would be folly to predict the Supreme Court's decision, at least two points are clear. First, the legal validity of the right of the voluntary psychiatric patient to refuse potentially harmful treatment is not really at issue. Rather, the debate concerns the ability of the involuntarily committed patient to exercise the right. For example, in its *amicus curiae* brief in the *Rogers* case, the American Psychiatric Association alleges the issue to be whether or not a patient committed pursuant to a legal civil commitment statute is incompetent *per se* to decide treatment issues, and that, therefore, consent to treatment (at least part of the rationale for commitment) should not be necessary.

Second, regardless of the legal analysis utilized by the Supreme Court in deciding the issues posed by *Rogers v. Okin* (now renamed *Mills v. Rogers*), mental health professionals have a difficult task before them as they attempt, frequently with the limited resources of state mental health institutions, to acknowledge and implement the legal rights of a class of patients long forgotten by society.

It is our hope that this text will help to provide the basis for an effective and meaningful understanding of the complex issues involved in the right to refuse psychiatric treatment, as well as underscore the need for multi- and cross-disciplinary dialogue among all concerned parties.

This book is divided into five sections, each of which is followed by a discussion between the conference faculty and the audience. The first, Treatment Decisions and the Courts, provides a general discussion of psychiatric treatment focusing on the use and efficacy of psychotropic drugs and a survey of the legal issues involved with a patient's right to refuse medication. Judge Stanley Brotman offers a unique perspective on the issues that he faced as the presiding judge in *Rennie v. Klein*, as well as his hopes for the future.

In the second section, Legal Reactions to the Courts' Decisions, two experienced attorneys, who stood on opposite sides in *Rogers v. Okin*, explore the oft-conflicting legal theories that support differing perspectives. Their debate is still going on, for both are the authors of briefs submitted to the United States Supreme Court in *Mills v. Rogers*.

The third section, *Clinical Implications of the Courts' Decisions*, includes contributions by three psychiatrists and one psychiatrist-lawyer. One details his personal involvement with and reaction to the Boston State Hospital case—a chapter that truly brings home the internal conflicts and problems faced by mental health professionals. Another, a state commissioner of mental health, explores some of the policy questions mental health professionals and society must confront and resolve. The last two chapters in this section discuss patients who refuse treatment and what happens to the clinical course of their illness, as well as some of the legal issues that must be resolved as we seek to treat the involuntarily committed patient.

The fourth section, *Commitment and Competency: Medical, Legal and Judicial Issues*, includes five chapters that examine the interrelationship between commitment and competency—two concepts often discussed but still in need of the multidisciplinary analysis provided by the contributors to this section.

The last section, *Treatment Decisions: Values in Conflict*, attempts to expand our focus on the issues by offering the perspective of a former mental patient who is active in the ex-patient's movement. Her views, which provided some sobering points of reflection for many of the mental health professionals in the audience and in the faculty, need to be heard. For, as some commentators have suggested, the right to refuse treatment is at least partly the result of psychiatry's failure to be concerned for the individual patient's needs or wants. Other chapters in this section discuss the role of the Federal government in advocacy programs designed to aid mental health patients, and the information still needed for professionals to more accurately and humanely treat the illness and help the patient.

A. Edward Doudera, J.D.
Judith P. Swazey, Ph.D.
December, 1981

Part I

Treatment Decisions and the Courts

1

Schizophrenia and Neuroleptic Drugs: A Biopsychosocial Perspective

Barry Blackwell, M.D.

Drug Treatment in Psychiatry

The history of drug treatment in psychiatry is repetitious. For over 300 years it has been marked by two recurring but opposing themes. First, there has been a recognition that chemical processes underlie brain function, and a belief that chemical agents have a logical place in the correction of mental disorder. For example, the expectation is that advancing knowledge would yield specific antidotes to aberrant functions.

> Many forms of insanity are unquestionably the external manifestations of the effects upon the brain substance of poisons fermented within the body. These poisons we shall, I have no doubt, be able to isolate after we know the normal chemistry in its uttermost detail.[1]

Second, there has been skepticism about whether chemical agents are appropriate to deal with emotional disorders and concern that easy availability or excessive use would infringe upon the patient's rights to privacy or discourage the use of safer forms of therapy.

> ... Coercion for the outward man and rabid physicking for the inward man ... jalap, syrup of buckthorn, tartarised antimony and ipecacuanha administered every spring and fall in fabulous doses to every patient, whether well or ill; spinning in whirligigs, corporal punishment, gagging, 'continued intoxication', nothing was too wildly extravagent, nothing too monstrously cruel to be prescribed by mad doctors.[2]

While every innovator in the care of the mentally ill has struggled with this paradox—Pinel, Tuke, Thudichum, Connolly, Maudsley, Freud— the prevailing balance between these opposing themes has often been more reflective of the social, political, and legislative climate than of the state of medical knowledge.[3] The fact that this controversy continues today is due not only to the intrinsically emotional nature of the discourse, but also to the tardy application of scientific principles and the experimental method to psychiatric practice. Our deeply culturally ingrained habit of reductionistic and dualistic thinking perpetuates the mind-body dichotomy and leads to "either-or" views of causality and therapeutic options.[4]

The goal of this chapter is to review current scientifically sound information on the place of drugs in the treatment of schizophrenia, and, within a holistic or biopsychosocial framework and avoiding polarizations of the past, cast some light upon the dilemmas resulting from a patient's right to refuse medication.

THE CONCEPT OF SCHIZOPHRENIA

When the great German psychiatrist Kraepelin first attempted to classify severe mental disorders at the turn of this century, he separated the psychoses into two groups: profound disturbances in mood known as manic-depressive disorders, and a second group characterized by remorseless progression and early onset that he named "dementia praecox." Ten years later, the Swiss psychiatrist Eugene Bleuler (Bleuler, 1913) renamed the second group "schizophrenia" to emphasize an even more fundamental aspect—a splitting apart of the normal integrated functioning of intellect, emotion, and behavior (Figure 1).

Individuals stricken with schizophrenia are often classified according to the differing degrees to which intellect, behavior, or emotion are most obviously affected. This diversity led Bleuler to speak of "the group of schizophrenias," in which the fundamental and common features were "disturbances in association, and affectivity, the predilection for fantasy as against reality and the inclination to divorce oneself from reality (autism)." Schizophrenia is a condition in which the sum of the disorder is greater than its parts; it is this splitting apart of intellect, feeling, and behavior that necessitates asylum or invites incarceration. It is also the disruption of logical thinking that calls into question individuals' capacity to give informed consent to the therapeutic procedures to which they are exposed and their ability to intelligently refuse medication or other treatments. Figure 2 outlines the defects in schizophrenic thought and speech. The following passage illustrates these defects:

> I have just looked up 'simplicity' and the dictionary says 'sim = one, plicare = to fold, one fold'. I told Dr. H_____ that I dreamed he returned to me the story I sent him which he had folded six times when I had folded it once making it double. Jesus said that the sheep he called would make one fold. I thought at the time that the Latin for six is sex, and that the number of the Beast is 666. Is sex then beastly? I think I will leave you to puzzle out the

Figure 1: Schizophrenia

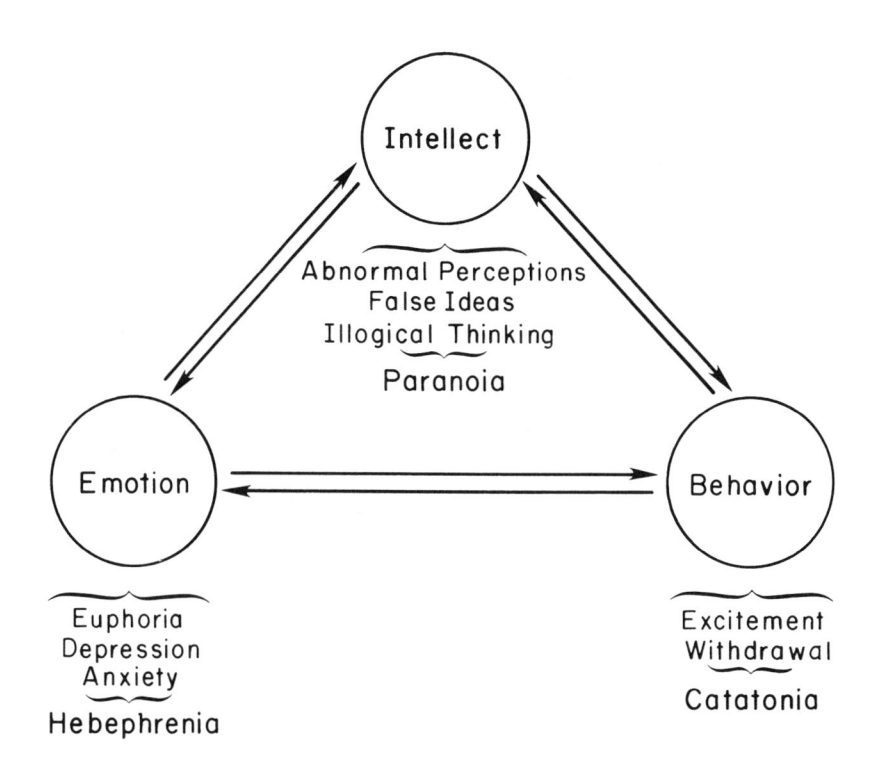

Intellect
Abnormal Perceptions
False Ideas
Illogical Thinking
Paranoia

Emotion
Euphoria
Depression
Anxiety
Hebephrenia

Behavior
Excitement
Withdrawal
Catatonia

Loss of intrapsychic equilibrium.
Splitting apart of intellect, feeling, behavior.

difference between 6 and 666 and 6 fold in substitution of one fold; for the number of the Beast is a mystery.[5]

THE CAUSES OF SCHIZOPHRENIA

From the earliest elucidation of the concept of schizophrenia, there were suggestions that genetic or biochemical disturbances might play some causal role and that physical methods might contribute to treatment. Some of the signposts suggesting a biologic basis to schizophrenia are:

1) Intractable deteriorating course
2) Universal incidence (1% of populations)
3) Genetic predisposition
4) Similarity to organic mental states (dementia, delirium)
5) Physical and physiological peculiarities
6) Discovery of biochemically determined mental illness (phenylketonuria)
7) Drug-induced psychiatric states (LSD, amphetamine)
8) Response to physical treatment (insulin, electroconvulsive therapy, drugs)
9) Resistance to psychological treatment

In reviewing the torrent of new biological information since 1959, Seymour Kety has spoken of the "numerous heroic but premature hypotheses based upon insubstantial foundation which attempted to bridge the gap and solve the clinical problem all at once."[6] The pace of discovery has quickened still further in the last decade as scientists have been able to isolate specific biochemical receptors and identify physiological peculiarities in the brain that lead to suggestions that schizophrenia may be linked to an abnormality in dopamine metabolism[7] and that there are disturbances in the left cerebral hemisphere that disrupt logical information processing.[8]

Whatever the precise nature of the genetically determined biochemical

Figure 2: Thought Disorder in Schizophrenia

Delusional content	Irrational ideas*
	Implausible ideas
Cognitive capability	Impaired abstract reasoning (proverbs)
	Thought disorganization*
	—Unpredictable utterances
	—Restricted vocabulary
	—Excessive repetitions
	—Blocking
	—Irrelevant associations
	—Competing associations (puns)

*Tends to be associated with arousal (poor attention span, sleeplessness) and to improve with drug treatment.

defect in the brain, it is triggered or unmasked by an individual's exposure and response to stress-provoking life predicaments.[9] Schizophrenia most often manifests itself in late adolescence and early adulthood, perhaps because individuals in this life "passage" are struggling with emancipation, intimacy, religious beliefs, sexuality, earning ability, and parenthood. There are considerable tensions both within the individual and between the person and significant others. Research into these role strains has focused on such issues as the double-bind communication defect[10] (where parents expect one type of behavior but demand another) and the degree of face-to-face contact between the person and relatives who are critical of his or her capabilities.[11] Not surprisingly, the most common but not the unique, symptoms of schizophrenia are anxiety and depression.[12]

While social, psychological, and biological factors are all involved in the etiology of schizophrenia, it would be a mistake to view these factors in a purely reductionistic cause-and-effect manner. They interact with one another in a nonlinear fashion as shown in Figure 3. An individual's normal capacities for dealing with stress may be eroded by the disorder, which in turn accentuates the stressful experience. For instance, bizarre behavior alienates social support. Disordered thinking disrupts psychological defenses. Delusional ideas impair the willingness or ability either to give informed consent to treatment or to cooperate with treatment.

Individual Variability and Vulnerability

Figure 4 suggests how individuals with schizophrenia may differ in the degree to which their vulnerability to psychosocial stressors and their biochemical or genetic vulnerability interact. This may also explain the variable response people show to drug therapy. A person with a high degree of exposure and susceptibility to environmental stress may develop schizophrenia despite a low genetic vulnerability.[13] Such an individual displays considerable emotion, falls ill suddenly after a clear-cut environmental upset, and responds rapidly to separation from the stressful environment with support in hospital and without any need for drugs. Less fortunate individuals who are highly vulnerable, both psychosocially and genetically, fail altogether to respond to medication and may require permanent asylum. The majority of individuals fall between these two extremes. For them, drugs appear to act as a buffer with their environment, but they are likely to relapse if they cease taking medication or if the level of stress increases either spontaneously or as a result of being

Figure 3: Interaction of Factors in Schizophrenia

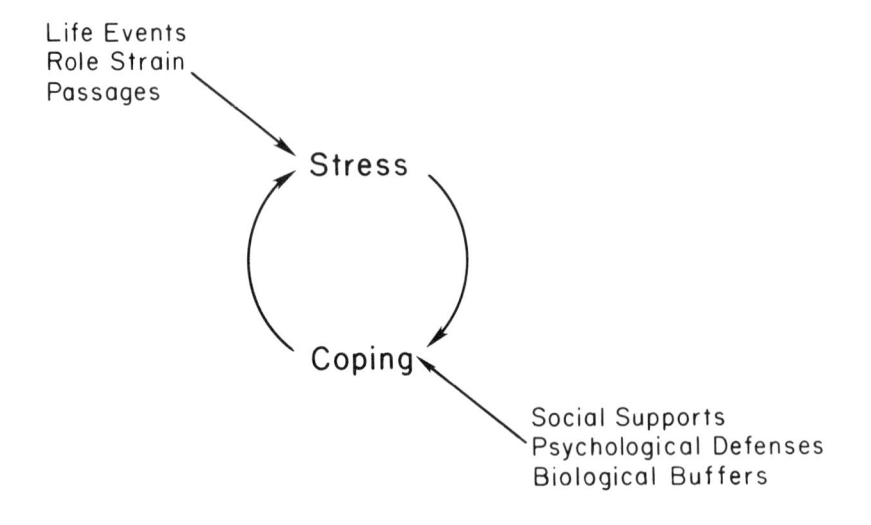

```
Life Events
Role Strain
Passages
         ↘
           Stress
         ⤺      ⤻
           Coping
                 ↖
                   Social Supports
                   Psychological Defenses
                   Biological Buffers
```

– The schizophrenic process erodes normal coping capacity.
– The sources of stress are aggravated by the condition itself.

moved from a protective hospital environment to a more hostile community one.

THE COURSE OF SCHIZOPHRENIA

The interaction of the social, psychological, and biological aspects of schizophrenia also explain the unpredictable course that the disorder takes over a person's lifetime. This is illustrated in Figure 5, which shows the progress of 228 patients followed over more than 35 years at the University Hospital of Lausanne.[14] The course of their psychoses did not appear to have been altered significantly by any of the different treatments to which these individuals had been exposed from the beginning of the century until 1962. The three factors that did appear to influence outcome were: well-adapted personality, acute breakdown in response to stress, and older age. These three factors seem to represent the psychological, social, and biological components already discussed.

Figure 4: Biopsychosocial Causality in Schizophrenia

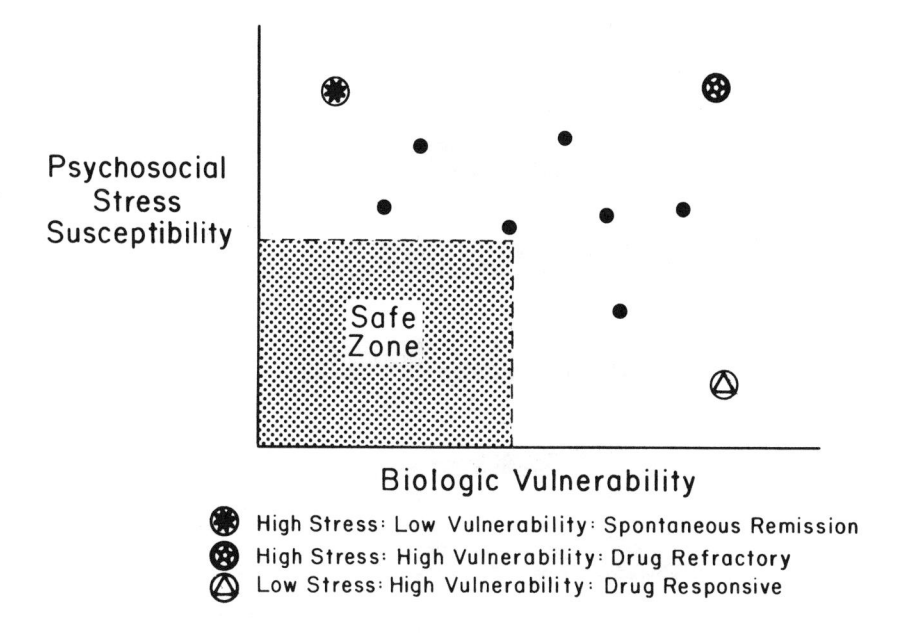

Psychosocial Stress Susceptibility

Safe Zone

Biologic Vulnerability

- ✹ High Stress: Low Vulnerability: Spontaneous Remission
- ✪ High Stress: High Vulnerability: Drug Refractory
- △ Low Stress: High Vulnerability: Drug Responsive

Drugs as Buffers

The concept of drugs as buffers between a schizophrenic and the environment is quite consistent with what is known about the way in which medications affect the schizophrenic process. Until the discovery of modern neuroleptic drugs, the only available chemical agents were sedatives like bromides and barbiturates. The sedatives were capable of exerting a temporary calming influence, but it was necessary to use amounts that put a person to sleep, and "sleep therapy" produced little sustained benefit and carried considerable risk.

In 1951, the French surgeon Laborit used chlorpromazine as a preoperative medication for his patients and reported that it provoked neither loss of consciousness, nor any change in the patient's mentality, but rather a slight tendency to sleep and "disinterest" for all that goes on around him.[15] Laborit recommended the drug to his psychiatric colleagues, Delay and Deniker, who gave it to psychotic patients and noted "obvious indifference or retardation of response to environmental stimulations, decrease of initiative and preoccupations without alteration of waking consciousness or of intellectual faculties."[16]

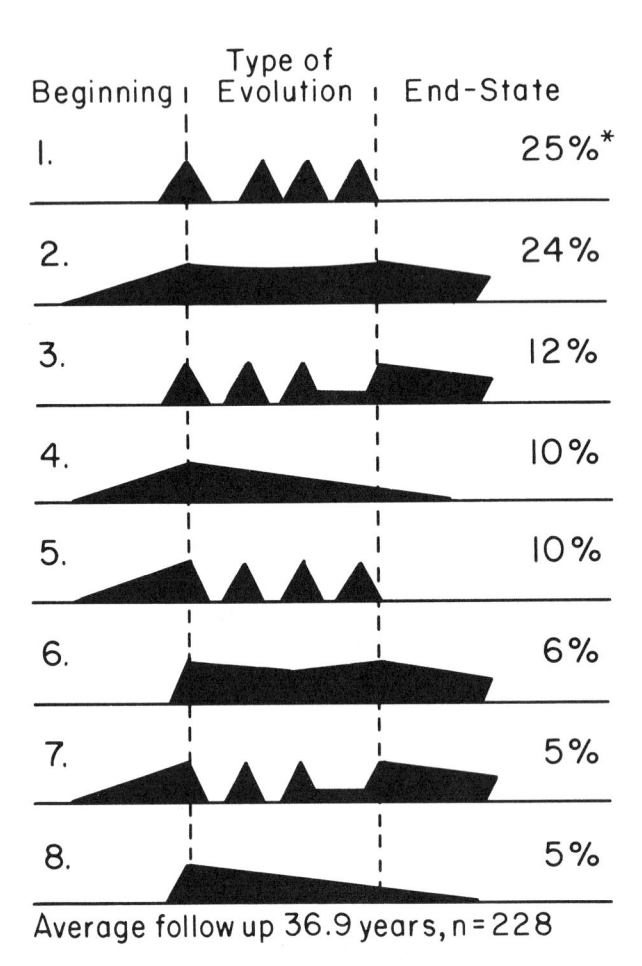

Figure 5: Long-Term Evolution of Schizophrenia

Beginning	Type of Evolution	End-State
1.	▲▲▲▲	25%*
2.	▬▬▬▬	24%
3.	▲▲▲▬	12%
4.	▬▬▬	10%
5.	▬▲▲▲	10%
6.	▬▬▬	6%
7.	▬▲▲▬	5%
8.	▬	5%

Average follow up 36.9 years, n=228

"There is no such thing as a specific course of schizophrenia."
(Ciompia, 1980)

Heinz Lehman first reported use of chlorpromazine in the United States in the May 1954 issue of the *American Journal of Psychiatry*. Lehman noted:

> other sedatives in small doses tend to produce disinhibition of affect with consequent loss of emotional control. Larger doses of ordinary sedatives

invariably bring about considerable clouding of intellectual processes. Chlorpromazine possesses the rather unique property of producing sedation without affective disinhibition and significant intellectual clouding.[17]

THE EFFICACY OF NEUROLEPTIC DRUGS

Over the next decade these early clinical observations were subjected to rigorous scientific scrutiny, despite the many obstacles to systematic evaluation of drug effects in schizophrenia. These problems included variable clinical picture, unpredictable natural history, "spontaneous" relapses and remissions, mixed patient populations, poor compliance with therapy, and difficulties in evaluation and follow-up. It was soon firmly established that chlorpromazine was more effective than either the barbiturates or an inert placebo in reducing the florid manifestations of schizophrenia.[18] A host of chemically related compounds were synthesized and became known as the major tranquilizers or neuroleptic drugs. Their impact on the care of mental patients was quickly likened to that of the antibiotics or insulin in medical practice. This enthusiasm contributed to the corollary effects that neuroleptic drugs had among both staff and patients—less violence, fewer restraints, less seclusion, and less crowding in mental institutions. The drugs became tools for the therapeutic milieu and community care.

UNREALISTIC EXPECTATIONS

The seductive nature of the advent of major tranquilizers is clearer in retrospect than it was at the time. Neuroleptic drugs were simplistically imbued with curative powers, side effects were sometimes minimized, and the hazards of chemical restraint were regarded somewhat complacently. This is in part because the effects of neuroleptic drugs on behavior are much more easily manifested and measured than their actions on cognitive processes. Yet one of the earliest articles in the American literature notes that "in chlorpromazine we had for the first time a drug that would tranquilize without stupefying."[19] Later in the same article, Bowes describes the administration of these drugs to a hard core of disturbed and aggressive patients and notes that "with the help of large doses of chlorpromazine and reserpine, we were soon able to reduce them to a state of benevolent stupor." Only recently has there been any serious attempt to examine the effect of the drugs on disorganized thought processes or to understand what implications this may have for the question of informed consent.[20] (Kay and Singh, 1979; Hymowitz and Spohn, 1980) In terms of speech and thought, the drugs have been found to increase verbal productivity, complexity of speech, and coherence, and to decrease pathological content.

> Antipsychotic drug treatment, rather than merely sedating patients, would seem to potentiate the kinds of ego capabilities and reality attunement that would allow them to participate in and benefit from verbally oriented psychotherapy.[21] (Hymowitz and Spohn, 1980)

Another consequence of the unrealistic expectations placed on the neuroleptic agents was the premature discharge of patients into communities ill-prepared to assimilate them. Figure 6 illustrates the way in which a declining hospital population was mirrored by an increasing rate of hospital readmissions. The fact that patients recovered rapidly when drugs were reinstituted paradoxically reaffirmed the faith in the drugs' curative properties and led to a belief that poor patient compliance following discharge was solely responsible for relapse. Only recently has it become clear that even when total compliance is assured by close supervision and the intramuscular injection of neuroleptic drugs, significant numbers of patients still relapse under social stress.[22] In this respect, psychiatric patients appear to be no different from those afflicted with other chronic medical conditions who live in deprived psychosocial environments.[23]

Figure 6: The "Revolving Door": Premature Deinstitutionalization

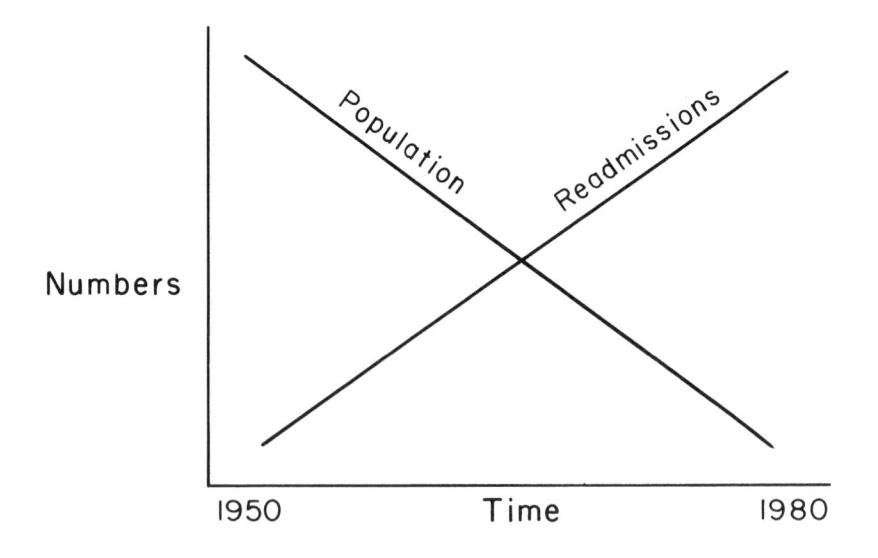

A Realistic View of Drug Therapy

A more realistic view of the capabilities and limitations of drug therapy is provided by the research illustrated in Figure 7. This displays the rate at which schizophrenic patients relapse within nine months of discharge from hospital after recovering with drug treatment.[24] If patients are discharged to live alone or with supportive uncritical relatives, they survive well and drugs contribute little. If patients live with critical relatives, their capacity to survive in the community is significantly improved by drugs, especially among patients who are in more frequent face-to-face contact with their relatives (over thirty-five hours per week).

Whatever the limitations of drug therapy, it must be viewed in the context that medication remains the most effective and parsimonious treatment available for a condition in which the basic disruption of thought processes, emotion, and behavior makes other forms of therapy equally or more ineffective. Figure 8 illustrates an evaluation of the degree to which drug therapy can be compared to social and supportive psychotherapy in forestalling readmission to hospital. The superiority of drug therapy is clearcut from the outset, and for the first six months after hospital discharge, social therapy adds nothing to either placebo or drug therapy. Only patients who survive beyond this point benefit from nondrug treatment, perhaps because their thought processes and general condition have stabilized.

Wanted and Unwanted Effects

The benefits of drug therapy must also be balanced by its unwanted effects. These are inevitable. The brain is a highly sensitive but well-protected organ. To reach the receptors that mediate emotion, behavior, and thinking processes a drug must be given in sufficient amounts to penetrate the gut and to exceed the highly individual ability of each person's liver and kidney to metabolize or excrete the compound. Accurate titration is difficult and the amounts administered act also on other receptors inside and outside the brain to produce a wide variety of unwanted effects. Figure 9 lists the diverse effects, some of which are frequent and troublesome, others of which are rare and occasionally fatal. Many of these unwanted effects were apparent from the earliest introduction of neuroleptic drugs while a few (such as tardive dyskinesia) only became apparent after prolonged administration or close observation of larger numbers of patients. The precise frequency, severity, and significance of unwanted effects is still unclear.[25] Attempts have been made to improve the therapeutic ratio between wanted and unwanted effects

Figure 7: Nine-Month Relapse Rates in 128 Schizophrenic Patients

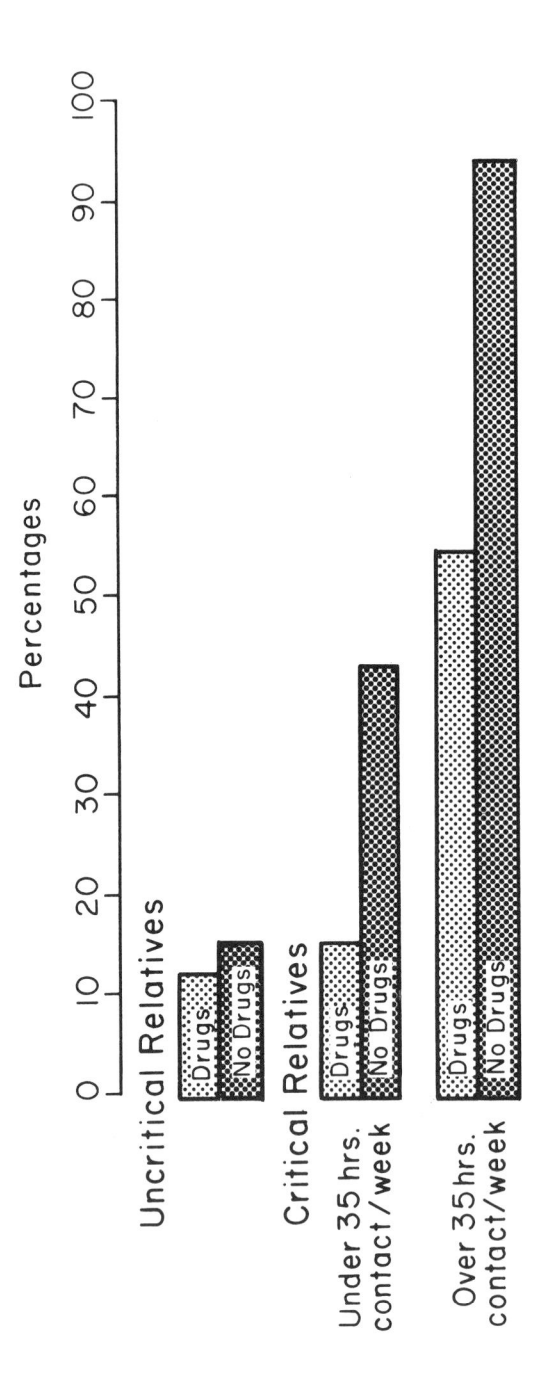

Source: Vaughn, C. E. and Leff, J. P., "The Influence of Family and Social Factors on the Course of Psychiatric Illness," *British Journal of Psychiatry* 129:125–137 (1976).

Figure 8: Relapse Rates of Patients Undergoing Drug Therapy and Social Therapy

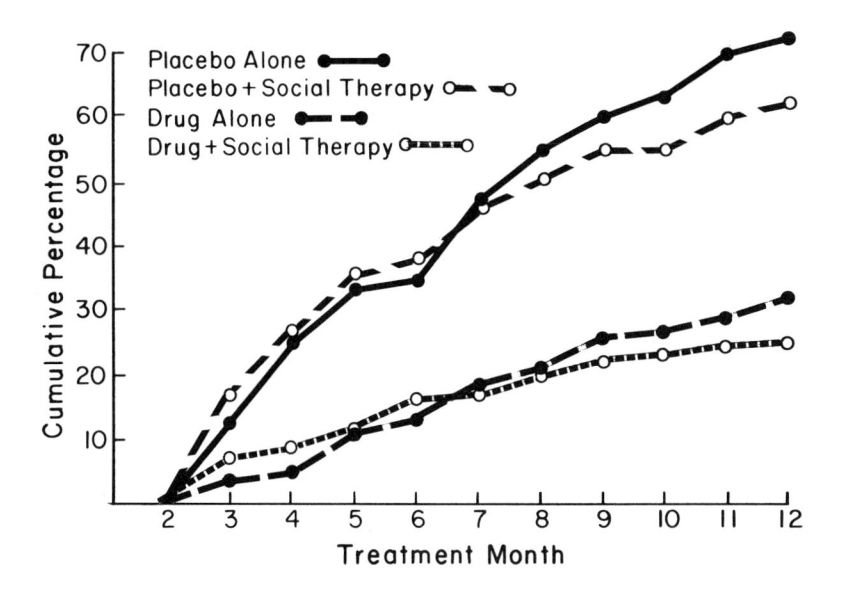

Source: Hogarty, G. E. and Goldberg, S. C., "Drug and Sociotherapy in the Aftercare of Schizophrenic Patients," *Archives of General Psychiatry* 28:54-64 (1980). Reprinted courtesy of *Archives of General Psychiatry*, copyright 1980, American Medical Association.

through the introduction of over 30 different neuroleptic drugs of differing chemical structures, but with limited success. The drugs still in widest use are those that have been available the longest.

A Balanced Perspective

A perspective on the use of neuroleptic drugs in the management of persons afflicted with schizophrenia is offered in Figure 10. This figure summarizes the opinions of Manfred and Eugene Bleuler, whose experiences at the Burgholzli Hospital in Zurich extend from the naming of the syndrome of schizophrenia to the present time. Manfred Bleuler

Figure 9: Unwanted Effects of Neuroleptic Drugs

Central Nervous System	*Blood*
Drowsiness	Agranulocytosis
Seizures	*Skin*
Movement disorders—restlessness, muscle spasms, Parkinsonism, tardive dyskinesia	Pigmentation
	Sun sensitivity
	Dermatitis
Cardiovascular System	*Gastrointestinal System*
Low blood pressure	Dry mouth
Cardiac irregularities	Constipation
Endocrine and Metabolic Systems	*Genitourinary System*
Weight gain	Delayed ejaculation
Breast enlargement and secretion	Urinary retention
Menstrual and sexual dysfunction	*Special Senses*
	Blurred vision
Liver	Retinal damage
Jaundice	

Figure 10: Effective Factors in Treatment of Schizophrenia (Bleuler)

Mobilization of healthy aspects in the patient
Mobilization of hidden resources by sudden change
Calming actions and influences
 —Talking
 —Togetherness
 —Asylum
 —Neuroleptic drugs

"A specific treatment for schizophrenia does not exist."

identifies three effective factors in the treatment of schizophrenia.[26] The third of these consists of calming influences such as talking and togetherness. It also includes neuroleptic drugs, although Bleuler is opposed to their regular, heavy, or prolonged use. He believes that each of the three major influences are at work in most treatment methods, but that "a specific treatment for schizophrenia does not exist." This is consistent with the view of schizophrenia as a very variable manifestation of each individual person's unique biological, social, and psychological vulnerability.

CONCLUSION

As biological agents, drugs can play a significant part in ameliorating the social and psychological causes and consequences of schizophrenia. Despite the tendency to overestimate "curative" effects and underestimate unwanted effects, drug therapies remain the most parsimonious intervention in a condition that is resistant to every other known therapy. Opposing viewpoints about the efficacy and appropriateness of drug therapy contribute to contemporary concerns about informed consent. These concerns are accentuated by our incomplete understanding of the degree to which the schizophrenic process erodes the capacity to give informed consent.

The resolution of this paradox will be enhanced by the adoption of a biopsychosocial model which avoids past polarizations, by a better definition of the psychological attributes necessary for informed consent, and by a clearer understanding of the effect of the disease process and drug therapy on those attributes.

NOTES

1. THUDICHUM, J. L. W., A TREATISE ON THE CHEMICAL CONSTITUTION OF THE BRAIN (1884).
2. CHARLES DICKENS, A CURIOUS DANCE AROUND A CURIOUS TREE (1852).
3. R. HUNTER and I. MACALPINE, THREE HUNDRED YEARS OF PSYCHIATRY (Oxford University Press, London) (1963).
4. Engel, G. L., *The Need for a New Medical Model: A Challenge for Biomedicine*, SCIENCE 196:129-36 (1977).
5. MAYER-GROSS, W. CLINICAL PSYCHIATRY, E. Slater and M. Roth, eds., 3rd Edition. (Williams & Wilkins, Baltimore) (1969) at 267.
6. Kety, S., *The Syndrome of Schizophrenia: Unresolved Questions and Opportunities for Research*. BRITISH JOURNAL OF PSYCHIATRY 136:421-37 (1980).
7. Creese, I. and Snyder, S. H., *Behavioral and Biochemical Properties of the Dopamine Receptor*. In Lipton, M. A., DiMascio, A. and Killain, K. F., eds., PSYCHOPHARMACOLOGY: A GENERATION OF PROGRESS (Raven Press, New York) (1978) 377-88.
8. Schweitzer, L., *Differences of Cerebral Lateralisation among Schizophrenic and Depressed Patients*, BIOLOGICAL PSYCHIATRY 14:721-33 (1979).
9. Birley, J. L. T. and Brown, G. W., *Crises and Life Changes Preceding the Onset of Relapse of Acute Schizophrenia*. BRITISH JOURNAL OF PSYCHIATRY 116:237-333 (1970).
10. Wynne, L. C., Singer, M. T. and Toohey, M. L., SCHIZOPHRENIA 75; PSYCHOTHERAPY, FAMILY STUDIES, RESEARCH, J. Jorstad and E. Ugelstad, eds. (University of Oslo Press, Oslo) (1976).

11. Vaughn, C. E. and Leff, J. P., *The Influence of Family and Social Factors on the Course of Psychiatric Illness*, BRITISH JOURNAL OF PSYCHIATRY 129:125-37 (1977).
12. Costello, C. G., *Classification and Psychopathology*, SYMPTOMS OF PSYCHOPATHOLOGY, E. G. Costello, ed.,(John Wiley & Sons, New York) (1970) at 1-26.
13. Leonhard, K., *Contradictory Issues in the Origin of Schizophrenia*, BRITISH JOURNAL OF PSYCHIATRY 136:437-444 (1980).
14. Ciompi, L., *The Natural History of Schizophrenia in the Long Term*, BRITISH JOURNAL OF PSYCHIATRY 136:413-420 (1980).
15. Laborit, H., *L'hibernation Artificielle*, ACTA-CHIR BELG 50: 710-15 (1951).
16. J. DELAY and P. DENIKER. METHODES CHIMIOTHERAPEUTIQUES EN PSYCHIATRIE: LES NOUVEAUX MEDICAMENTS PSYCHOTROPES (Masson, Paris) (1961).
17. Lehman, K., *Selective Inhibition of Affective Drive by Pharmacological Means*, AMERICAN JOURNAL OF PSYCHIATRY 110:856-57 (1954).
18. *See* Casey, J. F., Bennett, I. F., Lindley, C. J., et al. *Drug Therapy in Schizophrenia*, ARCHIVES OF GENERAL PSYCHIATRY 2:210-22 (1960).
19. Bowes, H. A., *The Ataractic Drugs: The Present Position of Chlorpromazine, Frenquel, Pacatal and Reserpine in the Psychiatric Hospital*, AMERICAN JOURNAL OF PSYCHIATRY 113:530-39 (1956).
20. *See* Kay, S. R. and Singh, M. M., *Cognitive Abnormality in Schizophrenia: A Dual-Process Model*, BIOLOGICAL PSYCHIATRY 14:155-76 (1979).
21. Hymowitz, P. and Spohn, H., *The Effects of Antipsychotic Medication on the Linguistic Ability of Schizophrenics*, J. NERV. MENT. DIS. 168:287-96 (1980).
22. Schooler, N. R., Levine, J., Severe, J. B., Brauzer, B., DiMascio, A., Klerman, G. L. and Tuason, V. B., *Prevention of Relapse in Schizophrenia*, ARCHIVES OF GENERAL PSYCHIATRY 37:16-24 (1980).
23. Blackwell, B., *Noncompliance with Psychiatric Drug Treatment*, TREATMENT OF DSM III DISORDERS, J. Griest, J. Jefferson and R. Spitzer, eds. (in press).
24. Vaughn, C. E. and Leff, J. P., *The Influence of Family and Social Factors on the Course of Psychiatric Illness*, BRITISH JOURNAL OF PSYCHIATRY 129:125-37 (1976).
25. Gardos, G. and Cole, J., *Public Health Issues in Tardive Dyskinesia*, AMERICAN JOURNAL OF PSYCHIATRY 137:777-81 (1977).
26. BLEULER, M., DEMENTIA PRAECOX OR THE GROUP OF SCHIZOPHRENIAS, translated by H. Zinkin (International Universities Press, New York) (1950).

2

The Psychiatric Patient's Right to Refuse Medication: A Survey of the Legal Issues

Richard J. Bonnie, LL.B.

Ethical considerations, as well as sound clinical practice, require the maximum possible participation by patients in the process of designing and implementing their treatment plans. The legal statements of this principle—in the doctrine of informed consent or in the codes of patients' rights—are indistinguishable from those expressed in position statements of the American Psychiatric Association or in the standards of the Joint Commission on Accreditation of Hospitals. All agree that patients have a right to participate in the decision-making process in the most meaningful manner consistent with their clinical conditions.

Of course, the patient's participation and even his *assent* does not assure the choice of sound or even adequate treatment. Only well-trained and well-informed clinicians who carefully assess the risks and benefits of available treatments can do that. But it is important to remember that the law places boundaries on therapeutic choice: sometimes it proscribes certain choices altogether, or conditions them on compliance with external review procedures. Experimental drug therapies provide the most obvious case in point, but the trend has been to subject even some customary practices, such as electroconvulsive therapy, to more rigorous external review procedures.

With respect to customary drug treatments, standard malpractice doctrine defines the traditional legal approach. Under this theory, the prescription and administration of medication must conform to accepted professional standards, and the choices made must take into account available information concerning the benefits and risks of alternative treatments. Recent developments in the law resulting from the so-called "right to treatment" litigation should be viewed as a process of specification rather than a departure from the traditional legal approach. For example, right to treatment regulations usually include statements forbidding the use of "unnecessary medication" or forbidding the use of medication solely for disciplinary or management purposes as opposed to therapeutic purposes. Even apart from a competent patient's right to refuse medication, every patient, whether competent or incompetent, whether assenting or recalcitrant, has a right to be free from unsound or abusive medication practices. Further, this right to adequate medical treatment implies a right to expect informed professional deliberation regarding the relative risks and benefits of alternative treatments.

These points merit attention at the outset because many of the so-called "right to refuse" cases are really "right to adequate treatment" cases. The goal for all of us, in law and in the mental health professions, is to improve the quality of care in our public psychiatric hospitals. We should not lose sight of this common ground in all the sparring over the "right to refuse."

THE COMPETENT PATIENT'S RIGHT TO REFUSE

In order to nurture and preserve the therapeutic alliance, the clinician will generally attempt to persuade a recalcitrant patient to take recommended medication rather than force such treatment upon him. Only if the patient's competency to make a rational decision is questioned and the therapeutic need is great will the clinician administer the medication against the patient's wishes.

From an ethical standpoint, the contours of the patient-therapist relationship may be defined in terms of duties, rather than rights. But these ethical duties, and sound clinical practice, rest upon a commitment to the dignity and autonomy of the patient throughout the treatment process. Indeed, the ultimate goal of psychiatric intervention is to restore to the patient the dignity and autonomy which are compromised by mental illness.

Even the most strident critics of the district court decisions in *Rennie v. Klein*[1] and *Rogers v. Okin*[2] do not oppose the principle of patient self-determination in the process of treatment decision making. Instead they oppose the idea that this principle should be characterized as a *legally enforceable right*. They would prefer that the process of therapeutic choice, and the problem of the recalcitrant patient, be left to the treatment team, to be resolved through the application of sound clinical judgment.

In my opinion, this position, when phrased this broadly, is legally unsupportable. First, the basic doctrines of medical malpractice impose outer boundaries on the therapeutic process. Thus, a possible private cause of action would lie for forcible administration of medication in situations involving a departure from standard medical practice. Second, and perhaps more to the point, the doctrine of informed consent gives legal substance to the principle of self-determination. As Judge Cardozo put it some seventy years ago: "Every human being of adult years and sound mind has a right to determine what shall be done with his own body."[3] Although informed consent litigation generally concerns a failure to disclose necessary information to the patient, the underlying principle is that a competent adult patient has the right to decide whether or not to undertake the prescribed course of treatment at all.

The current furor over the right to refuse psychiatric medication does not derive from the common law doctrines. Because these doctrines are linked to malpractice concepts, and because malpractice suits have traditionally been rare in the public sector, state courts have had few occasions to develop any law on the hospitalized psychiatric patient's right to refuse. In a sense, the case-by-case process of common law tort litigation has not defined the meaning of informed consent for persons of "unsound mind," and no one brings class action suits to enforce professional tort doctrines.

The psychiatric patient's right to refuse medication has been assimilated within a jurisprudence of constitutional rights that has developed only within the last decade. However, before discussing the constitutional basis for the right to refuse, I want to emphasize several points.

First, the current right to refuse litigation should not be viewed as an effort to fashion a legal right from whole cloth. It must be seen against the backdrop of the common law, which firmly establishes the principle of self-determination for competent patients. What *is* new is the application of that principle to patients involuntarily committed to state mental health institutions, and this development is directly attributable to the enlightened efforts of the mental health professions themselves to untie the legal concepts of commitment and incompetency.

Second, the constitutionalization of the right to refuse carries with it one of the distinguishing features of constitutional litigation: the wide powers of the federal courts (or of state courts applying state constitutions) to frame system-wide remedies to implement and protect rights of constitutional magnitude. There is much room for debate regarding the necessary and proper procedures which should be considered constitutionally required to protect the competent patient's right to refuse.

Third, the mental health professions in general, and institutional psychiatry in particular, will not successfully combat or deflect the excesses of public regulation, whether from courts or state legislatures, by resisting all regulation. It simply will not do to say, "Legislators and judges don't understand the problem. Leave us alone to do our job and treat the sick." In this sense, the right to refuse issue is no different from other regulatory intrusions into psychiatric decision making, whether they concern the process of admission and discharge, the quality of care, or specific types of treatments, such as electroconvulsive therapy.

In my opinion, we must accept in principle the *legal* right of the competent patient to refuse medication. I also think that judges who have been faced with this issue do no violence to the constitution by regarding this as a right of constitutional magnitude. I might note that I think the proposition that the right to refuse psychotropic medication derives from a First Amendment freedom of mentation is wholly without doctrinal foundation.[4] Instead, I believe this right rests securely in the jurisprudence of the constitutional right of privacy, specifically the individual's freedom from unwarranted governmental intrusions into his person.

Let me now turn to three substantive questions concerning the nature of the constitutional right to refuse medication. First, is there any necessary relationship between competency and the legal status of commitment? Second, can a competent patient's right to refuse ever be overridden? Third, what does competency mean and how should this be decided?

COMMITMENT STATUS AND COMPETENCY

Under current commitment statutes, it does not make either clinical or legal sense to argue that involuntarily committed patients are *per se* incompetent to make treatment decisions and, therefore, have no right to refuse medication, while voluntary patients are to be presumed competent and entitled to refuse. This could only be true only if *all* involuntary patients were incompetent to make *any* treatment decisions at the time of admission and would remain so during the entire period of their compulsory hospitalization. This was, of course, the legal assumption in an earlier day.[5]

The contemporary legal assumption is quite the reverse. A presumption of incompetency no longer flows from the fact of institutionalization or, in the mental health context, from commitment. The discernible trend in the law is toward the formulation of specific criteria for competency to make specific types of decisions; for example, in many states, guardianship proceedings need not result in a total determination of incompetency, and courts are recognizing that competency is a continuum. Competency determinations are increasingly contextual.

It still might be argued that a judicial determination that a person should be committed implies that he is incompetent to make a rational decision regarding his need for treatment. However, there are two serious problems with this argument. First, contemporary commitment statutes focus entirely on behavior rather than competence; that is, the focus is on danger rather than need.[6] Second, and even more important, even if incompetency to determine one's need for hospitalization were implicit in a commitment order, it does not follow that incompetency to make decisions regarding specific treatments is also implicit. To have legal significance a determination would have to be explicit.

One partial answer to this problem would be for commitment judges to make specific determinations regarding the patient's competency to consent to or to refuse particular forms of treatment, including medications, likely to be recommended to the patient. Then, if the patient is determined to be incompetent, an appropriate procedure for reallocating decision-making authority could be made at the "front end" of the treatment process. Such explict "front-end" judicial determinations should be encouraged.

But since this is not now done as a matter of course, involuntary patients cannot, as a class, be presumed to be incompetent to refuse medication. Moreover, a "front-end" decision would not, by itself, completely solve the problem. Treatment is a process, not an event, and the patient's condition will change, one hopes for the better. Thus, some procedure would have to be available for subsequent assessments of the patient's competence even if he were determined to be incompetent at the time of commitment—at least upon expiration of the period of the initial judicial order authorizing involuntary treatment.

It should be remembered, as well, that the institution would have to develop and implement a procedure for dealing with voluntary patients who refuse medication. Practically, there seems to be little point in insisting on different procedures for involuntary patients.

Exceptions to the Competent Patient's
Right to Refuse

In the *Rogers* case, Judge Tauro concluded, and counsel for the plaintiffs apparently conceded, that a competent patient could be forcibly medicated in an emergency. This was defined as "circumstances in which a failure to [medicate forcibly] would bring about a substantial likelihood of physical harm to the patient or others."[7] In the *Rennie* case, Judge Brotman expressed a similar view: "If a patient cannot be confined without endangering other patients and staff, and yet he refuses medication that would curb his dangerous tendencies, this would be one factor to weigh in overriding his decision to refuse."[8]

The assumption underlying either view is that a competent patient may be forcibly medicated if he is acutely dangerous. The doctrinal basis for this conclusion is the well-established principle that even fundamental constitutional rights are not absolute and may be overridden by what lawyers call a compelling state interest. For example, the freedom from bodily intrusions by the state can be overridden by the government's interests in preventing the spread of highly contagious disease, thus justifying quarantining the carrier or compulsory vaccination. In *Rennie*, in fact, Judge Brotman cited the 1905 case decided by the United States Supreme Court upholding Massachusetts' compulsory vaccination law.[9] It should be noted that the quarantine is the conceptual model for the prevailing constitutional analysis of the state's power to commit the mentally ill: the common idea is the need for confinement to prevent imminent harm to the patient or others. Judges Tauro and Brotman simply applied this same reasoning within the institutional walls: the patient's right to be free of forced medication, like his right to be free of seclusion or mechanical restraint, may be overridden by the need to prevent imminent harm.

I am troubled by this line of reasoning. Even if the police power prevails as the primary justification for commitment, I do not think it should be permitted to justify forced medication of competent but supposedly dangerous patients. I say this because the risks of indignity and abuse seem to me to be especially high when medication is used for behavioral restraint. In such cases, and there are surely not many where the patient is imminently dangerous but competent, the institution should rely only on restraints and/or seclusion, both because they are less invasive and because their use is more easily monitored than the use of drugs. Meanwhile, the so-called "emergency" exception to the right to refuse medication (and the correlative right to be free of forced bodily intrusions) should be tied explicitly to an assessment of incompetence.

Under this view, the institution's authority to administer medication forcibly in an emergency would derive from the same source as the traditional "emergency" exception to the common law informed consent requirement. Under the implied consent doctrine, when an incapacitated patient needs immediate medical attention, the physician is justified in assuming that the patient would have consented if he had been competent to do so. In the context of the psychiatric patient's "right to refuse," a bona fide emergency would justify forcible medication of a person thought to be incompetent to consent or refuse without the need to invoke the competency-determination procedures otherwise required. This traditional emergency doctrine would apply to voluntary as well as involuntary patients, but it would permit only short-term intervention. Continued treatment of a protesting patient would have to be authorized according to prescribed legal procedures. In the case of a "voluntary" patient, this would also require commitment.

Let me comment, in passing, on the broader definition of "emergency" offered by the state in *Rogers*. Under the state's definition, an "emergency" would include "property destruction," "bizarre behavior," or an "acute or chronic emotional disturbance having the potential to seriously interfere with the patient's ability to function on a daily basis." On its face, the definition is offered as an "exception" to the patient's prima facie right to refuse. However, it should be clear that it really represents a conceptual end-run around both the police power ideology that underlies the narrower definition and, more importantly, around the self-determination principle itself. In essence, it would authorize forced medication whenever the staff thinks the patient needs it without requiring an explicit assessment of the patient's competency. This would allow *parens patriae* to govern after the patient is committed, and reaches the same result as formally equating commitment with incompetency. As I mentioned earlier, provision for forced medication could be made by revising the criteria for commitment[10] or by requiring a "front-end" judicial determination of incompetency to make specific treatment decisions. But provision should not be made through the back door.

Competency Determinations

Absent imminent dangerousness, it seems clear that the clinical and legal principles do not diverge: the patient who is competent to make treatment decisions should be permitted to do so. Three difficult issues remain:

1) What does competency mean and how should it be assessed?
2) Who should determine whether the patient is competent and by what procedures?
3) Assuming the patient is determined to be incompetent, who should decide whether the recommended treatment should be undertaken and according to what criteria should this decision be made?

What Does Competency Mean?

The formulation of criteria for defining competencies and the development of clinical assessment protocols remain one of the most important frontiers in the law-psychiatry field. All of the refined discussion about the right to refuse medication is sheer nonsense if we have no meaningful and objective way to distinguish those patients who are competent to consent to or to refuse treatment from those who are not.

Dr. Roth will address this important subject later, but let me make a few comments. First, as Roth and his co-workers have noted, different "tests" of competency place varying emphases on the intellectual, affective, volitional, or integrative faculties of the mind. One might ask, for example, whether the patient is capable of understanding that a choice must be made and indicating such a choice. This question focuses on the cognitive process: does the patient understand the risks and benefits of alternative treatment, or of not being treated? Or, one could ask whether the patient's choice is a reasonable one judged solely by its outcome—that is, would a normal, reasonable person make such a choice? One also might ask whether the patient's choice is based on "rational" reasons, or whether the patient's reasoning is not logically linked to the real risks and benefits of the treatment. Or, one might ask whether the patient's assessment of the risks and benefits, which he does understand, is filtered through a prism of personal values which is symptomatic of his illness (such as thinking he is not worthy of treatment). These questions need study and deliberation.

Second, the standards of assessing competency vary, as Roth has suggested, according to the nature of the treatment and to whether the patient consents or refuses. As a practical matter, the threshold of competency for refusing electroconvulsive therapy is very low, while the threshold of competency for consenting (without substitution of a surrogate decision-maker) to this form of therapy is much higher. Conversely, the threshold for consenting to drug treatments, at least in acute situations, is *very* low—indeed there probably isn't one. For this purpose, most patients are regarded as competent to say "yes." However, the threshold for being competent to refuse is probably quite high; to put it the other way, for this purpose the threshold of incompetency is low, and most refusing patients are incompetent. As Roth suggests, this practical outcome reflects a strong social and professional bias in favor of treating patients with standard treatments so long as they are not thereby exposed to serious risks.

The law has not come to terms with the complexities of the competency question. This is one reason why the transfer of authority to judges to adjudicate an individual's "competency" to refuse medication is highly suspect—no one has told them yet what questions they are supposed to be asking.

WHO DECIDES?

Let me refer you to *Rogers v. Okin*. Having concluded that a refusing patient could be forcibly medicated only if he were incompetent, Judge Tauro decided, with no discussion of alternatives, that the competency decision must be determined judicially in a guardianship proceeding. He brushed aside practical objections that had been raised by the state. Although Judge Tauro rested his holding on Massachusetts law, it has been argued that the due process clause requires judicial procedures for incompetency determinations in connection with therapeutic choices, as well as in connection with other incompetencies, such as the management of one's own affairs.

I think this position is erroneous. It is by no means clear that a medical decision-making procedure for competency assessment would violate the due process clause. The Supreme Court's decision in *Parham v. J.R.*[11] concerning the commitment of minors, sanctions nonjudicial procedures. Although that decision is distinguishable on a number of grounds, the Supreme Court emphasized the clinical nature of the decision being made.[12] In the present context, the competency determination requires a subtle assessment of the patient's condition and its relationship to his "reasons" for refusing medication. Moreover, as I have noted, the practical meaning of competency draws on values of therapeutic need and relative risk. Thus, although "competency" is not a purely clinical judgment, it requires clinical expertise.

It does not follow from these observations that the competency decision should be left to the treatment staff. Due process does require some "neutral" or independent decision-maker. But I do not think that this decision-maker must be a judge or, after the initial guardianship appointment, a guardian. Judge Brotman's decision in *Rennie v. Klein* appears to endorse the use of an independent panel of psychiatrists.[13] I think this approach is constitutionally permissible and has many practical advantages.

Space will not permit detailed attention to the procedural aspects of this "external" review. However, I do not think that counsel must be appointed to represent any refusing patient before the independent panel. It is both more practical, and probably more helpful to the patient's assertion of his rights, if a clinically trained advocate (who *could* be a lawyer, but need not be) represents him. Clinical training and understanding are more valuable in this context than legal training.

I would like to say a word about the substantive aspect of this external review. Judge Brotman ruled that an independent reviewer should decide whether or not the medication should be administered by "weighing" four variables: (1) the patient's dangerousness; (2) the patient's competency to decide; (3) the availability of less restrictive treatment; and (4) the risk of permanent side effects from the proposed treatment. With deference to Judge Brotman, I do not agree. He has given the independent reviewer two very different functions. Even if both functions are appropriate, I believe they should be carefully separated.

The essential constitutional function is to assess the patient's competency. This is an evaluative role, not a therapeutic role. If the reviewer concludes that the patient is competent to refuse (a decision that inevitably will require an understanding of the patient's illness and the risks and benefits of the alternative treatments), then that should be the end of the matter. The reviewer should not "weigh" the patient's competency against the benefits of treatment. There is only one criterion here, not four. However, if the reviewer determines that the patient is not competent to decide, the question then becomes who should decide, and on what basis.

The Role of the Surrogate Decision Maker

One option is to return decision-making authority to the treatment staff. Another is to appoint a surrogate decision maker, such as a member of the patient's family, to make the decision after consultation with the staff and the independent reviewer.[14] Another is to transfer decision-making authority to the reviewer himself. This is what Judge Brotman did. In effect, Judge Brotman uses the patient's refusal, whether competent or incompetent, as a trigger for conducting an independent review of the staff's treatment decision. It is used as a mechanism to enforce and protect the patient's right to adequate treatment. This is actually a very significant step and one which should be carefully considered. If the judges, or those who administer state mental health institutions, lack confidence in the clinical judgments of the attending staff, then a review mechanism should be employed for medication choices for all patients, not only those who object. On the other hand, a review procedure need not involve the substitution of an outsider's clinical judgment for that of the treatment team. Requirements for second opinions and for consultation with the independent reviewer might be sufficient and would leave the authority where the responsibility lies—with the treating staff.

This whole question echoes the point that the patient's right to refuse medication is but a piece of a larger problem—the need to assure delivery of adequate psychiatric treatment.

Conclusion

I began with the principle of self-determination. There is no way around the simple proposition that a "competent" patient has the right to participate in the process of therapeutic choice and ultimately has the right to refuse medications that the therapist, exercising sound and reasonable clinical judgment, believes would improve the patient's condition. The question is how this principle is qualified by the process of involuntary psychiatric hospitalization. The answer is confounded by the conceptual ambiguities in prevailing legal doctrine: what are the purposes and justifying circumstances of civil commitment? To what extent does this decision modify and erode the self-determination principle? To the extent that the committed patient does not lose all control over the treatment process, according to what criteria should his participation be governed?

If, as I have assumed, the committed patient presumptively retains a right to decide, another set of issues arises. As I see it, the real challenge is to develop procedures for assessing a refusing patient's competency for making treatment choices that deal humanely and sensitively with the clinical realities of individual cases. I think this can be done without putting judges in the position of designing each patient's treatment plan—which was Judge Brotman's unenviable position in *Rennie v. Klein*. I also think it can be done without requiring a guardianship proceeding every time a patient refuses treatment. But it will *not* do to say the patient has no right at all.

Notes

1. *Rennie v. Klein*, 462 F. Supp. 1131 (D.N.J. 1978) (individual action for injunction); 476 F. Supp. 1294 (D.N.J. 1979) (class action for injunction); 481 F. Supp. 552 (D.N.J. 1979) (motion of defendants to stay order of temporary injunction pending appeal).
2. *Rogers v. Okin*, 478 F. Supp. 1342 (D.Mass. 1979), *aff'd in part, rev'd in part, vacated and remanded*, 634 F.2d 650 (1st Cir. 1980) *cert. granted* April 20, 1980.
3. *Scholendorff v. Society of New York Hosp.*, 105 N.E. 92, 93 (N.Y. 1914).
4. *Rogers v. Okin*, 478 F. Supp. 1342, 1366–67 (D.Mass. 1979). The District Court states that "The First Amendment protects the communication of ideas. That protected right of communication presupposes a capacity to produce ideas." *Id.* at 1367. The Court of Appeals found it "unnecessary in the present case to decide if this finding is correct." 634 F.2d 654, n.2. Similarly, the New Jersey District Court deciding *Rennie* declared that "the hospital's efforts to alter [Rennie's] thinking disorder cannot be seen as a first amendment violation. The court need not reach the question of whether ... disordered thought is within the scope of first amendment protection." 462 F. Supp. at 1144.
5. "[I]n those states which combine commitment and incompetency proceedings, the patient ... loses a number of rights, including control over his property ... to engage in business transactions, to make a will or gift, to vote or practice a profession." R. SLOVENKO, PSYCHIATRY AND LAW (Little, Brown, Boston) (1973) at 229.

6. California authorizes short-term commitment "[w]hen any person, as a result of mental disorder, is a danger to others, or to himself...." Calif. Welf. & Instns. Code §5150, 5250 (Deering Supp. 1973), but hospitalization beyond fourteen days may be imposed only if the person is dangerous to others (*Id.* §§5300, 5303).

In Massachusetts, involuntary commitment for more than ten days must be based on a hearing at which it is found that failure to institutionalize the person "would create the likelihood of serious harm by reason of mental illness." 104 Code Mass. Regs. 3.01(1).
7. *Rogers v. Okin*, 478 F. Supp. at 1364-65.
8. *Rennie v. Klein*, 462 F. Supp. at 1145.
9. *Id.*, citing *Jacobson v. Massachusetts*, 197 U.S. 11 (1905).
10. The prevailing legal approach to involuntary psychiatric treatment, including commitment criteria as well as the narrower right to refuse medication issue, is under a counterattack by the mental health professions. Drs. Stone and Roth and many others have argued that the "dangerousness" criterion for commitment should be supplemented, and perhaps replaced, by a "need for treatment" approach that links the state's power to intervene to a determination that the patient needs treatment, that treatment is available, and that illness deprives the patient of the capacity to appreciate the need for treatment. If the *parens patriae* approach to *commitment* were adopted, commitment itself should represent an explicit legal nullification of the self-determination principle. The commitment order would represent a transfer of the patient's decision-making authority to the treatment staff. Because the basis of commitment would be treatment, not containment, it would be counterproductive under this theory for the patient's objection to overcome sound medical judgment regarding the best way to treat the patient's condition.
11. *Parham v. J.R.*, 99 S.Ct. 2493 (1979).
12. *Id.* at 2507-11.
13. *Rennie v. Klein*, 462 F. Supp. at 1147.
14. If the patient is determined to be incompetent to decide—*i.e.*, as a practical matter, incompetent to refuse—it is not especially likely that a reasonable surrogate decision-maker would ratify the patient's refusal if the question were whether the recommended treatment is in the patient's best interests from a therapeutic standpoint. If the staff were not convinced of this, it would not have sought to override the patient's objection in the first place. However, some commentators have argued that the substitute decision-maker should use a so-called "subjective" approach, asking what the patient would have decided if he or she had the present capacity to decide. Under this approach, the family member, friend, or advocate would consider the patient's present view toward the treatment and his past attitudes when he was not so severely ill. I frankly think this is counting the angels on the head of a pin.

3

Behind the Bench on *Rennie v. Klein*

The Honorable Stanley S. Brotman

The *Rennie*[1] case has been on appeal to the United States Court of Appeals for the Third Circuit, and each day I expect its decision. Although I have the courage of my convictions, I, like any human being, am not infallible, and therefore have purposely left open to the last moment my options as to my remarks. I just checked with my office five minutes ago, and nothing has been received from the Third Circuit, so as of this moment, my opinion in *Rennie v. Klein* is still very much alive.[2]

Much has been written in various publications about the *Rennie* case. I have been provided with most of these articles and am aware of and can appreciate the reactions of all sides to my opinion. I hope my remarks will shed some new insights as we attempt to resolve the oft-conflicting values involved with the refusal of mental health treatment.

Based on the constitutional right of privacy, a mentally ill patient involuntarily committed to a state psychiatric institution has the right to refuse psychotropic medication in a nonemergency situation. That determination has been reached, initially in *Rennie*, and by the United States District Court for the District of Massachusetts,[3] the Supreme Court of Oklahoma,[4] the Supreme Court of Colorado,[5] and most recently in the United States District Court for the District of Ohio, Western Division.[6] The fact that these courts found as they did indicates that the factual basis for the determination exists in each state or district, and that continued litigation of this nature can be expected to bring the same result. But beyond that, the courts will define the right in terms of being absolute or qualified, and will fashion an appropriate remedy.

In *Rennie*, I found that the right to refuse treatment was a qualified right, not an absolute one. Before it can be enforced, there must be some type of a due process hearing afforded the patient at which time the right is considered against the following factors:

1) The patient's physical threat to other patients and staff at the institution
2) The patient's capacity to decide on his particular treatment
3) The existence of any less restrictive treatment
4) The risk of permanent side effects from the proposed treatment

What I have just stated is the basic holding of *Rennie v. Klein*. I recognize that this decision will affect a patient's treatment and will also change to an extent the patient-staff relationship. But does that mean the change is for the worse?

To put the subject matter into perspective in a summary manner, let me take you through the *Rennie* litigation from my side of the bench, working with the factual situation presented to me, and with the legal issues it raised. When Rennie's complaint was first filed in my court, I recognized its potential impact. I called in both the deputy attorney general and the public advocate and told them I would devote whatever time it would take to try this case completely and that they owed me the courtesy and responsibility of putting all the issues before me. They did, and my compliments go out to both the public advocate in the state of New Jersey as well as the deputy attorney general involved in this case, because both they and their staffs did an excellent job.

First of all, why was there judicial intervention? The answer is a simple one! Under our system everyone, no matter who, has recourse to the courts to define and protect his constitutional rights. In this instance, John Rennie challenged the State of New Jersey, alleging that his right to refuse medication was violated. Who is John Rennie and why was he forced to assert his claim in a courtroom rather than in some other forum which might have been more comfortable both for him and for the staff?

John Rennie, who is now forty years of age, is a highly intelligent, white, divorced male who, before the onset of his psychiatric difficulties, worked as a pilot and flight instructor. His first symptoms of mental illness appeared in December 1971, with serious problems commencing early in 1973 in the wake of his twin brother's death in an airplane accident. Between 1973 and 1978, Mr. Rennie had twelve admissions to psychiatric hospitals. His diagnoses ranged from paranoid schizophrenic to manic depressive, circular type. He exhibited aggressive and abusive symptoms, suicidal ideas, religious delusions, and even threatened to kill the President. He attempted suicide several times. He was given various antipsychotic drugs, including Mellaril, Thorazine, Haldol, Prolixin, Decanoate, and lithium to name a few. During his sixth admission, from April 9 to May 7, 1974, on a voluntary commitment, there was the first indication of his refusal to take medication. Throughout his subsequent hospitalizations, Mr. Rennie was inconsistent in his attitudes toward the various medications, refusing at times and cooperating at times. Even prior to the commencement of the lawsuit on November 17, 1977, Mr. Rennie reported that the evening shift attendants had beat him with sticks while he was tied to a bed. The next day he pointed out the sticks which were hidden at the nurses' station. The investigation that followed resulted in the suspension of one attendant for three days. Thereafter, Mr. Rennie and the attendant remained together in the same ward.

There was no mechanism available to Mr. Rennie within the institutional system to test his position. Although the public advocate entered the picture on Mr. Rennie's behalf, he was met with resistance and distrust and outright hostility by the staff. The Division of Mental Health and Hospitals of New Jersey had not formulated Administrative Bulletin 78-3 nor its implementing order.[7] As a result, judicial intervention was sought, which resulted in considerable cost in terms of time and resources—costs that were, however, necessary under the circumstances.

During trial, the subject of psychotropic medication was well covered by the experts, who were of considerable assistance in educating me about the role of these medications in the treatment of the mentally ill. Mr. Rennie's mental condition changed throughout the two years of litigation, and I was faced with conflicting medical opinions as to treatment, since the staff was hesitant to force medication upon him. Once, early in the proceedings, counsel for the parties reached an agreement, after consultation with the state psychiatrist, that Mr. Rennie, except in an emergency, would not be medicated against his will beyond a maintenance dosage. In another instance, the state psychiatrist and plaintiff's outside psychiatrist reached a consensus about Mr. Rennie's treatment.

At no time, and I stress this, did the court on its own order specific treatment. Although it was necessary for proper control of the case to require that Mr. Rennie's refusals to take medication and attempts to medicate him be brought before the court, it was apparent to me that a better forum had to be found in which these matters could be aired quickly by the medical people. In this respect, after I gained more familiarity with the subject matter, my thinking changed from my first opinion.

The conversion of the *Rennie* case into a class action afforded me the opportunity to go beyond my finding of the right to refuse medication in a nonemergency situation, and provided a nonjudicial forum to test and determine that right against the factors outlined previously. Some excerpts from the testimony and case history may help you to understand why I mandated in detail the relief contained in the September 14, 1979 order.

Ms. A. was a twenty-three year old woman who was involuntarily committed to Ancora Psychiatric Hospital in 1978. She had a history of mental illness and hospitalization since she was ten. At Ancora, she was given psychotropic drugs which often blunted her consciousness to such an extent that she would spend much of the day sleeping. Heavy doses were probably given in response to her quarrelsome and sometimes violent relationship with ward staff, which could, in large measure, be attributed to the fact that she felt unneeded and idle on the ward and was sometimes subject to physical assault from the attendants. Until January 1979, Ms. A. usually took her medication without objection, and, on occasion, even requested it. However, she was also threatened with forced injection of medication when she expressed reluctance to take the drugs. In January, she began openly resisting drugs because she had become pregnant and "did not want to hurt my baby." In disregard of her pregnancy and of her opposition to drugs, the treating physician persisted in prescribing psychotropics, and the patient was forced to complain to the public advocate's office, which interceded in her behalf. Nevertheless, with the approval of the hospital's medical director, she was given Haldol, a psychotropic, on March 16, 1979. One week later she ingested a small amount of detergent and was transferred to the hospital's medical unit. That unit immediately stopped her use of Haldol, because of her pregnancy and because her diagnosis did not require use of psychotropics. The medical unit also allowed her to do small chores on the ward. Her general condition rapidly improved and she became very cooperative with ward staff. On May 16 she was discharged and has remained off medication. Her demeanor when she testified in the courtroom was excellent. In summary, despite the patient's hesitance and outright refusals during her pregnancy, Ancora physicians on the psychiatric ward persisted in medicating Ms. A. by force or intimidation when a simple change in environment apparently was the best and least restrictive treatment indicated.

Another woman, Ms. G., was sixty-six years old. She had been an involuntary patient for ten years at Greystone, another state psychiatric institution in New Jersey. Plaintiff's expert diagnosed her illness as manic-depressive psychosis. The hospital had given her diagnoses of both manic-depressive psychosis and schizo-affective schizophrenia at different times. The patient began refusing doses of Thorazine, although she accepted lithium, which is the drug of choice for manic-depressive illness. Her refusal was, according to plaintiff's expert, "very good judgment." The expert credibly characterized the Thorazine prescription as grossly irresponsible because of the reasonable success of lithium alone, her symptomology, and particularly the fact that the patient had tardive dyskinesia. In fact, a neurologist's report from 1975 in her medical record indicated that she had a classical case of tardive dyskinesia, but that report was apparently lost from her record. A January 1979 note in her record indicated that Ms. G. was "faking" her mouth movements, although plaintiff's expert testified that her movements were "so gross as to be unable to be fake." Indeed, because of her gross mouth movements from this disease she cannot be fitted with dentures, and is forced to subsist on a diet of ground food. She was also subjected to taunts from the hospital staff implying that the deformity was her own fault. Not only was Thorazine inappropriately prescribed, it was forced upon this patient by injection at least once in January 1979. Here again, a psychotropic drug was involuntarily administered where there was little medical justification for the drug and a great danger of creating or enhancing irreversible side effects. The side effects were blatantly ignored by the doctors.

A third woman, a voluntary patient at Greystone, sixty years old, refused medication in August 1978 and was thrown onto a bed by attendants and injected with a long-acting form of Prolixin. The drug caused the patient severe discomfort. The plaintiff's expert credibly testified that this was improper medication in this case, and that the open ward privileges then given her were inconsistent with the suicidal diagnosis appearing on the patient's record. The expert believed that many of her psychotic symptoms stemmed from her frustration with hospital staff and delays encountered in her discharge planning. The hospital medical director was involved in the decision to forcibly medicate this patient and upheld the treating physician's decision based on the physician's reports. Review by an independent hearing officer before the forced injection might have aired this patient's complaints and might have prevented the questionable use of Prolixin.

There were other cases indicative of poor charting, failure to follow through on consultations, and absence of visual observations clearly indicative of tardive dyskinesia. I have given you these examples because I want you to understand what it is like to be a judge who has to try a case with which he has no experience. Day after day, testimony by experts and by patients, as well as the arguments of counsel are offered and the judge has to arrive at a decision. All that testimony has to bear on that decision. That's why I want you to sit behind the bench with me and understand my thought processes and the procedures I went through in reaching the result that I did.

The plaintiffs in *Rennie v. Klein* did not seek to prohibit the administration of psychotropic drugs to any particular patient. Rather, they sought sweeping changes in hospital practices to protect their rights. Defendants Klein and Rotov never acknowledged the right found by the court. But these defendants contend that the procedures instituted by them in Administrative Bulletin 78-3[8] and Administrative Order 2-13[9] meet any constitutional requirements. In other words, although they did not admit that there was this right of privacy, they felt that the Bulletin and Order satisfied any constitutional mandates relative to a right to refuse treatment.

The testimony clearly indicated shortcomings in those procedures which may be summarized as follows: (1) failure to adequately inform patients of their rights and of the effects of drugs, particularly long-term side effects; (2) failure to seek written consent to the administration of specific drugs; and (3) inadequate review of decisions to forcibly medicate.

In framing my procedures for the state hospital, I found that a review by an independent psychiatrist, rather than by a judge or administrative hearing officer, would be more satisfactory. I analogized that the judge will sit and hear testimony, and on the basis of that testimony, will reach a fact-finding, and from that fact-finding, will determine a remedy. A doctor listens to his patient, gets all the facts, reaches the diagnosis, and then prescribes. I felt that in this instance a psychiatrist could hear and make a determination better than a judge could.[10]

Similarly, there was no system for providing representatives for patients who wanted to appeal decisions of staff psychiatrists. I felt that a "patient advocate system" should be established. I felt that an attorney would not be as effective, because when we start talking with attorneys we generally think in adversarial roles, and I felt that the adversarial role did not really belong in decisions concerning refusals of psychiatric medications. The policies and procedures of the defendants were ineffective because the defendants failed, as earlier stated, even to acknowledge and instruct their staff that involuntary patients have a qualified right to refuse treatment.

What does the final order in *Rennie* require, and how intrusive is it? The order has five components. First it requires the use of an affirmative consent form.[11] The form must contain the information on drug side effects and patients' rights so that the consent will be informed. The second component is a system of patient advocates which is essentially the full implementation of an idea initiated on a limited basis by the New Jersey Division of Mental Health. Patient advocates are given two areas of responsibility: they analyze cases in which the treating physician certifies that a patient is incapable of providing informed consent, and they serve as informal counsel to patients who wish to refuse treatment. The third component requires informal review by an independent psychiatrist before the hospital may forcibly medicate an involuntary patient. The next part of the order is enforcement of voluntary patients' rights to refuse treatment under state law. The last component is a provision for forced medication in emergency situations which, the court holds, not only qualifies the constitutional right to privacy but also the rights of voluntary patients under state law.

To date, I have received monthly reports respecting compliance with the order, which indicate that the various state psychiatric hospitals have attempted to comply. Consent forms have been developed and new procedures evolved. But problems with a patient that cannot be attributed to anything or anyone else are blamed on "the Brotman order." To give you an idea of these reports, one, from July 1980 from Ancora Psychiatric Hospital, notes that

> during June there were twenty emergency certifications for the first 72 hours. There were no second 72-hour certifications by the medical director during the month of June. All cases of first 72-hour certifications were reviewed by the medical director, hospital liaison, and the advocate with no disagreements. There were 11 certificates of functional incompetency received by the Advocate during June; all such certificates were reviewed by the Advocate with none going beyond medical director review. All necessary documentation is being reviewed by the Advocate, medical director, and hospital liaison with no problems in this area. Team meetings are ongoing in all units of the hospital with input from all necessary disciplines with the individual patient as a member of his or her treatment team. There was one hearing scheduled for the independent psychiatrist in June. This particular report also discusses staff morale, noting that it continues to be an up-and-down problem.

The report goes on to state that

> the hospital has tried to develop some data on the following areas: (1) patient-to-staff confrontations—verbal or physical; (2) patient-to-patient confrontations—verbal or physical; (3) patients missing at census; (4) patients found with injuries due to self-abuse or accident; (5) patients found to have injuries after patient-to-patient confrontations; (6) staff found to have been injured after patient-staff confrontations; (7) incidents of fire-related activities, such as smoking in bed, fires; and (8) incidents of destroyed or damaged property, with the comment that although we are unable to directly attribute this to the Brotman decision, it is the opinion of the administration that a greater number of these cases could and can be attributed to the Brotman decision.

I also like this remark: "Decrease polypharmacy."

Another report, dated August 26, 1980, also from Ancora, states that there "continues to be no problems in obtaining informed consent." According to this report, "both physicians and other disciplines have utilized the medical director, Advocate, and liaison in advising residents of their rights in regards to signing consent forms." Again, polypharmacy has been decreased. This report indicates that no severe staff morale problems attributable to the *Rennie v. Klein* decision exist at the hospital at this time.

Shortly before the November 1980 conference, I invited Steve Wallach, a deputy attorney general of New Jersey who represents Mrs. Klein, and Linda Rosensweig, the public advocate who now represents Mr. Rennie, to meet with me in my chambers and informally discuss their views about the implementation of my order and whether any modification is warranted. Let me quote some of the colloquy which took place:

JUDGE BROTMAN: Let me direct this to you, Linda, how do you feel the order is being carried out?

Ms. ROSENSWEIG: I think it's being carried out better in some of the looser run hospitals. It's probably working best in Ancora, due to the fact that the initial scrutiny was focused there. One of the major problems I see is that the doctors have become "gun-shy," for lack of better words, of people who are not medicated and for whom medication is a desirable part of the treatment plan. I think that the doctors take the position that the order, your injunction, stands in the way of medicating people. I addressed the problem with Dr. Pepernik [Medical Director at Ancora], and he claims that he tried to educate the staff as to what the procedure is. I think there is undue reluctance to follow the procedure.

MR. WALLACH: I should tell you that Dr. Pepernik is no longer Medical Director.

JUDGE BROTMAN TO MR. WALLACH: What is your comment on Linda's statement just now about the gun-shyness of the psychiatrists? How do you feel about that?

MR. WALLACH: It's absolutely true. We get this kind of resistance right away from all the hospitals. I think [Linda's] right that it's obviously much more apparent at Ancora for the reason I'm sure that everyone understands. We are trying to deal with it [resistance to the order] and have had numerous situations go from the office of the Public Advocate up to me about a problem and the answer always is, tell the people there is always a way to medicate somebody if they want to medicate somebody. This order never prevented us from medicating someone if they need the medication. It may require us to do something new, but there are procedures we can follow. If it's necessary to medicate somebody, you just have to follow this procedure. I think it is an objection we have to keep grappling with. I think the good doctors have come to accept it; for example at Marlborough, it was a big problem at the beginning; but it has settled down. At Ancora, however, I would say, it will take longer.

JUDGE BROTMAN: Now how are the patient advocates doing?

Ms. ROSENSWEIG: It works very well at Ancora because of Rose Swelto [a patient advocate]. I do not know how well it is working out at the other hospitals, since there the advocates tend to take the position that the doctor knows best and tend not to be advocates as much as neutral bystanders. They don't seem to be applying the test properly.

JUDGE BROTMAN TO MR. WALLACH: What do you think?

MR. WALLACH: I guess I got really contrary information. There have been tremendous internal battles between the Division of Mental Health and Hospitals, at central office level particularly but also at the hospital level with the patient advocate, which I take as some indication that they are attempting to act independent.

JUDGE BROTMAN: Anything else you want to talk about?

Ms. ROSENSWEIG: One thing you may be interested to learn is that the expenditure for medication at Ancora went from $191,000 in calendar year 1979 to $98,000 in calendar year 1980.

JUDGE BROTMAN: Interesting statistic.

JUDGE BROTMAN TO Ms. ROSENSWEIG: Have we lost any patients?

Ms. ROSENSWEIG: The census is down by about 75 patients. I checked to see if there are any statistics on the average length of stay going up or down. However, there's such a time lag in compiling the data—two years from now we'll know the answer.

JUDGE BROTMAN: Is there anything else to talk about?

Ms. ROSENSWEIG: We've had some problem with the independent psychiatrist. It is difficult getting them at Ancora. That is a problem. It takes too long to get them to come. Each one devotes about half a day a week. There seems to be a scheduling problem. Another problem I have observed is that a doctor has a hard time regardless of what guidelines are given to him. He has a hard time really knowing the kinds of legal balancing required under the Order.

JUDGE BROTMAN: When he sits as a hearing officer?

Ms. ROSENSWEIG: Right. I think that when he says this patient should have medication in his judgment, it is really the kind of best-interest judgment that any doctor in private practice would make. They also don't go through recommended factual findings, they just speak informally to the doctor and informally to the patients without ascertaining the information called for in the objectives. That is an educational problem.

JUDGE BROTMAN: Perhaps the psychiatrist should have legal counsel to advise him as to the type of order to prepare and to give him the guidelines upon which to make the requisite factual findings? But that's a mechanical matter and that can come about through education, too.

Ms. ROSENSWEIG: There has also been a problem in getting attorneys to come to hearings.

JUDGE BROTMAN: Why do you need attorneys?

Ms. ROSENSWEIG: For two reasons. If the patient advocate function was a true advocate, counsel would not be required. The other problem is that if the independent psychiatrist does not have the necessary factual records, it is important that someone be there to say "Doctor, this patient has had a problem on the medication before."

MR. WALLACH: That doesn't require legal services.

Ms. ROSENSWEIG: It requires that somebody has to make sure.

JUDGE BROTMAN: I stayed away from having lawyers at that level. I felt that a patient advocate should be the person because as soon as you inject an attorney you think of an adversary proceeding, and I just thought it wasn't the right thing. It doesn't necessitate the presence of an attorney.

Ms. ROSENSWEIG: I do not see it as a problem with the Order; it's the mechanics.

MR. WALLACH: I think there could be more, you know, to the extent that you and your office want to get more involved in making the patient's advocate better. As far as I'm concerned, that will help make it a better system; I'm in favor of that.

Let me offer a word of caution about overreaction by the court, the state, the public advocate, and the medical profession. Legal decisions are based upon factual determinations made after exposure to direct and cross-examination of witnesses and the review of evidence. The factual pattern in cases such as *Rennie* appears to be set. It is demonstrated by the decisions of five courts in different jurisdictions, with other cases in the pretrial stage. There is a challenge here to all of us. The courts must balance the constitutional right of the patient against the treatment and provide for medical judgments to be made by medical people. *Rennie* supports that framework and, in so doing, affords due process to John Rennie. The medical professional must quickly develop new techniques and systems. The public advocate must continue to monitor and protect the rights of the patient, and the state must implement procedures to assure the exercise of those constitutional rights.

In closing, I quote a comment Professor William Curran made in the *New England Journal of Medicine*:[12]

> The New Jersey decision, actually passed down shortly before the Massachusetts case finally moved out of the system, is, in my judgment, the more imaginative in suggesting administrative methods for allowing greater scope to patients' refusals of treatment and yet allowing medication under controlled conditions for patients clearly in need of such treatment. It also seems that the New Jersey court was more willing to allow (or to prod) the professional system to readjust itself and to meet the new demands placed on it. The order of Judge Brotman contains a series of steps to safeguard patients but it also allows necessary medication in controlled situations without the need to obtain courtroom or judicial review of each case or to seek general guardianship that could for indefinite periods deprive patients of a right to refuse.... There is no doubt that these courts have (with perhaps overreactive zeal) suggested a solution that itself may create havoc on the wards as it seeks to redress serious patient problems. I am not sure of the wisdom of this judicial confrontation.

It may well be that there is perhaps a bit of overreaction, but then that is the stimulus to spur the reforms that are so badly needed. There is also a need for compromise. In *Rennie*, I believe that in the balancing process I have provided that compromise, by providing a due process mechanism to satisfy the public advocate, an independent psychiatrist as the ultimate hearing officer to satisfy the medical profession, and better patient care to satisfy the demands of society.

Notes

1. *Rennie v. Klein*, 462 F. Supp. 1131 (1978); 476 F. Supp. 1294 (1979); 481 F. Supp. 552 (1979).
2. *Rennie v. Klein*, 653 F.2d 836 (3d Cir. 1981). The United States Court of Appeals for the Third Circuit substantially upheld Judge Brotman's decisions, and held that involuntarily committed mental patients have a constitutional right to refuse antipsychotic drugs that may have permanently disabling side effects. Agreeing that the state may override that right when the patient is a danger to himself or others, the court held that the degree of procedural due process required was less than the formal adversary hearing before an independent psychiatrist, which was imposed by the federal district court.
3. *Rogers v. Okin*, 478 F. Supp. 1342 (D.Mass. 1979), *aff'd in part and remanded*, 634 F.2d 650 (1st Cir. 1980), cert. pet. filed, No. 80-1417 (Feb. 23, 1980), granted April 20, 1980.
4. *In re Mental Health of K. K. B.*, 609 P.2d 747 (Okla. 1980).
5. *Goedecke v. State Dept. of Institutions*, 603 P.2d 123 (Colo. 1979).
6. *Davis v. Hubbard*, 506 F. Supp. 915 (N.D.Ohio 1980).
7. N.J. Div. of MH Ad. Bul 78-3. The Administrative Bulletin was a belated attempt to establish some guidelines for the administration of psychotropic medications. It is appended to the first *Rennie* decision. 462 F. Supp. at 1148-51.
8. *Id.*
9. Ad. Order 2-13.
10. Conceivably, the psychiatrist as the hearing officer may need the assistance of legal counsel in the preparation of his determination, *i.e.*, type of order and guidelines.
11. *See* consent forms in appendix.
12. Curran, W. J., *The Management of Psychiatric Patients: Courts, Patient's Representatives, and the Refusal of Treatment*, New England Journal of Medicine, 302(23):1297-99 (June 5, 1980).

Discussion

Neil L. Chayet, J.D., Moderator

Ms. JUDI CHAMBERLIN (Conference Faculty): My question is to Dr. Blackwell. When I was a patient, I was diagnosed as a chronic schizophrenic and told that I could not exist without institutionalization and drugs. Yet for the past fourteen years I have not partaken of any kind of psychiatric treatment. I believe that at least part of my ability, and that of many, many ex-patients, to survive in the community is through involvement in ex-patient mutual support or self-help groups such as the Mental Patients' Liberation Front in Boston. What I inferred from your presentation was that anyone who comes into a mental hospital is sick, is disordered, and can't make these decisions or judgments for himself. Yet it seems to me that this is precisely the question that needs to be decided. Is this person indeed suffering from that sort of a problem or is it just an attribution that's being made? I think this is an overriding problem, that anybody who is being labeled a mentally ill, sick, schizophrenic, hospitalized patient is thereby assumed to have these problems, these disabilities.

DR. BARRY BLACKWELL (Conference Faculty): I'm not sure if that was a question or a statement—I really don't find myself in disagreement with anything that you said.

Ms. CHAMBERLIN: The question is, don't we need to adjudicate whether, in fact, a person is schizophrenic, ill, unable to make decisions, incompetent? Currently, this is just a medical attribution.

MR. CHAYET (Moderator): In other words, when a person comes into the hospital there is an assumption that the individual is ill. Is there a way of approaching this more impartially than perhaps is done in some institutions?

DR. BLACKWELL: I imagine that would lead to a due process hearing around the issue of diagnosis, rather than drug treatment, and I think that would be a very cumbersome system.

Discussion

Ms. GAY LESTER: I'm also a former mental patient. When you're in a hospital, and you're allowed to do nothing except sit around, you start fantasizing, thinking about what you wish you could have said to Dr. So-and-so, when you were nice enough to grant him an interview and he called you a whore in front of all his students because you've been to a nudist colony. You're demeaned by the people who are working in the hospital. You're feeling tense because you lack exercise. The drugs that you're given make you feel lethargic so you don't want to do anything. It seems to me that mental illness is created or a tension is created from these drugs. I wonder how many psychiatrists realize that. Also, as far as patients who seem to want to go back to the hospital, or don't want to get out, it's difficult to go out on your own when you're conditioned to think that you can't survive without the help of certain people, when you're constantly intimidated by people working in those institutions, and when you're different. I'm very different from most people. I have a high energy level. I speak the truth. I'm very strong. Yet I have been charged with being schizophrenic and a number of other things because people in authority refuse to accept my personality differences. Why does that make me mentally ill? Why doesn't it just make them stupid, because they refuse to understand me?

MR. EVAN GOODMAN (Probate Court Commissioner, Indianapolis, Indiana): Two questions for Dr. Blackwell. I didn't understand your graph, on the critical relatives versus no drugs. Second, I didn't quite understand when you said that drugs help for six months, and after that drugs were of no help. Please explain that.

DR. BLACKWELL: The studies show that drugs do have some role in buffering the patient who has schizophrenia from the critical relative. If the patient continues to take the drugs on an outpatient basis, he or she is less likely to be readmitted to the hospital. The illustration of the relapse rates of patients undergoing drug therapy and social therapy [see fig. 8] shows that social therapy did not improve the relapse rates during the initial six months that the patients were released from the hospital. After that point, there was a marginal increment as a result of patients' being given both social therapy and drug therapy. That's consistent with a considerable amount of literature. The various forms of psychotherapy alone really don't benefit the patient who has schizophrenia, at least not until the patient is well stabilized and has been out of the hospital and in the community for some months.

DR. KENNETH KAUFMAN (Assistant Professor of Psychiatry, University of Southern California School of Medicine): I'd like to address these questions to Mr. Bonnie. First, would you comment further on the role of the independent clinical expert. Next, if the patient does refuse treatment, who then pays for the hospitalization?

MR. RICHARD J. BONNIE (Conference Faculty): Assuming that there ought to be some form of review—either of treatment decisions generally, or of a person's competency to refuse recommended treatment—the process should be a practical one. It should not, for example, require the treatment staff to spend every other day in a courtroom, and it should be designed to maximize the clinical understanding of the decision that's being made. That's why, at least after the person has been institutionalized, I look for medical decision-making procedures, rather than judicial ones. Most jurisdictions have begun to develop advocacy systems to deal with the general issues of adequate treatment and the protection of patients' rights. I would hope that it is possible to build on the systems that are already in place to provide access to some independent decision-making authority who is not in the hierarchy or on the particular treatment team. I know that it would be quite costly if we were required to have independent commissions review treatment decisions. But if that were the only way to do it, I think it would have to be done. The state, of course, would have to bear the burden of paying for it. It would be another cost of operating the public system. My own hope would be to design such a system with people already employed in the public sector, or who are affiliated with it as consultants, so long as they are not part of the treatment team for that particular patient. But again, I think the problem is one of education and role definition. I think it is not beyond the capacities of the people who are trained to be therapists to make independent judgments that take these other considerations into account.

MR. CHAYET: The second question was, who pays for an involuntarily committed patient who refuses treatment?

DR. KAUFMAN: In California, Medicaid/Medicare will suggest that a patient be discharged from the hospital if the patient is receiving no form of treatment.

MR. BONNIE: This is a large question, which I did not touch upon. I realize that the instinctive reaction of many people who are in the business of treating is that their hands are tied if a patient refuses treatment. They feel that the patient who needs treatment and can't get it is going to deteriorate, or at least not improve, and that there is no purpose of having him in the hospital. My assumption—which I think is borne out in the experience of implementing Judge Brotman's order—is that when there's a strong belief in therapeutic need, the medication will be ordered in a significant number of cases. I don't believe this involves substantial numbers in terms of the census of the institution, however.

Discussion

Patients whose right to refuse has been vindicated propose a substantial and unanswered question: what then is to be done? Do you release the person? If the person is no longer committable, release might be the legally appropriate action. The payment question, I feel, is beyond my expertise.

PETER STURGES (Regional Counsel for the Department of Mental Health, Commonwealth of Massachusetts): My question involves practice as I understand it in New York. It came to my attention at an annual review involving my brother who is a profoundly retarded Down Syndrome adult at age 40. My brother is, without question, mentally incompetent to make any kind of decision regarding his personal affairs, and certainly medical affairs. I'm told that in New York, were he competent, there would be no question about his right to refuse treatment, except in extraordinary circumstances where there might be injuries to himself or others. Because he is incompetent, our parents are his guardians. Yet a right to refuse treatment is not afforded to him or my parents unless there should be a surgical operation. Additional medication is prescribed within an annual or quarterly period without the guardian's consent or knowledge, except after the fact at an annual or quarterly review. I'd be interested in Professor Bonnie's or Judge Brotman's thoughts or comments.

MR. BONNIE: The traditional system is one that delegates to the treatment team all decisions relating to the rehabilitation or treatment of the patient or resident. As you look at existing practices, particularly for the mentally retarded, you begin to realize that what is done now may not comport with what one might think are the applicable legal principles. You've raised an example of that. Many mentally retarded persons have guardians for something other than decisions about care and treatment. Maybe that ought not to be the case, and I imagine that because the issue has begun to surface it will get some additional attention.

MS. ELLEN FINKELSTEIN (Legal counsel to Clifton T. Perkins Hospital, Maryland's maximum security state hospital for the criminally insane): I'd like to address this question to Professor Bonnie and perhaps to Judge Brotman. Under either a *parens patriae* or police power theory of treating a patient who does not wish to be treated, the constitutional right of the patient is balanced against the compelling state interest. As far as I know, all the cases that deal with this issue, including *Rennie*, have involved populations of involuntarily committed patients. I'd like to speak of another group of patients who comprise a significant proportion of the patients at Perkins, those sent to the hospital for pretrial evaluation who may remain there for years, incompetent to stand trial. They may be very sick, and yet they have not been adjudicated to be incompetent, nor have they been committed. Is there any legal justification for treating such a category of patients, and does the consideration which influenced Judge Brotman in deciding *Rennie* include such a category of patients as well?

JUDGE STANLEY S. BROTMAN: I can't answer that question, because I can't give advisory opinions. I'm not faced with the case. So I'm going to let Professor Bonnie answer this question.

MR. BONNIE: Professors love to give advisory opinions, right? That's a large question, as you know. There is literature on this question, and I think that there are some cases as well. My understanding is that the line of constitutional thinking, stemming from the Supreme Court's decision in *Jackson v. Indiana* in 1972, would be that the substantive justification for hospitalizing people who are charged with crime as being incompetent to stand trial is to restore them to competency. It might be regarded as implicit, and perhaps ought to be made explicit again, that the commitment order authorizing the state to use accepted medical interventions to restore the person to competency permits forcible medication. Obviously that means treatment without the person's consent. A related question is, if treatment can be given without consent, can the person then stand trial when he has been medicated, because the medication is necessary in order to restore the person to competency in order to stand trial? I think that the trend is for the court to hold that that person can't stand trial even though he or she has been chemically restored to competency.

MR. CHAYET: In Massachusetts we can no longer hold people found incompetent to stand trial any longer than they could have been held had they been found guilty of the crime with which they are charged. At the end of that period of time there is still the question of what happens next. If the individual is dangerous he can continue to be held civilly; if not he is released.

Part II

Legal Reactions to the Courts' Decisions

4

Patients' Rights: Too Much Courting, Not Enough Caring

Eugene J. Comey, J.D.

The decisions in *Rennie v. Klein*[1] and *Rogers v. Okin*[2] are the focal point of much of the debate over the newly recognized constitutional right to refuse psychiatric medication, which has sparked such controversy in the medical and legal professions. Yet despite the common reliance of these cases on a constitutionally protected right to refuse psychiatric medication, there are important differences between them, both in terms of the factual background against which the decisions must be evaluated, and in terms of the scope of the relief mandated by the courts to correct the alleged constitutional violations. I would like to discuss briefly, but critically, the common element in *Rennie* and *Rogers*—namely, the newly created right to refuse psychiatric medication—and then focus on the differences in facts and remedies and the corresponding implications for the operation of state mental health systems.

I turn first to the newly created right to refuse treatment. The American Psychiatric Association (APA) filed amicus curiae briefs in the appeals in both *Rennie* and *Rogers*, arguing that civilly committed patients do not have a constitutional right to refuse psychiatric medication in nonemergency situations. The APA's position is simply this: civil commitment of the mentally ill in both Massachusetts and New Jersey should occur only after an individual has been accorded full due process protections including a judicial hearing at which the individual is represented by counsel. At the commitment hearing, the state must establish that the prospective patient is mentally ill and dangerous to self or society. Significantly, in both Massachusetts and New Jersey, mental illness is defined in terms of need for care and treatment. Thus, the state's decision to hospitalize a person necessarily includes a determination that the person requires care and treatment. In short, in both Massachusetts and New Jersey, treatment, not confinement, is inherent in the rationale for commitment. As a result, the protection that the federal Constitution extends to an individual's privacy—the right to be free from unwarranted governmental intrusion into fundamental personal matters—is lawfully overcome by the state's decision to commit the patient.

The APA argued that the fatal flaw in the district court opinions in *Rennie* and in *Rogers* is the failure to explain why the decision to commit a person against his will is not a sufficient constitutional predicate to justify the provision of that treatment for which the person was committed. It is well established that the state may commit mentally ill patients for involuntary treatment. Indeed, the United States Supreme Court recently noted that the state has "a legitimate interest under its parens patriae powers in providing care to its citizens who are unable because of emotional disorders to care for themselves."[3] Therefore, the APA argues, once a patient is properly committed, the state may treat his mental illness even if he objects.

The federal district courts in *Rennie* and in *Rogers* nonetheless attempted to separate the decision to commit from the decision to treat. This separation is without support. For persons committed under the state police power because they are dangerous to others, both Massachusetts and New Jersey act with a dual purpose—the welfare of the community and the care and treatment of the patient. For persons committed under the *parens patriae* power because they are likely to harm themselves, the sole justification for commitment is to help the patient. Thus, for both police power and *parens patriae* commitments, the state's lawful purpose, in whole or in part, is to treat the committed patient.

By separating treatment from commitment, the district courts not only misunderstood the law in their respective states, they also undermined the constitutional basis for commitment itself. The United States Supreme Court has made it clear that with respect to civil commitment, the power of the state is not exercised in a punitive sense. Yet, this is precisely what *Rennie* and *Rogers* allow by authorizing continued commitment of patients who reject treatment. Since the alternative to accepting treatment may be permanent custody in the hospital, psychiatric hospitalization in such circumstances impermissibly becomes equivalent to placement in a penitentiary where one could be held indefinitely for no convicted offense. In short, treatment is an essential ingredient in hospitalization, and the decision to commit properly overcomes any right to refuse appropriate medication that a person might otherwise possess.

Obviously, given this position, the APA opposes the decisions in both *Rennie* and *Rogers* for their reliance on a separate constitutional right to refuse treatment after involuntary commitment. But, especially with respect to the scope of the remedy mandated by the courts, there are significant differences between *Rennie* and *Rogers*. As a result of these differences, the cases are likely to have significantly different effects on the operation of state psychiatric hospitals.

Patients' Rights

The factual background in *Rennie v. Klein* certainly weighed heavily in the court's evaluation of the asserted right to refuse treatment. In *Rennie*, Judge Brotman confronted a serious problem of misuse of medication in New Jersey state hospitals. Judge Brotman found that decisions about medication often were made by nurses and ward staff rather than physicians; that patient records were poorly documented; that medication was sometimes used for purposes other than treatment of patients' medical problems; and that many medicated patients suffered from both transient and permanent side effects that were not properly detected or treated.

These conditions, I suggest, motivated Judge Brotman to order relief aimed at assuring, in his own words, that "medication will be used more wisely."[4] Thus, though relying on a constitutionally protected right to refuse treatment, *Rennie* is in reality a right to treatment case, that is, a case in which the court attempted to improve the level of patient care.

To implement its constitutional holding, the court issued a detailed injunction mandating a rather complex administrative procedure. Under this procedure, before any patient can begin receiving antipsychotic medication, he must sign a written consent form advising him of his right to refuse the medication and listing all of the drug's known long- and short-term side effects. If the patient refuses to sign, or later orally objects to the medication, the necessary procedures for resolving his rights depend on his status in the institution. Involuntary patients not found legally incompetent by a court or functionally incompetent by their treating psychiatrists are entitled to an informal hearing before an independent psychiatrist (that is, one that does not work at the patient's facility) before medication may be given over the patient's objections. The independent psychiatrist must issue a written opinion, based on certain factors identified by the court, for deciding whether to accept or to override the patient's qualified right to refuse in each case. This opinion is effective for at most 60 days. Involuntary patients deemed incompetent by a court, or those whom the treating physicians find incapable of giving consent, may be forcibly medicated, but an independent patient advocate must be given an opportunity to assess the patient's feelings and condition and to initiate a hearing before an independent psychiatrist if the advocate deems it warranted.

As a practical matter, the essence of this remedy is the establishment of a system of peer review. Although the American Psychiatric Association has challenged this remedy on appeal as being constitutionally inappropriate, the APA has noted that these procedures *might* be a sensible part of an administrative solution to this problem. From the APA's point of view, there are two difficulties with Judge Brotman's injunction. First, as a constitutional remedy, the court's order locks in a single model when greater flexibility is needed. A flexible administrative system, rather than a constitutional rule, is needed if an institution is to find a comprehensive solution to the overall problem. Second, notwithstanding the evidence in the record before Judge Brotman of serious deficiencies in New Jersey state hospitals for the mentally ill, the court's scrutiny of these problems was applied in a case invoking a right to refuse medication. Consistent with that constitutional claim, the court fashioned relief that aims largely at reviewing patients' refusals. Surely, a comprehensive solution to the problem of abuse in medication practices through peer review should not turn on whether the patient is sufficiently assertive of his right to treatment.

In sum, *Rennie* is a case in which the facts showed serious problems of abuse with respect to psychiatric medication in New Jersey state hospitals. To assure adequate treatment, the court unfortunately relied on the notion of a right to refuse treatment. As a result, the procedure employed as a constitutional remedy, though not in itself objectionable, may frustrate the evolution of a sensible and effective system of psychiatric care and peer review.

Rogers v. Okin, the Massachusetts case, differs markedly both in terms of the treatment conditions at the defendant hospitals and in the scope of the remedy. At issue in *Rogers* was the medication program used at the May and Austin Units of the Boston State Hospital—both teaching units of distinguished medical schools. Judge Tauro acknowledged that the medication practices at these units were consistent with good medical practices and generally beneficial to patients. Thus, the record before the court in *Rogers* would not on its face appear to trigger even the informal peer review mandated by the court in *Rennie v. Klein*.

Nonetheless, to implement the constitutionally protected privacy right to refuse psychiatric medication that it found to exist, the court prohibited the administration of medication unless the patient was declared incompetent at a judicial hearing, a guardian was appointed, and the guardian consented to the medication.[5] The American Psychiatric Association takes strong exception to this broad remedy which interposes the courts and judicially appointed guardians between the patient and the treating psychiatrist. Even assuming, contrary to the APA's position, that there is a constitutional right for committed patients to reject medication, the APA maintains that the Constitution allows a psychiatrist to decide when such a patient is incompetent to exercise that right.

This conclusion flows directly from the United States Supreme Court's recent decision in *Parham v. JR*.[6] In that case, the Court held that an objecting child has a due process liberty interest at stake when his parents attempt to place him in a psychiatric hospital. The Court made clear, however, that "[d]ue process has never been thought to require that the neutral and detached trier of fact be law-trained or a judicial or administrative officer.... Surely, this is the case as to medical decisions for 'neither judges nor administrative hearing officers are better qualified than psychiatrists to render psychiatric judgments.' "[7] While recognizing the fallibility of medical and psychiatric decision-making, the Court nevertheless noted that common human experience and scholarly opinions suggested that the supposed protections of the adversary proceeding utilized to determine the appropriateness of medical decisions for the commitment and treatment of mental and emotional illness may be more illusory than real. Accordingly, the Court concluded, due process is satisfied when the decision to hospitalize the objecting child is made by "a staff physician . . . so long as he or she is free to evaluate independently the child's mental and emotional condition and need for treatment."[8] The *Parham* case thus makes clear, as Judge Brotman clearly recognized in *Rennie v. Klein*, that the due process determination of whether a committed patient is competent to refuse medication is exactly the kind of medical decision that must be left to the judgment of physicians in each case.

Moreover, even assuming, contrary to the ruling in *Parham*, that the decision as to the patient's competence to reject medication must be made at a judicial hearing, there is no constitutional basis for requiring that a guardian be appointed to decide whether the patient should accept or reject medication. The *Rogers* court never explains why the Constitution requires that a guardian, rather than the treating physician, must approve medication even after an initial declaration of incompetence.

The district court's solution of competency hearings and appointment of guardians not only lacks a constitutional basis, but it would also prove needlessly costly and wasteful. Typically, the patient will have had a commitment hearing recently, and the competency hearing will thus be largely duplicative, with the patient's attorney again arguing that the patient should not be treated involuntarily. The costs of such hearings, in terms of treatment staff diverted from the hospital, as well as the costs of lawyers and court time, will be significant.

Moreover, these competency hearings will not assure ongoing effective treatment. Under the best of circumstances, it will take time—weeks, if not months—before notice is provided, an attorney appointed, and the hearing completed. During this period, absent an emergency, the patient's refusal cannot be overridden. This hiatus in treatment, which often will occur at the beginning of commitment when the patient's illness is likely to be the most acute, can have serious consequences, including significant deterioration of a patient whose illness might have been treated quickly and effectively. As a result, the procedure required by the district court in Massachusetts will require the state to expend significant resources to warehouse patients who might have been released before the time for their competency hearings arrives.

Little comfort can be taken from the fact that the district court's order allows forced medication in emergency situations; that is, when there is a substantial likelihood of physical harm to the patient or others.[9] First of all, absent an actual violent episode, the patient cannot be forcibly medicated because psychiatrists cannot otherwise predict when physical harm is likely to result. Second, in view of a possible suit for damages if his judgment is wrong, it can be expected that a psychiatrist will be especially reluctant to make such predictive assessments. Third, once the violence occurs, it is, unfortunately, often too late to treat with medication, and seclusion may be necessary. If medication is administered, it is used essentially as a restraint until the patient is calmed, at which point he presumably can refuse medication again.

In sum, *Rogers* is a case in which the use of forced medication was found to be in the best interests of the patients; indeed, it may have helped many for whom Boston State Hospital was the end of the treatment line. Yet the court strained to create a constitutional rule that replaced psychiatric discretion with a court hearing and a disinterested guardian. Presumably, the *Rogers* court believed that anyone but a psychiatrist could be trusted to act as a substitute decision-maker for committed patients.

This comparison of *Rennie* and *Rogers* should demonstrate to all parties concerned with the level of patient care the need to focus not only on the *existence* of a constitutional right to refuse treatment, but also on the *method of implementing that right if it indeed exists*. Although there are some difficulties with the independent peer review system imposed in *Rennie v. Klein*, it nonetheless is a system that allows for, and indeed depends on, medical discretion and flexibility. The competency hearing/ appointment of guardian approach implemented in *Rogers*, on the other hand, poses a serious threat to the quality of mental health care and treatment, especially if these court-imposed requirements deter competent physicians from seeking employment in state psychiatric hospitals.

NOTES

1. *Rennie v. Klein*, 462 F. Supp. 1131 (D.N.J. 1978); 476 F. Supp. 1294 (D.N.J. 1979).
2. *Rogers v. Okin*, 478 F. Supp. 1342 (D.Mass. 1979), *aff'd in part, rev'd in part, and vacated and remanded for further proceedings*, 634 F.2d 664 (1st Cir. 1980). These remarks were prepared and presented prior to issuance of the First Circuit's decision on November 25, 1980.
3. *Addington v. Texas*, 99 S.Ct. 1804, 1809 (1979).
4. *Rennie v. Klein*, 476 F. Supp. at 1306.

5. Certain aspects of the federal district court's decision in *Rogers v. Okin*, including the necessity of appointing a guardian, were modified by the United States Court of Appeals for the First Circuit. *See* Chapter 5, "Patients' Rights vs. Doctors' Rights: Which Should Take Precedence?" by Richard Cole, J.D.
6. *Parham v. JR*, 99 S.Ct. 2493 (1979).
7. *Id.* at 2506-2507, *quoting In re Roger S.*, 19 Cal. 3d 921, 941, 569 P.2d 1286, 1299 (1977) Clark, J., dissenting.
8. *Id.* at 2507.
9. *Rogers v. Okin*, 478 F. Supp. at 1371.

5

Patients' Rights vs. Doctors' Rights: Which Should Take Precedence?

Richard Cole, J.D.

The Boston State Hospital case has been highly criticized by certain members of the psychiatric profession. It is considered by some to be an unwarranted intrusion into the practice of medicine. The patients' attorneys, including myself, have been described as "naive," "unrealistic," and ignorant of the effects of medication and of the needs of hospitalized patients. Our position has been characterized by a number of doctors as "anti-drug." In addition, some doctors firmly believe that the establishment of the right to refuse treatment will be harmful to patients. One article declared that patients provided with the right to refuse will "rot with their rights on."[1]

I am aware that if you strongly oppose the district court's or court of appeals' decisions in the Boston State Hospital case, this presentation is not likely to change your opinion. However, I hope that those of you who have open minds will begin to reexamine your own and your colleagues' practices in light of the legal and medical principles raised by both sides in the Boston State Hospital case. Primarily, I will address the misperceptions some doctors have about the patients' position.

In April 1975, two attorneys, on behalf of seven named patients and the class of patients at Boston State Hospital, filed a lawsuit in the United States District Court in Massachusetts. The court was asked to prohibit the forced medication of both voluntarily admitted and involuntarily committed patients in nonemergency situations. An emergency was defined as the serious threat of, or an instance of, extreme violence, personal injury, or attempted suicide. The patients' position was that under Massachusetts law they were legally competent to refuse drugs, and that unless specifically adjudicated incompetent by a court, they had a legal right to refuse treatment. Prior to the Massachusetts Supreme Judicial Court's decision in *In the Matter of Guardianship of Richard Roe III*,[2] if a patient was declared incompetent by a court, under

Massachusetts law a guardian had to be appointed who would then decide on behalf of the patient if the patient must accept or might refuse the drugs. Since *Roe*, Massachusetts law requires prior court approval before an incompetent person may be treated with antipsychotic drugs.

The patients focused on the use of antipsychotic drugs for two reasons. First, these medications were the most commonly used and, in the patients' opinion, the most abused drugs at Boston State Hospital and elsewhere. Second, when these drugs are ingested they can cause serious, painful, and at times permanent side effects, which the patients believe are too often minimized by their doctors.

Is Forced Medication in the Patients' Best Interest?

Many psychiatrists agree that the first step in the therapy of the patient is to persuade the patient to participate in and cooperate with the individualized treatment plan. These same doctors, however, assert that if the patient persists in refusing treatment, then that refusal should be ignored. The amicus curiae brief of the Massachusetts Psychiatric Society in *Rogers v. Okin* describes the view of some psychiatrists concerning the informed consent doctrine in mental institutions:

> Hospitals have not merely a right, but a judicially recognized duty, to provide involuntary patients with treatment, including forcibly administered medication, when such is considered appropriate in a competent doctor's best judgment.

Will Antipsychotic Drugs Be Beneficial or Detrimental?

Psychiatrists have long recognized that administration of antipsychotic drugs has specific pharmacological effects on the physiology of patients. There are numerous "nonspecific" factors, however, which determine whether such administration will be beneficial or detrimental to a patient. These include the race, age, and sex of the patient; the intellectual, emotional, and psychodynamic aspects of the patient's personality; and the patient's ego defense structure and attitudes and expectations about treatment, the treating staff, and the therapeutic setting.[3]

This has led one noted psychiatrist to state:

> Psychotropic medications, given in adequate dosage, have clinically observable, specific, pharmacologic profiles, but are therapeutically non-specific. The therapeutic effects depend on the patient's psychodynamic constellations

and factors including the patient's personal situation, the physiologic effects of the drug, the relationship with the physician, transference and countertransference, the total milieu, etc.[4]

The interaction of all these variables, particularly the patient's subjective reaction to the medication, determine whether or not the pharmacologic effect of the drug will cause improvement in the patient's mental condition. As Dr. Sarwer-Foner has noted:

> The patient may be visualized consciously and unconsciously reviewing his situation and all that is done to him in the following terms: "What is this doing to me?" "Am I in the doctor's power?" "If I am, is this good or bad?" "Is this helping me?" "Why is this being done to me?" "Is this for the doctor's or the institution's benefit, or for mine?" "Do the doctors, the nurses, the occupational therapists, etc., really care about me?" "Are they really interested in me?" "Are the staff my friends or my enemies at any one moment?"[5]

Drugs produce an internal alteration which the patient has to accommodate and comprehend. If the patient perceives the drug therapy as a helping tool in controlling impulses that threaten to overwhelm him, the patient will integrate the pharmacologic change caused by the drug into his egostructure, thereby improving his mental condition.

On the other hand, if the patient perceives the drug as destructive and malignant, the pharmacologic effect will cause a reaction which is antitherapeutic, worsening the patient's mental state:

> Conversely, I have reported dramatic worsening of the patient, including development of panic reactions, marked anxiety, further psychotic disorganization in those already psychotic, body image changes, increased agitation, and development of anxiety as a result of drug administration. These adverse reactions result from the physiologic effects of the drug being interpreted by the patient to mean that he has been made a less adequate human being, having lost something to the action of the drug.[6]

IS A THERAPEUTIC ALLIANCE ESSENTIAL?

The concept of the "therapeutic alliance" is central to the treatment of emotionally disturbed or psychiatrically disabled patients. The essence of the therapeutic alliance is a trusting relationship in which there is two-way communication between the therapist and patient. This alliance must be established and maintained in order to achieve behavioral and emotional change in the patient.

The coercive use of antipsychotic medication is antithetical to psychiatric treatment and hinders or destroys the establishment or maintenance of a therapeutic alliance. Many psychiatrists agree that a basic principle of psychiatric training and practice is that a patient should not be involuntarily medicated in nonemergency situations.

The psychiatric residents, who had primary treatment responsibility on the wards of Boston State Hospital, testified at trial in *Rogers v. Okin*[7] that it was their practice to respect a patient's refusal in nonemergencies. The testimony of most of the expert witnesses about the respecting of and the abiding by a competent mental patient's wishes concerning medication, led the court to conclude that the practice would not undermine the ethical integrity of the profession.[8] One of the defendant's expert witnesses testified that because of the district court's order issued in 1975, psychiatric practice had changed statewide with beneficial results.[9]

The success of any antipsychotic drug in relieving mental distress substantially depends on the patient's attitude about the drug being administered. Consequently, the physician must take into account not only the pharmacological and therapeutic effects of the antipsychotic drug itself, but also the effect that the administration of the drug will have on the therapeutic alliance.

IS INVOLUNTARILY ADMINISTERED ANTIPSYCHOTIC MEDICATION COUNTERTHERAPEUTIC?

Involuntarily administered antipsychotic medication undercuts rather than fosters the patients' needs to control their behavior, to trust their own judgment, and to validate their own feelings. For example, to disregard patients' subjective complaints about the antipsychotic drugs they are receiving, or to ignore patients' requests to change their medication, serves only to reinforce the patients' feelings of incompetence. Patients' dependence upon the staff for decision making increases, often resulting in patient passivity. Furthermore, forcible medication is often demeaning and humiliating. Picture being forcibly restrained, having your pants removed, and being injected with antipsychotic drugs through a hypodermic needle in the buttocks, at times in full view of the other patients or staff of the opposite sex. This often causes patients to view medical personnel not only as unresponsive to their personal needs, but also as persons who actually create distress. As the district court found:

> Given a non-emergency ... it is an unreasonable invasion of privacy, and an affront to basic concepts of human dignity, to permit forced injection of a mind-altering drug into the buttocks of a competent patient unwilling to give informed consent.[10]

IS THE RIGHT TO CONSENT OR REFUSE ANTIPSYCHOTIC MEDICATION THERAPEUTIC?

For patients to return successfully to the communtiy, they must reattain their self-respect and independence. It is therapeutically essential for hospitalized patients to be allowed and encouraged to make decisions about their own treatment, as well as other important decisions in their lives. During institutional care, many patients become infantilized by a pervasive staff attitude that patients are unable to make their own decisions. When translated into how the staff relates to patients, this attitude reinforces patients' own sense of incompetence, dependence, and lack of self-respect.

Although the Boston State Hospital case has been characterized by some commentators as being "anti-drug," this position unfairly and inaccurately depicts the patients' position. The patients agree that drugs, used consensually and consistently with recent medical advances, can be and are effective in treating patients.[11] However, substantial evidence was also introduced, through expert witnesses at trial and through articles in the medical literature, that these drugs are often overused and their efficacy is exaggerated.[12]

Although substantial evidence of the high risks and of the effectiveness of antipsychotic drugs was introduced at trial, the real focus of the case was the right of patients to decide for themselves whether the risks outweigh the benefits of drug treatment. As indicated by the evidence presented at trial and by the district court's findings, when patients were provided the right to refuse and when doctors were required to seek the cooperation of patients, most patients agreed to submit to some form of medication, although not necessarily the medication that the doctor had originally prescribed.[13] What changed was that the court order required the doctors to listen to and respond to patients' complaints about the pain and discomfort caused by the medication.

An example of this change in practice was typified by the treatment of plaintiff R.R., a 39-year-old patient diagnosed as chronic schizophrenic, who had a lengthy history of hospitalization. R.R. received Haldol, against her express wishes, for two years. R.R. was informed that if she refused oral administration of the drug, she would be confined in seclusion and injected with Haldol, although she complained that the drug caused her severe physical pain and discomfort. Her medical records indicate that she was subjected to serious drug-induced motor restlessness, shakes, stiffness, fatigue, nausea, and at times immobility. The medical staff failed to respond to her complaints and requests to change her medication until the issuance of the district court's order in April, 1975. As a result of the staff's unresponsiveness, R.R. not only distrusted and feared them, but felt that they were actually causing her distress. After the court issued its order, R.R.'s refusal of Haldol was respected. When approached as a full participant in her treatment, R.R. voluntarily agreed to take a new drug, Moban, as long as it did not cause the painful or discomforting effects she experienced with Haldol. This transformation of the hospital into an environment fostering discourse rather than force in treatment, with resulting positive effects, "speaks well for the confidence in a doctor's judgment that may be established given the effort to establish a strong therapeutic alliance," as Judge Tauro stated.[14]

DO PATIENTS REFUSE DRUGS FOR RATIONAL REASONS?

Another argument articulated by the defendant doctors in *Rogers v. Okin* was simply that patients' refusals should not be respected because they are based on irrational reasons and are symptoms of their mental illnesses.[15] However, this position was unsupported at trial, where evidence was presented that many patients refuse for rational reasons.[16] First, the court heard testimony from the patients themselves, who stated their reasons for refusing. Second, expert witnesses testifying on behalf of both the patients and the doctors, and articles written by medical experts rebutted the contention of irrational refusal. The evidence attributed drug refusal to various rational reasons, including patients' finding extrapyramidal symptoms unbearable, or reacting adversely to the sedative effects of the drugs. Other patients experience dysphoric responses to the neuroleptic drugs: feelings of psychological distress and discomfort; feeling drugged, drowsy, tired or slow; or having no drive or ambition. Some patients view the drugs as an external dominating agent and resist them because they desire to be in complete control of their lives. Sarwer-Foner, a pioneer in exploring the dynamic aspects of drug response, has emphasized that the sedative, extrapyramidal, or other physiologic effects of antipsychotic drugs can precipitate panic reactions, further psychotic deterioration, and increase somatization.[17] Finally, some patients refuse antipsychotic drugs because of the realization of the serious long-term risks of the drugs, such as tardive dyskinesia.

ARE DOCTORS OR GUARDIANS BETTER ABLE
TO SERVE THE PATIENT'S INTEREST?

Clearly, some patients refuse drugs for irrational reasons. If that occurs in a nonemergency, the patients argued, the doctors should seek the appointment of guardians to make substituted judgments on behalf of these patients. The doctors asserted, however, that they can better serve the individual patient than can guardians, whose loyalty must as a matter of law be undivided. In fact, one ground for removal of a guardian is the existence of an interest in conflict with his or her duty to the ward.[18] The defendants virtually conceded an inherent conflict of interest: "A guardian cannot be allowed to refuse medication for one patient when the result of that refusal is increased violence and tension affecting all patients."[19] The patients did not question the doctor's obligation to protect all of the patients on the ward, even if it means sacrificing the interests of one patient, as long as there is an emergency. Because of this conflict in responsibility, however, a doctor cannot be expected to monitor the treatment of the individual patient in the same way that the guardian is obligated to do under the law. Not only is the doctor's loyalty to a patient diminishd by the competing concern for the entire ward, but the loyalty is also reduced by staff pressures to maintain "peace and tranquility."

For example, one defendant testified that when he began his psychiatric residency on the May Unit on January 6, 1975, he questioned whether a patient should remain in seclusion. Some of the staff demanded and "threatened" that the doctor keep the patient in seclusion.[20] The doctor acceded to staff pressure and, the district court found, continued to so confine the patient illegally for another 17 days.[21]

The inability of doctors to resist staff pressure is even more acute when the doctors who make the medication decisions are inexperienced and have had little training in dealing with the substantial pressure from the staff to keep patients "manageable and tranquil." For example, in the Austin Unit, it was the psychiatric residents, not the supervising psychiatrist, who made the medication decisions, including the decision of whether a patient should be forcibly medicated. The residents, just graduated from medical school, were immediately given total responsibility for medicating patients. In addition, their supervision was only marginally adequate. One supervisor/psychiatrist in the Austin Unit testified that he supervised the residents for only an hour to an hour-and-a-half per week, or approximately two minutes per patient.[22] This is the environment in which the defendants requested the power to medicate forcibly in nonemergencies and the power to act with virtually unbridled discretion as the patients' guardians.

Another reason that independent guardians are needed is because some doctors are disciples of certain schools of psychiatric practice that believe in one particular treatment to the exclusion of all others.[23] Independent guardians are essential to protect the patients' interest by insuring that all treatment alternatives are considered. Otherwise, patients may be subjected to a particular treatment because a particular doctor is committed to it, not because it is appropriate for the individual patient.

Was Forced Medication Supported by the Literature and Based on Fact?

Is there any scientific basis for the psychiatric claim of the proven therapeutic value of involuntarily medicating patients in nonemergencies? No expert who testified at the trial or with whom I consulted could cite any study in the medical literature which used a nonconsenting patient population as subjects. Furthermore, no expert could cite any study which attempted to determine the short- or long-term efficacy of antipsychotic drugs on mental patients who are involuntarily medicated in nonemergencies, or the effectiveness of drugs in assisting these patients to successfully reintegrate into the community.

Since the studies upon which the medical community relies to demonstrate the efficacy of antipsychotic drugs did not use nonconsenting participants, it must be seriously questioned whether their results can be applied to patients who have been medicated involuntarily.[24] The need to distinguish between consenting and nonconsenting patient populations is especially important in view of the fact that nonspecific factors play a crucial role in the success or failure of drug treatment. The therapeutic importance of voluntariness has been recognized judicially.

The District Court in *Rogers v. Okin*, when addressing the right of patients to refuse antipsychotic drugs, stated:

> [A] fundamental concept for treating the mentally ill is the establishment of a therapeutic alliance between psychiatrist and patient. Implicit in such an alliance is an understanding and acceptance by the patient of a prescribed treatment program.[25]

This is consistent with Chief Justice Burger's statement in his concurrence to the opinion of the United States Supreme Court in *O'Connor v. Donaldson*:

> [I]t is universally recognized as fundamental to effective therapy that the patient acknowledge his illness and cooperate with those attempting to give treatment; yet the failure of a large proportion of mentally ill persons to do so is a common phenomenon.[26]

The impact of involuntary medication on the success of therapy was also addressed in *Rennie v. Klein*. Following the testimony of a number of national psychiatric experts, the District Court for New Jersey stated that:

> [A] trusting relationship or therapeutic alliance between psychiatrist and patient is essential for a drug regimen to succeed. Plaintiff has demonstrated that psychotropic drugs are less efficacious in a hostile or negative environment. As a corollary to this, even if the best drug is prescribed, if the patient is unwilling to accept it, the positive effects are greatly lessened, especially in terms of long range benefits.[27]

Did the Court's Order Cause Chaos, Violence, and Deterioration?

Some psychiatrists believe that the district court's temporary restraining order (TRO), issued in April 1975, created institutional chaos, caused a substantial increase of violence at Boston State Hospital, and the serious physical and mental deterioration of numerous patients. These claims were made by the hospital's two unit directors during the course of the lawsuit. The allegations were later publicized in certain prestigious medical publications and by psychiatrists who were not connected with Boston State Hospital.

At first, these allegations caused the patients' attorneys great concern. Were we in fact causing havoc and seriously harming patients by asserting patients' legal rights? Although inconsistent with the reports from our staff and patient contacts at Boston State Hospital, we agreed that these claims required further investigation. We were unsure initially of how to determine whether the claims were valid. The unit directors must have recognized that their allegations, if true, would have dramatic impact on the lawsuit. Yet they felt it unnecessary to base their conclusions on anything but what they described as their own "clinical impressions."

After discussions with expert consultants, we decided to adopt a "medical model" approach. Any medical study requires the use of the scientific method. The patients' attorneys also pointed out that conclusions based upon the impressions of biased observers would be considered by most medical experts and journals to lack scientific validity. Certainly, scientific method should not be discarded merely because members of the profession believe that forced medication of patients is not a substantial intrusion into their minds and bodies, or does not create a high risk of painful side effects and permanent harm.

Measured by the standards of the scientific method, the defendants' allegations are clearly invalid. The defendants admitted that they were strongly opposed to the court's order and wanted it dissolved. They realized that strong evidence of its adverse impact would be necessary either to convince the court to dissolve its order, or to have the order overturned on appeal. These doctors filed affidavits and testified that it was their belief that violence and deterioration on the part of patients on their wards were caused by the court's order. Yet, the unit directors admitted that they did not control any of the other variables which may have caused the alleged changes in patients' behavior or mental states. They also admitted that they did not use a data base from which they made comparisons of behavior and mental status, nor did they document the behavioral or mental status changes that they alleged occurred after the court order was issued. One unit director simply declared that he did not believe in "quantification." In addition, though admitting that their conclusions amounted to a study of the effects of the court's order, the unit directors felt it unnecessary to use the "double blind" method to control the variable to be studied and to eliminate other variables, including experimenter bias.

In fact, during cross-examination one of the unit directors admitted that there were a number of variables to consider in determining the cause of patients' violence or deterioration occurring after the court's order. This doctor agreed that without controlling the variables, one could not reasonably determine whether it was the court's order that caused any given change in a patient's behavior or mental status. He also agreed that one would have to study patients' behavior for a long period of time to determine the cause of any change in their behavior.[28]

From the evidence, it was clear that at least two factors may have had a dramatic impact on patients' behavior after the court's order was issued. First, mental health workers and nurses at Boston State were involved in a statewide strike over a contract dispute during the early period that the court's order was in effect. Second, because of large funding cuts by the governor in 1975 and 1976, there was a statewide freeze on hiring that resulted in severe staff shortages in at least one of the two units involved in the Boston State Hospital case.

As a Result of the Order, Did Many Patients Refuse Drugs for Prolonged Periods?

Another part of the misinformation concerning the Boston State Hospital case was the claim that many patients refused drugs for prolonged periods after the court's order was issued. When the defendants were asked prior to trial to document this "fact," they were able to document only 20 out of 1,000 patients over a two-year period who refused their drugs for a prolonged period after the court's initial order.[29] One of the two unit directors testified that:

> Right after the TRO, a great many patients began refusing the medication, testing their right to do so, some of them to a great disadvantage. Most patients would do this more than they had before, but eventually when they found out from the staff, yes, you don't have to take your medication, if you don't want, the next day they would. However, there were [sic] a core of patients who decided to stay off the medication.[30]

This defendant testified that eight patients out of the approximately 1,200 to 1,600 patients in his unit were the core of patients who refused drugs for a prolonged period.[31] However, at the trial one of the other unit directors claimed that in fact 89 patients from the unit had deteriorated because of their refusal to take antipsychotic drugs.[32] Although a search of all the records was impossible, given the number and size of the records, a summary of some of these records was introduced to the court, and was considered as evidence by the court. These records in no way supported the defendant's testimony and in many cases directly contradicted it.[33]

Therefore, it was not surprising that this defendant's testimony was given little weight by the court:

> Also to be borne in mind is that the great majority of patients have not declined their psychotropic medication during the pendancy of the TRO. Most of those who did changed their mind within a few days. This speaks well for the confidence in a doctor's judgment that may be established given the effort to establish a strong therapeutic alliance.[34]

Did the Order Cause an Adversary Relationship between Staff and Patients?

Another serious allegation was that providing patients the right to refuse medication at Boston State created an adversarial relationship between staff and patients, making treatment impossible. However, the evidence demonstrated that only when the order initially went into effect was the treatment relationship affected by the order. During this "adjustment period," there was an alteration in the power relationship between the doctors and patients. One of the unit directors said:

> There seemed to be an adversary relationship set up between the patients and staff by the TRO, by the suit. Staff were afraid to intervene with the patients for fear that the patients might take this to mean that they are trampling on their rights, the rights of patients. Again, these situations quieted down in time.[35]

In fact, the unit director admitted that most of the deleterious effects caused in his unit, allegedly by the TRO, were caused by the defendants' own conduct.[36] It was admitted that the defendants failed to read the court's order until a week after it was issued, and that the staff panicked because it misinterpreted the court's order as a prohibition from medicating or secluding in all circumstances. As the unit director declared: "Once this was clarified, things calmed down in that respect somewhat."[37]

Are There Important Societal Issues in Right to Refuse Cases?

Some doctors believe that the only issue in patients' drug refusals is whether it is better medical practice to forcibly medicate patients than to respect their refusal. Such doctors believe that they should have the power to medicate forcibly, without lawyers and courts being involved. Although I have already addressed at length the issue of whether or not it is in fact good medical practice to medicate patients forcibly, I now wish to discuss the larger societal issues involved.

Patients' Rights vs. Doctors' Rights

The "right to refuse" doctrine must be considered in light of the constitutional and common law principles which serve as the fundamental basis of our political system. It is a system, however imperfect, of limits and checks on the power of state officials and state institutions over persons. This system has developed and embodied the "right to be left alone"—a value forcefully enunciated by Justice Brandeis in his seminal dissent in *Olmstead v. United States*:

> The makers of our Constitution undertook to secure conditions favorable to the pursuit of happiness. They recognized the significance of man's spiritual nature, of his feelings and of his intellect. They knew that only a part of the pain, pleasure and satisfactions of life are to be found in material things. They sought to protect Americans in their beliefs, their thoughts, their emotions, and their sensations. They conferred, as against the Government, the right to be let alone—the most comprehensive of rights and the right most valued by civilized men.[38]

Justice Burger, elaborating on Justice Brandeis' "right to be let alone" philosophy, has stated that:

> Nothing in this utterance suggests that Justice Brandeis thought an individual possessed these rights only as to *sensible* beliefs, *valid* thoughts, *reasonable* emotions, or *well founded* sensations. I suggest that he intended to include a great many foolish, unreasonable and even absurd ideas which do not conform, such as refusing medical treatment even at great risk.[39]

One of the ways in which this philosophy has found its development is through the informed consent doctrine.

> The very foundation of the doctrine on informed consent is every man's right to forego treatment or even cure if it entails what for him are intolerable consequences or risks, however warped or perverted his sense of values may be in the eyes of the medical profession, or even of the community so long as any distortion falls short of what the law regards as incompetency. Individual freedom here is guaranteed only if people are given the right to make choices which would generally be regarded as foolish.[40]

There has been a traditional tension between medical doctors who believe that it is their moral responsibility to treat patients whom they believe are ill and those asserting the fundamental constitutional and common law rights of individuals to make their own decisions. Medical doctors have come, in general, to accept their role as expert advisors to their patients, providing diagnosis and prognosis and recommending the course of treatment. Most doctors would not consider coercion as a legitimate treatment technique for their medical or private psychiatric patients. It is assumed that if a medical or noninstitutional mental patient rejects the recommended course of treatment, the law protects that patient's decision, no matter how unwise, so long as the refusal is not what the law considers incompetent.

> A medical doctor, being the expert, appreciates the risks inherent in the procedure he is prescribing, the risks of a decision not to undergo a treatment, and the probability of a successful outcome of the treatment. But once this information has been disclosed, that aspect of the doctor's expert function has been performed. The weighing of these risks against the individual subjective fears and hopes of the patient is not an expert skill. Such evaluation and decision is a nonmedical judgment reserved to the patient alone.[41]

However, some psychiatrists seek a power which other medical doctors do not have. Because these doctors view mental patients as different from medical patients, they do not accept the limited role of advisor to the patient, but seek the power to make decisions for the patient. There is tension between these doctors' belief in their right and duty to treat and society's interest in the liberty of its citizens.

Is there a factual basis for the distinction between the treatment of medical patients and the treatment of hospitalized psychiatric patients? One should first recognize that many patients who are physically ill have limitations in their mental competency. For example, in a case of a 77 year old woman suffering from gangrene, who refused to consent to the amputation of her leg, the Massachusetts Appeals Court affirmed her right to refuse to submit to this treatment, even though this decision would lead to her death. The court stated that the law protects the right to make decisions to accept or reject treatment, whether the decision is wise or unwise. The court stated that even though one doctor said that this woman could not make a "rational choice," this was not sufficient to prove incompetency in the legal sense, even though

> [h]er testimony ... showed that she is lucid on some matters and confused on others. Her train of thought sometimes wanders. Her conception of time is distorted. She is hostile to certain doctors. She is on occasion defensive and sometimes combative in her responses to questioning.[42]

The position that psychiatric patients, whether institutionalized or in the community, are unable to make competent treatment decisions has been rejected with virtual unanimity by both the medical profession and the courts. Under the law of many states, even psychotic patients are not considered incompetent *per se*. Many patients are incompetent only in limited areas which do not necessarily affect their ability to make treatment decisions. Of course, some patients who refuse drugs may continue to suffer. But that is true of patients who are suffering from physical ailments as well as of patients who are suffering from psychiatric ailments. As the Supreme Judicial Court of Massachusetts declared:

> The constitutional right to privacy, as we conceive it, is an expression of the sanctity of individual free choice and self-determination as fundamental constituents of life. The value of life as so perceived is lessened not by a decision to refuse treatment, but by the failure to allow a competent human being the right of choice.[43]

It has also been stated by some members of the psychiatric profession that any discussion of infringement of First Amendment rights is totally irrelevant in discussing the use of antipsychotic medication. They state that drugs enhance the capacity to think, and liberate the mind by freeing it from mental illness. They assert that any discussion of First Amendment violations in the context of "right to refuse" cases is totally inappropriate. However, the doctors and lawyers who argue this fail to understand the true thrust of the First Amendment. Assume for the sake of argument that antipsychotic drugs only alter thought processes, mood, personality, and behavior in a clinically desirable therapeutic direction. The question presented to the courts would still be whether the state has the right to alter a patient's thought processes.

If the First Amendment protects the communication of ideas, then it certainly protects the privacy of mental acts of patients, even though those thoughts may not be as competent as yours or mine. To permit doctors to determine whether or not to alter a legally competent patient's thoughts and emotions, even in a therapeutic direction, would set an extremely dangerous precedent. A recent Massachusetts case is a shocking example of how far the rationale for the power to treat forcibly may be extended. In the case of a 21 year old man living at home with his family and diagnosed as psychotic, the court authorized his forced treatment (although the man had been steadfast in his opposition to taking drugs for at least three years) based on the justification that:

> *Each state has a vital interest in seeing that its residents function at the maximum level of their capacity.* The interest of the state in this regard outweighs the right of the individual to remain free from the possible side effects of antipsychotic drugs. The individual in the circumstances of this case does not have a constitutional right to remain in the twilight zone of mental illness.[44]

However, the nonconsensual use of antipsychotic drugs raises an even more dangerous precedent and a more fundamental First Amendment issue. Antipsychotic medication, especially in higher dosages, has the capacity not only to alter the thought processes but to immobilize both body and mind. Many patients taking these drugs complain of feeling "like a zombie," dulled, slow. Some doctors may reject these complaints as merely a subjective, irrational, or insignificant response on the part of patients. But too many patients complain about this reaction to the drugs for this response to be discounted. In addition, the literature clearly supports the fact that antipsychotic medication causes in some patients a decrease in perception, cognition, speed of response, organization, and problem-solving ability. In addition, for some patients, medication contributes to institutionalization by reducing drive, initiative, and planning ability, as well as by causing patients to be more passive.[45] Furthermore, antipsychotic drugs may also cause adverse reactions similar to some of the symptoms of psychosis, called "paradoxical reactions." As a result, the District Court in *Rogers v. Okin* found that "[i]t is clear from the evidence in this case that psychotropic medication has the potential to affect and change a patient's mood, attitude and capacity to think,"[46] and that these drugs are powerful enough to immobilize both the body and mind.[47]

Speaking and communication require the thought processes, and it is these which must be protected by the First Amendment. The privacy of mental acts has intrinsic value in our society, and is considered to be a foundation of democratic institutions. If the First Amendment does not protect legally competent patients from drugs with the capacity to immobilize or slow thought processes, then the First Amendment becomes meaningless.

Right to refuse cases should not be seen as a new area of societal conflict between doctor and lawyer, but should be recognized as part of the prolonged and sometimes bitter political disagreement over the extent of power that institutions in our society should have over persons. Although many doctors do not consider themselves state officials, doctors working in institutions should recognize that their power and authority to admit, commit, or treat patients is derived solely from the law. Without statutory or judicial authority, patients could not be hospitalized and have their freedom revoked. Part of my responsibility as a civil rights lawyer is to scrutinize the ramifications of permitting a particular segment of our society to have powers that other segments of our society do not have. Lawyers are concerned with precedents, and the effect that one decision will have on future decisions. The struggle between patients' rights and doctors' beliefs in their own rights is not different from other struggles involving state power versus individual liberty. Seen in this light, the role of the lawyer in right to refuse treatment cases becomes more understandable.

As one court has stated:

> The individual who is the subject of a medical decision must have the final say and that must necessarily be so in a system of government which gives the greatest possible protection to the individual in the furtherance of his own desires.[48]

Even with judicial recognition of the right of patients to refuse antipsychotic medication, there is no guarantee that this right will be respected by all members of the psychiatric community. As long as some psychiatrists are convinced that this right is antithetical to good medical practice, violations of the right will be commonplace. Patients' right to refuse and right to participate in their treatment will not be fully guaranteed until psychiatric attitudes towards those rights change. I hope that this presentation will be one step in that direction.

NOTES

1. *See, e.g.*, Gutheil, T.G. and Appelbaum, P.S., *The Patient Always Pays: Some Reflections on the Boston State Case and the Right to Rot*, MAN AND MEDICINE 5(1):3-11 (1980).
2. *In re Guardianship of Richard Roe III*, 421 N.E.2d 40 (Mass. 1981). The plaintiff-patients in the Boston State Hospital case intervened as parties in *Roe* and argued in support of prior judicial approval before an incompetent patient could be forcibly treated with antipsychotic drugs.
3. *See*, Sarwer-Foner, G.J., *Psychodynamics of Psychotropic Medication—An Overview*. In A. Dimascio and R. Shader, eds., CLINICAL HANDBOOK OF PSYCHOPHARMACOLOGY (Science House, New York) (1970) [hereinafter cited as Sarwer-Foner, *Psychodynamics*]; Fisher, S., *Non-Specific Factors as Determinants of Behavioral Response to Drugs*, CLINICAL HANDBOOK OF PSYCHOPHARMACOLOGY, *supra*.
4. Sarwer-Foner, *Psychodynamics, supra* note 3, at 168.
5. *Id.* at 169.
6. *Id.* at 171. *See also* the important experimental work of DiMascio, A. and Klerman, G.L., *Experimental Human Psychopharmacology*. In G. J. Sarwer-Foner, ed., THE DYNAMICS OF PSYCHIATRIC DRUG THERAPY (Charles C. Thomas, Springfield, Ill.) (1960); DiMascio, A. and Rankel, M., *Prediction of Clinical Effectiveness of Psychopharmacology Agents from "Drug Action Profiles" in Normal Human Subjects*. In J. Wortis, ed., RECENT ADVANCES IN BIOLOGICAL PSYCHIATRY (Grune & Stratton, New York) (1960).
7. *See Rogers v. Okin*, 478 F. Supp. 1342, 1370 (D.Mass. 1979), 634 F.2d 650 (1st Cir. 1980). *See also* Sovner, *et al.*, *Tardive Dyskinesia and Informed Consent*, PSYCHOSOMATICS 19(3):173-77 (March 1978) (it was only some of the supervisory psychiatrists, who had virtually no primary treatment responsibility at the hospital, who testified that they could not practice medicine at the hospital if patients were provided the right to refuse in nonemergencies).
8. *Rogers v. Okin*, 478 F. Supp. 1342, 1370 (D.Mass. 1979).
9. Transcript of Record, at 63-71, *Rogers v. Okin, supra* note 8.
10. *Rogers v. Okin, supra* note 8, at 1369.
11. Transcript of Record, at 31-30, 47-51; 34-4, 7-8, 13-14, 19; 30-65-66, *Rogers v. Okin, supra* note 8.

12. See, e.g., Bockoven, J.S. and Solomon, H.C., *Comparison of Two Five-Year Follow-Up Studies: 1947 to 1952 and 1967 to 1972*, AMERICAN JOURNAL OF PSYCHIATRY 132(8):796–808 (August 1975); Carpenter, Jr., W.T. et al., *Treatment of Acute Schizophrenia Without Drugs: An Investigation of Current Assumptions*, AMERICAN JOURNAL OF PSYCHIATRY 134(1):14–20 (January 1977); Crane, G., *Clinical Psychopharmacology in its 20th Year*, SCIENCE 181:124 (July 1973); PRIEN, SYMPOSIUM: ACTIVE TREATMENT OF CHRONIC SCHIZOPHRENIA (United States Government Printing Office, Washington, D.C.) (1974). See also the court's findings in *Rennie v. Klein*, 462 F. Supp. 1131 (D.N.J. 1978), 478 F. Supp. 1294 (D.N.J. 1979), 481 F. Supp. 552 (D.N.J. 1979), which starkly demonstrates how some doctors disregard the standards of practice articulated in the medical literature.
13. *Rogers v. Okin, supra* note 8, at 1369–70.
14. *Id.* at 1370.
15. *See Id.* at 1361.
16. Transcript of Record, at 6-13-14, 28-8-16, 33-99; Exhibit 31; 38-45-47; 58-96, *Rogers v. Okin supra* note 8.
17. See, e.g., Van Putten, T., *Why Do Schizophrenic Patients Refuse to Take Their Drugs?* ARCHIVES OF GENERAL PSYCHIATRY 31(1):67–73 (January 1974); Van Putten, T. et al., *Drug Refusal in Schizophrenia and the Wish to Be Crazy*, ARCHIVES OF GENERAL PSYCHIATRY 33(12):1443–46 (December 1976); Van Putten, T. and May, P. R., *Subjective Response as a Predictor of Outcome in Pharmacotherapy: The Consumer Has a Point*, ARCHIVES OF GENERAL PSYCHIATRY 35(4):447–80 (April 1978).
18. *Introductory Commentary*, Mass. Gen. Laws Ann., ch. 201, at p. 11.
19. Brief for Defendants at 59, *Rogers v. Okin, supra* note 8.
20. Transcript of Record at 20–22, 24–61, *Rogers v. Okin, supra* note 8.
21. *Rogers v. Okin, supra* note 8, at 1376–77.
22. Transcript of Record at 11-27-28, 11-54-55, 3-28-30, *Rogers v. Okin, supra* note 8.
23. *See, e.g., id.* at 34-2-3.
24. Tosti, D. et al., *The Concerns of Statistics*, INDIVIDUAL LEARNING SYSTEMS (Beginning Systems, Inc., San Rafael, Calif.) (1971).
25. *Rogers v. Okin, supra* note 8, at 1361.
26. *O'Connor v. Donaldson*, 422 U.S. 563, 584 (1975).
27. *Rennie v. Klein*, 462 F. Supp. 1131, 1141 (D.N.J. 1978) (citations omitted).
28. Transcript of Record, at 58-104-106, *Rogers v. Okin, supra* note 8.
29. *Rogers v. Okin, supra* note 8, at 1369.
30. Transcript of Record, at 48-32-33, *Rogers v. Okin, supra* note 8.
31. *Id.* at 58-88-89.
32. *Id.* at 66–70, 68-33.
33. *Id.* at 68-31-51.
34. *Rogers v. Okin, supra* note 8, at 1370.
35. Transcript of Record at 58-33, *Rogers v. Okin, supra* note 8.
36. *Id.* at 58-32-33.
37. *Id.*
38. *Olmstead v. United States*, 277 U.S. 438, 478 (1928).

39. *In re Application of President and Directors of Georgetown College,* 331 F.2d 1010, 1017 (D.C. Cir. 1964).
40. 2 HARPER and JAMES, THE LAW OF TORTS 61 (1968 Supp.)
41. *Cobbs v. Grant,* 502 P.2d 1, 10 (Cal. 1972).
42. *Lane v. Candura,* 376 N.E.2d 1232, 1234–35 (Mass. App. 1978).
43. *Superintendent of Belchertown State School v. Saikewicz,* 370 N.E.2d 417, 426 (Mass. 1977).
44. *In re Guardianship of Norman Loring III,* No. 50205 (Mass. Prob. & Fam. Ct., Franklin County, August 13, 1980), *aff'd in part and rev'd in part sub nom. In re Guardianship of Richard Roe III,* 421 N.E.2d. 40 (Mass. 1981).
45. *See, e.g.,* DiMascio, A. *et al., Behavioral Toxicity of Psychotropic Drugs, III: Effects on Perceptual and Causative Functions; IV: Effects on Mood States,* CONNECTICUT MEDICINE 32(8):617–20 (August 1968); Van Putten, T., *Drug Refusal and the Wish to Be Crazy, supra* note 17.
46. *Rogers v. Okin, supra* note 8, at 1366.
47. *Id.* at 1378. *See* discussion of plaintiff Bybel, n.49.
48. *Erikson v. Dilgard,* 252 N.Y.S.2d 705, 706 (N.Y. 1962).

Discussion

William J. Curran, J.D., LL.M., S.M.Hyg., Moderator

WILLIAM J. CURRAN (Moderator): The great emphasis is on whether or not there is a right to refuse treatment, and the primary focus is the consenting party himself: is there or is there not a right to consent? Yet if we can encourage dialogue, participation, and decision making involving different views and more than one party, then there can be only improvement. A refusal to cooperate is only one way that a patient can participate in his or her treatment, and such a refusal is not always a manifestation of the patient's illness. It may, in fact, be a useful contribution to successful treatment. One hopes that successful treatment can be designed without a black-and-white decision of whether the patient's rights or the doctor's rights are paramount. I think both parties would lose in such a bold decision.

RAY BILODEAU (Western New England College School of Law, Developmental Disabilities Law Clinic, Springfield, Massachusetts): I'm rather amazed at Professor Curran's statement. I was not aware that the lawyers on the panel had any disagreement about the right to refuse treatment. The question is whether a person is incompetent, and then whether he has the right to refuse treatment. I'm not aware of any disagreement whatsoever about a competent person; the questions are what constitutes incompetency, and under what conditions can you medicate forcibly? In *Parham* there is de facto a guardian, or a parent or parents, and the Supreme Court is not saying you don't need a competent person to make those decisions. The Court in *Parham* is really saying that there is a parent who has a legal responsibility and a long history of being entrusted with the care of a child, and that the court should not second guess the parent. This, to me, leads to the inevitable conclusion that the Supreme Court will say in *Rennie* and in *Rogers,* "That's right, you need someone who is competent to make decisions as a legal matter."

Discussion

DR. THOMAS G. GUTHEIL (Conference Faculty): Attorney Cole, wouldn't you agree that in the medical situations you describe, the difference in some ways is not commitability, but what you might call, for want of a better word, dischargeability? The medical patient who refuses, let's say, a cardiac bypass operation may in fact be sent home because he or she is not going along with the prescribed treatment. The doctor in some sense has no more obligation to treat the patient. I felt that your presentation did not address the ways that the doctors might be affected at a place like Boston State, by still having an obligation to care for people and yet not being allowed to use one of their several treatments.

MR. RICHARD COLE (Conference Faculty): If voluntary patients refuse all forms of treatment and they are not commitable, the hospital obviously has the right to discharge them. The parties in the Boston State Hospital case agreed on that. In terms of an involuntary patient, you have to remember that he or she has not decided to go to the institution in the first place. The state has decided society's needs require that person to be hospitalized. If after commitment a patient refuses treatment, then in terms of constitutional doctrine the state must care for that patient because it has decided to take away his or her liberty. On the other hand, the state can't take a further step and intrude into the patient's body and mind without a compelling interest.

Our position has been that if patients refuse all forms of treatment, the hospital may have to create some separate wards for custodial care. But the Boston State evidence is that very few patients refuse for any length of time once they're asked to participate in treatment decisions. I want to reinforce this point, because I think there is a great deal of fear about the right of patients to refuse treatment. Initially, a lot of patients did refuse, until they found that they could indeed exercise this right. But once there was some cooperation, very few patients refused for a prolonged period of time.

MR. CURRAN: Would you say that the person who is put into a custodial ward would have to be dangerous as well?

MR. COLE: I wouldn't limit the criteria for custodial care to dangerousness. I think custodial care would apply also to patients who might be causing a substantially adverse impact on the treatment of other patients. We need to consider what real treatments are available in a state hospital besides the use of restraints and medication.

UNIDENTIFIED SPEAKER: I'd like to relate an experience that makes me seriously question the capacity of psychiatric professionals to decide whether or not a person's behavior is uncontrollable. I was in a rehabilitation center in a nursing home, the kind you hear horror stories about. I was seriously angry about something and I think rightfully so. I needed time and space by myself so I could cool off. Instead, this frustrated nurse provoked me, telling me that I ought to think her way, telling me that she thought I was in the wrong without explaining why or giving me a chance at it. I begged her to go away but she didn't, and I finally just blew up. I thought I'd never see the day when I'd actually smash a window, but when people are constantly harrassing you, telling you you're stupid, you're crazy, you're wrong, you're this, you're that—constantly abusing you emotionally and physically—well, I broke a window.

MR. COLE: There was evidence in the Boston State Hospital case concerning the creation of patient violence through the violence of the staff. The staff does act in some ways as a role model for some patients. When patients see the staff using force rather than discussion to get cooperation, some turn to violence. There was testimony about one patient who attempted to set herself on fire in order to get to a regular hospital where she would not be forced on medication and locked in seclusion.

MORT COHEN (Professor of Law, Golden Gate University Law School, San Francisco): I have a question for Mr. Comey. I'm not sure I understand your argument about the consitutional right. From what I understand, you are saying that due process protections in the commitment procedure for purposes of treatment would be sufficient to protect the individual thereafter as to the form of treatment, in particular, medication. It seems to me that the United States Supreme Court, in a relevant context having to do with the incarceration of an accused criminal who is eventually convicted for purposes of punishment, treatment, or rehabilitation, has already said no: you cannot simply institutionalize that person. A person still retains a number of constitutional rights in prison, even to the extent of not being put into solitary confinement without some form of hearing. It would seem that that is a constitutional value, comparable to what we're dealing with here. You cannot simply put people into institutions, even if they need to be institutionalized for treatment, and thereafter give them whatever form of treatment that you want.

EUGENE J. COMEY (Conference Faculty): The American Psychiatric Association's position in its briefs is that, to the extent that there is an intrusion into a constitutionally protected interest, procedural requirements are needed. Nobody disputes that. The due process clause of the Constitution does not allow the state to interfere with constitutionally protected rights, absent some form of a hearing to determine the risks and balances. The APA's position in the two federal cases, *Rennie* and *Rogers*, is that the risk-balancing approach takes place at the initial commitment hearing.

MR. COHEN: Without there being any consideration of the nature of treatment? So that can be done as well for ECT?

MR. COMEY: No, under that position the medication issue can be brought up at the initial commitment hearing.

MR. COHEN: Then I don't understand you. Are you saying that if somebody cares to bring up the issue, fine, but if not you can forcibly medicate these individuals?

MR. COMEY: Under the New Jersey and Massachusetts laws, once there is a decision that the individual is to be committed and there has been a determination of the risks and benefits after a full hearing, we then rely upon reasonable medical judgment as to what's best. We're not going to have a due process hearing every time some sort of treatment is to be provided.

MR. COHEN: And there even could be psychosurgery thereafter?

MR. COMEY: Correct me if I'm wrong, but many states have specific limitations on other forms of treatment.

MR. COHEN: But, I'm asking about your constitutional position, not the states' legislation. Is it your constitutional position that once a commitment hearing has been held, you can give an individual medication, psychosurgery, or ECT without other hearings?

MR. COMEY: No.

UNIDENTIFIED SPEAKER: Assuming that the United States Court of Appeals for the First Circuit upholds the district court decision in *Rogers*, do you see an affirmative obligation on the part of the state to have a guardian or substitute decision-maker appointed to make the treatment choice for persons who seem clinically incompetent but for whom there has been no judicial determination?

MR. COLE: If *Rogers* remains good law and there is a right to refuse treatment, there has to be a substitute decision-maker. No court is going to allow a patient who is incompetent to make treatment decisions.

DR. JOHN FELBER (Attorney and psychiatrist, Hartford, Connecticut): I would like to tell those who don't know that *Parham* is not the unanimous decision of the Supreme Court. The opinion in *Parham* was written by Chief Justice Burger in direct contradiction of his previous opinion in *O'Connor v. Donaldson,* in which he expressed disdain for psychiatrists' power to make decisions. Further, the APA is not undivided in their mandate to Mr. Klein to write a brief as an amicus curiae. The American Orthopsychiatric Association and the Mental Health Associations of the

United States are both on the side of the plaintiff and not on the side of the defendants. I hope the Supreme Court takes this into consideration.

DR. JEFFREY GELLER (University of Massachusetts Department of Psychiatry, Northampton State Hospital): My question to Mr. Cole is about obtaining a legal guardian for an individual who is, in fact, incompetent but may become competent through treatment. Given the fact that the appointment of a guardian is a rather cumbersome process, and given the fact that the removal of the guardian is an extremely cumbersome and often time-consuming process, doesn't the appointment of a guardian for an individual significantly interfere with the individual's right to free determination and his right to exist without those guardians?

MR. COLE: There are two separate issues. One is the question of the power of the guardians. The Supreme Judicial Court of Massachusetts has made clear that a court can authorize a limited guardianship to take away only a limited aspect of a patient's power to decide. Second, there is the difficulty involved in appointing guardians. We are now involved in a statewide coalition to deal with some of the problems that have been raised by the employment of guardians. The court essentially said in *Rogers* that if in fact there are problems in appointing guardians, people should be directing attention to the legislature. We are doing that by attempting to get a number of professions to work on legislation dealing with this issue. We hope members of the psychiatric profession can work together in setting up, for example, an independent corporation to have guardians appointed so that is an easier and less cumbersome process. Appointing a guardian in fact is very easy. Removing a guardian is not that easy.

MR. COMEY: Guardianship procedures seem to be an issue peculiarly appropriate to legislation, as opposed to a judicial remedy.

Part III
Clinical Implications of the Courts' Decisions

6

Side Effects of a Right to Refuse Treatment Lawsuit: The Boston State Hospital Experience

Michael J. Gill, M.D.

The Austin Unit at Boston State Hospital applied the principles of therapeutic community articulated by Maxwell Jones[1] in order to develop an environment in which all of the psychiatric patient's time in the hospital could be viewed as treatment. According to Jones, "the social milieu in which social learning can occur is as important as the skills required to analyze interpersonal interactions within the group, to uncover latent content, and to examine the various solutions to problems raised in such a group."[2] He lists six principles fundamental to establishing and maintaining a therapeutic community: (1) face-to-face confrontation, (2) timing, (3) skilled neutral leadership, (4) open communication, (5) appropriate level of feeling, and (6) participant attitudes conducive to growth.

The Austin Unit applied these basic principles to its structure and daily functioning of the unit, and it was into this atmosphere of open communication regarding clinical approaches—an atmosphere receptive to feelings of trust and mistrust, growth and regression, change and stagnation—that the *Rogers v. Okin* case burst like a bombshell. I and the other defendants from the unit were unbelieving at first, then stunned, and then all too aware of the meaning of the legal action. Other staff and patients gradually realized the significance of the case during the weeks after the suit was brought.

THE LOSS OF THE THERAPEUTIC COMMUNITY

The first painful fact of public interest litigation in a public institution that confronted me is that the physician-defendants are required to continue to administer treatment to the class of individuals—involuntarily committed patients—bringing suit against them. Private practitioners terminate treatment of their legal adversaries. The defendants in *Rogers v. Okin* were collecting evidence concerning the ill effects of the temporary restraining order on the class of plaintiff-patients, while trying to provide that same population with effective psychiatric treatment. These conflicting goals need to be addressed more carefully by those who seek to improve conditions in mental hospitals through litigation.

I described in an affidavit the condition of the unit after suit was brought. The affidavit noted incidents of serious violent attacks on twelve staff members and similar attacks on eleven patients, carried out by ten different patients. General conditions were described as follows:

> staff under threat of litigation and criminal contempt of court are very reluctant to take actions necessary to limit patients' dangerous activities, to remove them from excessive stimulation characteristic of mental hospital wards, and to administer appropriate medications, etc. Interventions are made but are made timidly with a great deal of ambiguity and half-heartedness which leads to inadequate treatment, lack of structure and limits, panicky violence in the patients, and uncontrolled spread of anxiety to other patients and to staff trying to help them. In short, attendants feel it is an exhausting, frustrating hell to work in and frequently seek reassurance from supervisors. Tension fills the air, twenty-four hours a day, seven days a week.

These conditions prevailed throughout the hearing on the temporary restraining order, the attempts at settlement that followed, the discovery process, the trial, and the announcement of Judge Tauro's opinion four-and-one-half years after litigation was begun. Maintaining our therapeutic community was impossible. An adversarial quality entered relationships between patients and staff. Suspicion and overt, bitter hostility cropped up in staff relations. For example, a rather ambiguous and provocative remark that "psychiatry is above the law," delivered by me among colleagues and supposed friends as a rather untimely joke, was repeated in court by one of the nursing staff as if it had been said in all seriousness by a haughty and autocratic leader playing God. My misguided attempts to make people aware that the qualities I consider to be the essence of psychiatry—concern, patience, dedication, perseverance, understanding, loyalty—are in fact above the law fell on deaf ears as adversary relationships established themselves. The darker, erroneous meaning, which in the courtroom atmosphere sounded very dark indeed, was all the court heard.

I relate this incident to convey to you the degree of suspicion that grew among caregivers who had previously used their home turf, their therapeutic community, to settle disputes. Now there seemed to be spies in our midst. One had to be careful of what one said, as it might come back to haunt one in court. Many members of the staff and former staffers seemed quite friendly with plaintiff's counsel, and they offered evidence in court that was damaging to the defendants. Friendliness and relaxed comfortable exchanges to relieve staff frustrations and to bolster morale were abandoned in favor of restrictive formal agenda and concrete items of information. The patients were cared for by a staff that was tense, on guard, and unable to provide the wards with effective models for settlement of disputes.

The various parts of the pretrial discovery process were experienced as a further intrusion by staff. This was especially true of the depositions, which were multiple and lengthy, and which stimulated tremendous anxiety in many of those deposed. Those giving depositions sought support and advice, but despite getting both, including excellent and plentiful legal advice, they experienced sleepless nights and numerous fears. The supervisory staff, some of whom were defendants, were sorely stretched. The abundance of requests for unit admissions and sets of interrogatories and affidavits seemed to descend on us like confetti and did little to help. I wondered what was done in such cases before the invention of the copying machine, and then realized that they didn't have these cases before the copying machine and found at least something I could blame for our troubles that could not sue me for defamation of character!

The stresses and strains experienced by staff, however, were small in comparison to the difficulties manifested by our patients. Study of patients' reactions to the case is extremely difficult because of (1) the overwhelming scope of the multiple, interrelated, and complex issues; (2) the lack of objectivity; and (3) the style of record keeping. The Austin Unit's patient records were standard individual medical records, of acceptable but not excellent quality. It was not our practice to log various incidents in the unit that might indicate a change in overall climate. There is, however, a strong impression among staff that property destruction, stealing, fire setting, inappropriate sexuality, elopements, and staff injuries increased greatly after issuance of the temporary restraining order. The increase in disturbed behavior was related to patients' refusing medication and other treatments, to the uncertainty of the staff, and to an increase in the level of anxiety created by the stress of the lawsuit. How much the restraining order provoked unrealistic wishes and their accompanying disappointments and frustrations in the patients, or how much fear was stimulated in the staff by the threat of contempt or the threat of damages uncovered by insurance remains unclear. But it is clear from the frequently expressed views of both patients and staff that all of these factors, and more, were involved.

There were also some harder data on the numbers of patients refusing medication or other treatment, and on a switch to a more management- rather than treatment-oriented approach to the care of refusing patients.

This switch in the style of care was regrettable and most discouraging, and the leadership of the unit felt helpless to counteract the adversary quality obvious in patient-staff relations.

MEDICATION REFUSALS

Four types of refusals were identified, all of them manifested by patients who were denying their illness:

1. Consistent, absolute refusals for weeks or months at a time (15–20 percent)
2. Episodic absolute refusals for days at a time (35 percent)
3. Consistent single-dose refusal (30 percent)
4. Sporadic single-dose refusals (15 percent)

After the suit was filed, a survey was made of approximately 1,400 patient evaluations entered in the Evaluation-Admission Unit logbook, during a 26-month period. Approximately 1,000 of these entries, or 70 percent, were evaluations made of patients on their admission to the unit. The 70 patients hospitalized at the time the suit was started were also surveyed. In this way everybody who was either hospitalized when the suit was started or evaluated for admission during a two-year period after that time was surveyed by a group of experienced staff who met together for this purpose several times. The average census of inpatients was 70. On several separate occasions, a count of patients refusing medication in any of the four categories described above averaged around ten, with extremes as high as 18 at times of stress and as low as 6 during relatively peaceful periods.

Our survey identified a total of 159 patients who refused medication and fit at least one of the categories. It was apparent to us also that many other patients were not being medicated at all or were being medicated inadequately. Fifty-six of those refusing medication neither deteriorated nor improved. Since these patients were too disturbed to be discharged from the hospital, their hospitalizations were more prolonged than on previous occasions or more lengthy than one would ordinarily anticipate.

The condition of 89 patients who refused medication *did* deteriorate, often into states of physical emergency in which they resorted to physical assault on themselves or others, or became self-destructive through refusal of food. Medication would then be forced, and the patients would receive it, mostly involuntarily by the oral route, and sometimes by injection. Any patient whose deterioration did not constitute an emergency would go untreated until a guardian could be appointed. No individual who experienced the terrors of psychotic turmoil and psychological emergency could be treated without proper authority under the conditions imposed by the restraining order.

The remaining 14 of the 159 refusing patients evaluated for admission were refused entry into the hospital. They were patients well known to the unit. They had refused medication in the past and presented difficult management problems. Some of this group of 14 deteriorated in the community, causing distress and great concern in their homes and to our related agencies. One such patient was an intelligent man in his early twenties, with a paranoid schizophrenic psychosis and delinquent behavior. Having been refused admission, he left the state angry, stole a truck, and was later shot to death by police who were pursuing him.

Patients who deteriorate for lack of medication often become violent. Only then, according to the court order, can they be medicated forcibly. Unfortunately, the order leaves it unclear whether force may be used on a single-dose basis or a longer therapeutic trial of medication. As our experience and that of others has borne out, guardians are not a feasible solution to the problem of consent decisions. Guardians may have self-serving motives that are antitherapeutic or motives that interfere with building an alliance between psychiatrist and patient. They are simply unavailable for many patients such as the skid row population, and they may also be unreachable for consent decisions when needed.

SECLUSION RECORDS

The monthly restraint and seclusion reports submitted by the unit chief to the department of mental health were another source of data. These reports included: (1) the number of patients restrained or secluded during the month, (2) the number of occasions of seclusion for each individual, and (3) the total seclusion time for each individual. Keeping in mind an average admission rate of 40 patients per month and an inpatient census of 70, the number of patients secluded each month from April 1974 through March 1975—the 12 months preceding the suit—averaged 20. Some of these patients required long-term care and repeatedly engaged in threatening and/or violent behavior requiring seclusion. Other patients were new admissions arriving in a disturbed and often violent state. The total number of secluded patients for that year was 244. Over the year following initiation of the lawsuit, the average number of patients secluded per month increased from 20 to 27.6, with a total of 332. For the next 12 months, the monthly average increased to 32.6, with a total of 392. Similarly, during those years the total number of hours in which patients were secluded increased from 5,868 before the suit to 11,855 in the second year after it. Thus, during the two years after the suit was filed the number of patients secluded greatly increased, and the average number of seclusion hours per patient also increased. More patients were secluded for longer periods of time.

It should be noted that seclusion was limited to the strictest and most conservative definition of the law. Patients were seldom secluded for "threats," even of extreme violence, personal injury, or suicide, as allowed by the applicable Massachusetts Department of Mental Health regulation. Rather, we generally waited until the incidents actually occurred. Plaintiff's counsel kept a close watch on our unit as his clients were still hospitalized there, and he threatened contempt of court action because of our seclusion practices. He did not charge us with contempt on this particular issue, but he later charged contempt on the issue of forced medication. This contempt charge (which seemed a major stimulus in actually getting the trial underway) concerned the forced medication of a psychotic young woman who refused food on pseudoreligious grounds and was physically deteriorating.

TRANSFERS TO MAXIMUM SECURITY

During the five years prior to the *Rogers v. Okin* suit, the Austin Unit at Boston State Hospital transferred only five dangerously disturbed patients to the maximum security facility at Bridgewater State Hospital. Such transfers were considered treatment failures by the staff. Every effort was made to maintain patients in the unit in order to prevent the stigma of incarceration at Bridgewater, and to provide them with continuing psychotherapy and pharmacotherapy aimed at rehabilitation and return to the community. After the suit was filed and because of the enormously increased level of violence, general disturbances, and tension, the unit found itself unable to contain dangerously disturbed patients, and the transfer rate escalated to about six or seven per year. In addition, the psychiatrist at the major court clinic in our area screened out difficult patients and had the court refer them directly to the Bridgewater facility, because he was aware of our hospital's difficulties. It is possible that the increase in violent patients is attributable to a general increase in violence, to a change in the hospital's population, to the policy of deinstitutionalization, or to the fact that Bridgewater is obliged to release patients earlier because of crowding and because of Massachusetts regulations, revised in 1971, which call for annual review and recommitment of patients. Nonetheless, the dramatic increase in the number of patients transferred to Bridgewater after the lawsuit is quite remarkable, and to my mind, inappropriate.

Discussion

It is apparent that the Austin Unit, as a result of this suit, was subjected to many negative side effects, and the question of positive effects from the suit is very difficult for me to answer. The lawsuit did bring to the attention of the public the plight of the mentally ill and the many complications involved in their treatment. It caused the staff to be careful with their definitions of psychosis, of retardation, of incompetence, of voluntary and involuntary, of forced treatment, of management as distinct from treatment, and of physical emergency as distinct from psychiatric emergency. It taught both the legal and psychiatric professionals something of the others' profession. But the benefits of this legal action to the people it was designed to help, or to the institution it was designed to guide, remain obscure, and the plaintiffs throughout the long and arduous process did not produce a shred of evidence that the suit helped any patient.

Notes

1. MAXWELL JONES, THE THERAPEUTIC COMMUNITY (Basic Books, New York City) (1953).
2. MAXWELL, JONES, BEYOND THE THERAPEUTIC COMMUNITY (Yale University Press, New Haven) (1968).

7

Should There Be a Right to Refuse Treatment?

Scott H. Nelson, M.D., M.P.H.

Should there be a right to refuse treatment? This question is being debated with increasing intensity and frequency in this time of heightened concern with patients' rights and due process. In my view, the responsible answer to this critical question, when posed relative to an involuntary patient who is committed with a diagnosed and treatable mental disorder, is no. Even though criminals are at times deemed not guilty by reason of insanity (NGRI), I do not believe that involuntarily committed patients with mental disorders should be able to be not treated by reason of insanity (NTRI), or that overriding such patients' refusal should be allowed only in "psychiatric emergencies."

THE PHILOSOPHICAL ARGUMENT

In *Rennie v. Klein* and *Rogers v. Okin*, the courts held that patients have a constitutional right to privacy, and therefore, under certain circumstances, may refuse treatment, particularly psychotropic medication. An analogy is often made by advocates of the right to refuse treatment between the nonpsychiatric medical patient who makes a decision about his treatment and the involuntary psychiatric patient. These situations are not analogous, however, because of the difference in competence. The medical patient presumably makes his decision unimpeded by mental illness. The psychiatric patient, involuntarily committed to a hospital because of a mental disorder which affects his judgment about

---

Dr. Nelson is Deputy Secretary for Mental Health, Department of Public Welfare, Commonwealth of Pennsylvania, and Vice-President, National Association of State Mental Health Program Directors. The views expressed in this paper do not necessarily reflect the policies of the Commonwealth of Pennsylvania or the NASMHPD.

his mental condition and his need for treatment, is usually not competent to make an informed decision.

Patients do have a right to privacy. However, they also have a right to the pursuit of happiness. As a physician, I seriously question whether a patient who is allowed to refuse the treatment needed to restore his mental and emotional functioning is truly being guaranteed his right to pursue happiness.

Few would deny that there have been abuses of involuntarily committed psychiatric patients in the past. Prior to the advent of the major tranquilizers, patients were often routinely placed on back wards with little opportunity for social interaction or treatment. However, commitment statutes in most states now provide patients with protections against abuses in three ways:

First, patient "bills of rights" have been enacted which guarantee a patient a healthful and safe environment, access to the least restrictive treatment via an individualized treatment plan, the ability to communicate by phone or letter with family or friends consistent with the patient's clinical condition, and other protections.

Second, patients are entitled to legal due process. No longer can they be committed to hospitals for an indefinite period of time; instead, regular hearings are required to determine the patients' conditions and whether or not treatment in a hospital is the least restrictive alternative.

Third, most states have now made some form of "dangerousness" the criterion for involuntary commitments, at least for adults. While many psychiatrists and others believe that this is an unnecessarily restrictive criterion, it does provide protections for mentally ill persons who are being considered for involuntary commitment and increases the likelihood that the patient will remain in the more restrictive environment of a hospital only for the period of time necessary to alleviate the mental illness that produced the dangerous behavior. A right to refuse medication, however, goes too far in protecting patients and inhibits the administration of necessary treatment.

THE PRACTICAL PROBLEMS

The argument against involuntary mental patients having a right to refuse treatment can be made on legal as well as practical grounds. Several state statutes have expressly *required* treatment of individuals who have been committed after being found to be dangerous to themselves or to others. This is consistent with the state's responsibility, through the police power, to protect society and individual citizens from harm to self or others. At the national level, the advocacy title of the newly-passed Mental Health Systems Act does not provide a federal right to refuse treatment; rather it leaves the resolution of the issue up to the individual states.

It seems apparent that serious clinical and programmatic consequences can occur if patients must consent to any form of treatment, particularly medications, or if a drawn-out legal or administrative process is involved to obtain that consent through petitioning of guardians or through other legal means. From the clinical point of view, patients who exercise their right to refuse medication will be treated later in the course of their mental disorder than they otherwise would have been, if they are treated at all. Therefore, such a right will lead to chronicity of the psychosis of many patients who otherwise could have been helped. This in turn will lead to longer hospital stays, and poorer functioning in the community, if and when the patient is able to be discharged. Studies have shown that the earlier that treatment is provided, the greater the chance of improvement of a person's mental disorder. Research also indicates that medication is the single most effective treatment for psychotic disorders. Therefore, a psychotic patient's refusal to take a medication which is known to be effective against psychoses seriously limits his ability to improve, although because of his mental illness, he may not recognize that this is the case. This is not meant to say that each and every patient who receives a medication will respond to it, nor that there are not other factors, such as a trusting relationship, which can be helpful adjuncts to the efficacy of medications. In most instances, however, medications are found to improve the patient's mental condition, and this fact makes it reasonable in my view to mandate the responsible use of medications when patients are committed for treatment, even if they object.

In addition, untreated hospitalized patients will be more difficult to care for. Some hospitals where patients have been allowed to refuse medication have experienced serious problems with unmedicated and, therefore, uncontrolled patients who have inflicted serious injuries on other patients or on hospital staff. Violent or dangerous patients who are left untreated in hospital settings will continue to be dangerous to themselves or to others. In the absence of medication, their treatment will consist of more staff for patient control, and more deprivation of liberties through restraint and seclusion in the hospital, which is precisely opposite to the intent of most commitment statutes. Therefore, by allowing patients the right to refuse appropriate treatment, the more fundamental right to treatment in the least restrictive environment is violated.

Program Issues

Programmatically, it seems safe to predict that the census at most state hospitals will increase as a result of a right to refuse treatment mainly because of larger numbers of untreated patients and longer lengths of stay. The census also would increase because patients in the community who have similar rights will require admission to hospitals more frequently.

Since hospitals will not be able to apply the least restrictive alternative principle either in fact or in spirit, some patients will simply end up in "preventive confinement" because of the severity of their mental disorder combined with their refusal to take medication. It is also likely that, should a right to refuse medication become widespread, separate units for uncontrolled violent patients will be created, with specialized programming, high staff-to-patient ratios and, as a result, higher costs. Higher costs will also result from longer hospital stays and the increased hospital census, particularly since inpatient care is the most expensive kind of treatment.

There will be other serious problems in operating state mental health programs if patients are allowed to refuse standard treatments, particularly medication. Quality superintendents, psychiatrists, and other professionals of the mental health staff will be increasingly reluctant to seek employment in state mental hospitals when they assess the clinical and legal risks of working there. An adversarial atmosphere will be created in inpatient treatment units that will potentially inhibit the development of relationships between staff and patients and will thereby alienate and drive away competent clinical staff.

If a right to refuse treatment is established, the courts may be creating a curious "triple bind" for clinical personnel, particularly psychiatrists. Mental health professionals will not be allowed to treat involuntary patients without the patients' consent. At the same time, the professionals may be prevented by the courts from keeping untreated patients in the hospital. Yet there may be legal liability if patients are discharged, particularly if the patient is felt to be likely to engage in violent behavior towards self or others. Legal provisions for assigning a treatment guardian can help this situation, but the process of establishing guardianship can be a lengthy, complex, and expensive one. In addition, guardians are increasingly unwilling to take on the responsibility of making an alternative treatment decision for a patient who is mentally ill, particularly when their own legal liability may be increased.

What Needs to be Done?

In a few states, mental health professionals have discharged involuntary patients who refuse treatment, arguing that there is no further basis for their professional relationship. I believe that this approach does not provide an effective solution to the problem, especially when patients need treatment and when the status of the law and the consequences of refusal of treatment are at issue as they are now. However, this stance does demonstrate a legitimate concern of clinical mental health professionals both for liability and for being allowed to take appropriate responsibility for their patients' care.

It is my view that several courses of action can be pursued to improve the current situation with regard to a patient's refusal of treatment. Some of these have been implemented in various states, and some were incorporated in the result of *Rennie v. Klein*.

The principle should be affirmed that when patients meet the criteria for involuntary commitment to a mental hospital, they should be treated. For example, Dr. Loren Roth has suggested that commitment should specifically involve a determination of competency. In addition, a clear diagnosis of mental disorder and a reasonable probability of successful treatment should be expected from the hospitalization. This seems consistent with the intent of many, if not most, state involuntary commitment statutes.

In addition, it is important to realize that the *Rennie v. Klein* decision came about not only because of questions about the constitutional rights of patients, but also because of legitimate concern about the way intrusive treatments, particularly medications, were actually being applied in state hospitals. This concern emanates from the lack of adequate clinical and administrative supervision and poor documentation of treatment that occurs in some state hospitals, and from the belief that the quality of physicians in state hospitals, as reflected in part by their prescribing practices, is inferior. The concern also comes from the knowledge that certain psychotropic medications, such as the major tranquilizers, produce side effects such as tardive dyskinesia which are resistant to amelioration, and there is a desire on the part of courts to protect patients from such side effects.

As a remedy for concerns about quality of care, I suggest that every state mental hospital and all other inpatient mental health treatment programs develop and implement the following:

1. A practical plan for recruiting and maintaining professional personnel who meet standards of quality practice. Such recruitment and retention is often difficult in state hospitals because of the low professional status of those who treat chronically ill patient populations, the geographic isolation of the institutions, and the low salaries paid to professional staff. In Pennsylvania, we recently documented the impact of our low salaries on the recruitment and the retention of physicians, particularly psychiatrists, in our state system.

    Related to recruitment and retention of psychiatrists are the selection and training of psychiatric residents, regardless of the location of their training. Deficiencies in residency programs may lead to the graduation of substandard psychiatrists who lack the preparedness to respond to the complex medicolegal requirements of psychiatric hospital policies, state laws, and court decisions. The willingness of local psychiatric societies and state licensing boards to police their members who engage in incompetent practice is also an issue in some parts of the country.

2. Programs for the regular review and improvement of the prescribing practices of physicians in the hospital. These should include:
   a) An active system of peer review;
   b) A regular continuing education program for physicians, particularly targeted to prescribing psychoactive medications and documenting the patient's need for such medications in the record;
   c) The development and regular updating of policies and procedures related to the prescription of medications, and evidence of how such policies and procedures are working;
   d) A regular procedure for monitoring side effects in all patients on medication;
   e) Medical audits to review on a regular basis the prescribing practices of physicians; and
   f) The routine opportunity for patients and/or patient advocates to obtain second opinions regarding the type and amount of medications required for treatment of patients' mental disorders.

3. Programs for other hospital treatment staff concerning the doses and side effects of psychotropic medications.

4. A system for meaningful involvement of patients in their treatment. This system should include:
   a) Participation of patients in preparation of their treatment plans;
   b) Conveying information to the patient regarding the proposed treatment and, if medications are involved, what effects and side effects can be expected; and
   c) The availability of meaningful patient advocacy.

Even these provisions will not ensure that there will be no mistakes, but such procedures would help to reduce the number and magnitude of errors.

In addition, clear policies and procedures should be developed in relation to treatment of children, including how the family should be involved in treatment decisions. Similar guidelines and policies need to be developed for intrusive treatments which are controversial, such as electroconvulsive therapy, aversive conditioning, and psychosurgery.

SUMMARY

In summary, I do not believe that patients who are involuntarily committed to psychiatric hospitals should have a right to refuse medication. Patients should have the right to an opportunity to ameliorate their mental illnesses and to the pursuit of happiness that successful treatment can afford. Almost all state commitment statutes now provide patients with rights and regular due process hearings which should keep many of the past abuses in mental hospitals from recurring.

If patients are not treated early, they may not be able to be treated at all. This will lead to longer if not indefinite hospital stays, higher hospital census, more deprivation of liberties, and higher costs. Particularly in state hospitals, it will lead to deterioration of the quality of staff, require more staff to control patients' violent behavior, and create a programmatic need for specific units for the preventive confinement of untreated patients.

The basic issue in requiring treatment is not patients' rights, but quality of care. I have suggested some ways in which such quality can be improved. We do need to develop and implement new and better ways to provide protection from treatment abuses. We in the state mental health agencies want to work with attorneys, advocates, and the courts; but in the process, let us not deprive patients of the major psychiatric treatment modalities they need to get better.

8

Clinical Approaches with Patients Who Refuse Medication

Thomas G. Gutheil, M.D. and
Mark J. Mills, J.D., M.D.

Sam Goldwyn, a very colorful character on the Hollywood scene, once requested that a flower garden be prepared for him. Much effort was spent in trying to see that all the flowers were in full bloom at the time that Goldwyn would visit the garden. When Goldwyn arrived, the various flowers indeed were in full bloom. Supported by his cane, he walked with great pride through his garden, but when he rounded a corner, he saw one rose in bud rather than in bloom. He turned crimson with rage and began smashing the rosebud with his cane, screaming, "Bloom, damn you, bloom!" This image of attempting to bludgeon rosebuds into bloom seems to us similar to the effect on state hospital conditions created by suing a psychiatrist. That would, needless to say, excoriate the bud; the psychiatrist will leave, but it really won't change the condition of patients in those hospitals. The answer is that something must be done through the legislature.

We would like to dedicate this presentation to a young patient, David S. His death through suicide is one of the consequences of a delay in treatment caused by the *Rogers v. Okin* political activity. David is also a reason for our own interest in this topic.

One of the things not fully underscored in the discussions thus far is that medication refusal is again being singled out; clinically, it is quite common for the patient refusing medication also to refuse food, showers, change of room, change of clothing, and the like. The clinical entity, refusal (or in some instances negativism), is a category with many elements. Another difficulty in the area is the so-called "one punch—one shot" rule. This term depicts the clinician's sardonic view of the chemical restraint theory. Under the chemical restraint legislation, if a patient is violent, he gives one punch—that's the proof of violence—and you give him one shot of medicine. One shot of medication does extremely little good; it wears off and is metabolized, and then the patient is back to square one. He again gives one punch, and again he gets one shot. This sequence may continue indefinitely. This scenario indicates the difficulty in looking at medication as a legal event rather than as a clinical one in the context of ongoing patient care.

There are three major categories of factors that are clinically involved in drug refusal. The first consists of *illness* factors, which, in sum, are the symptomatology of the illness, and, of course, represent a Catch-22: The very illness for which the patient requires treatment is the factor preventing treatment from occurring, because of refusal based on that illness. An example would be a patient's refusing medication because of the delusion that it is lethal poison.

Then there are factors inherent in *treatment* itself, factors that are frequently not given full attention. Remember, in some ways, there are no real problems in psychiatry, there are only solutions that are not working well. Thus, psychosis is itself a solution to an impasse, an irresolvable dilemma with which the patient is faced. For many patients, psychosis is in a sense an alternative to suicide or homicide and represents an attempt to resolve the irresolvable. Consequently, patients may refuse the alleviation of their psychotic state because it seems to represent the only solution that is accessible to them at that moment. A common example is the grandiose patient who would rather be sick and the Messiah than be well and ordinary—quite an understandable preference but a problem for the ethical clinician. There is also the component which psychiatrists call secondary gain. This may be hard to understand, because what possible secondary gain could there be in being an inpatient at a state hospital, where the cockroaches are outnumbered only by the mice? The answer, as one serious clinician has stated, is that with all its chaos, the state hospital may be the most sane and orderly place a particular patient has available to him. It is a question of the individual's life experience. The secondary gain, the advantages of being ill and being cared for—or as one patient put it, "three hots and a cot"—sometimes outweighs even the need for adequate treatment and the potential for cure in the patient's value system.

The third major category in treatment refusal is factors stemming from the doctor-patient relationship. These include transference—the phenomenon where the doctor is experienced as someone other than who he is. The same patient who refused spoon-feeding by his mother may refuse medication by the doctor who is perceived or experienced as the mother. Another more realistic factor is that the doctor who is exploitive, nonsupportive, or unavailable may have his treatment refused in an attempt by the patient to communicate with him. Next, intimacy is one of the byproducts of a close working relationship in psychotherapy. Intimacy is a wonderful thing to have, except that for many people, it is an intolerable strain. This is a point frequently missed in considering the patient's experience of being cared for, and for many people it is the grounds for refusal, on the basis that refusal decreases intimacy by increasing distance.

Finally, family pressure can contribute to refusal of treatment. It may be difficult to envision a patient on a ward being troubled by family pressures, but clinicians are aware that for many families, a family member's illness may become a very competitive situation. The family wants to be in charge of the patient's care, but the patient wants to be in charge of his own care. The autonomy struggle between the patient and the family is recapitulated by the autonomy struggle between the patient and doctor and between the patient and staff. Families may actively or passively sabotage treatment plans because of their wish to be more involved with the patient than are the treatment staff.

Let me now turn to a whirlwind summary of the clinical approaches to the management of a patient's treatment refusal. The first approach may seem somewhat banal, but is frequently forgotten in overly legalistic discussions. It is the exploration of the issues. The psychology of an individual patient's refusal of treatment is just as much a legitimate topic of therapeutic investigation as are the matters that brought the patient to the hospital. The patient's posture of denial, for example, his persistence in repetitive patterns of self-defeating behavior, or his delusional guilt should be explored in the customary manner—that is, viewing the treatment refusal as a symptom. At times the legalistic atmosphere now surrounding the right to refuse can obscure the fact that refusal is at base far more nearly a psychological problem than a legal one.[1]

The second component is maintaining the alliance posture. I was enormously gratified to hear attorney Richard Cole use the words "therapeutic alliance," as I thought it was a term barely comprehended in the legal profession; however, one clarification must be made: The therapeutic alliance is between the therapist and the *healthy* part of the patient against the illness that resides within the patient, but at the same time, the therapist is in opposition to another aspect of the patient. The therapist must oppose the patient's violence, for example, in an apparently oppositional way while actually maintaining his interest in the patient's healthier side—the side that would want *not* to be violent.

In the present instance, the patient's refusal of the therapist's recommended treatment places the two parties in an oppositional stance. It represents most significantly a threat to the therapeutic alliance. Faced with this problem the clinician must address and recruit the healthiest level of the patient's function which remains available, and ally himself with that level. Practically, such an approach requires seeing refusal as a problem facing the dyad—the patient and therapist—not the therapist or the patient alone. Typical expressions in actual work with patients would be, "What are *we* going to do about this problem we have in agreeing?" or "*We* have seen how this helped your last three hospitalizations, why can't *we* try to make it work this time?"

A third clinical approach involves the amelioration of causative influences. In addition to therapeutic investigation or intervention, specific influences provoking refusal may be identified and ameliorated directly. Subjectively troublesome side effects may be managed in the usual way, ventilation of unexpressed hostility may be encouraged, misinformation about medicine may be corrected through education, conflict and impasses on the ward may be resolved, and various forms of interpersonal attention may be provided. All of these responses may correct the problematic situation that sparks refusal. Once again, I am presenting refusal as a symptom with underlying causes rather than as an abstract legal principle.

The role of the ward staff in treatment refusal also needs to be recognized. Therapeutic work, reassurance, coaxing, and persuasion on the part of the medication nurse and other staff are pivotal influences in overcoming medication refusal. A positive, caring relationship between staff and patient can play a vital role in reversing a treatment refusal. In our institution, we have a social worker working with the family. This alliance is absolutely critical in the total management of treatment refusals, and for that matter, treatment as a whole, because the patient frequently cannot get better until the family can understand it.

Should these approaches fail, involuntary treatment may be necessary and effective. One of the most formidable challenges to the clinician is maintaining the therapeutic alliance even in the face of an overriding treatment refusal. Even in a clearly oppositional situation, the therapist still attempts to speak to the healthy side of the patient's ego, emphasizing the rationale for the recommended course of action, and exploring the patient's feelings and reactions. The patient's attention is directed to previous positive effects of medication, if any, and the importance of treatment in achieving a rapid release from the hospital. Efforts directed toward involuntary treatment should be candidly described in terms of their purpose in serving the patient's *interests,* even though they are contrary to the patient's *wishes.* The clinician must take an unequivocal stand against psychotic distortions of the treatment situation and continue to maintain a realistic view of the patient's medical needs. I emphasize as a footnote that all aspects of involuntary treatment require the most excruciatingly detailed documentation.

If involuntary treatment is necessary, as soon thereafter as it is clinically feasible, the patient should be invited again to participate voluntarily in treatment. This change should be discussed in anticipation of its arrival, and the subject should be kept open during the changeover. The opportunity should not be lost to explore in detail the dynamic and environmental bases for refusal and to render them explicit, exploring them as symptoms after the fact as one does in ordinary treatment situations. This is important not only for therapeutic understanding but also for future reference in case of relapse or rehospitalization.

In sum, while legal remedies may exist, the clinical issues challenge the treater to continue to see the patient's *needs* through all the obscuring factors, which regrettably occasionally consist of unilateral attention only to the patient's rights viewed in a vacuum.

NOTE

1. *See* Applebaum, P. and Gutheil, T. *Drug Refusal: A Study of Psychiatric Inpatients.* AMERICAN JOURNAL OF PSYCHIATRY 137:3 (March 1980).

9

Legal Approaches to Treating the Treatment-Refusing Patient

Mark J. Mills, J.D., M.D. and
Thomas G. Gutheil, M.D.

Whatever powers the Constitution has granted our government, involuntary mind control is not one of them....[1]

How real is the promise of the individual autonomy for a confused person set adrift in a hostile world?[2]

This presentation considers legal approaches to treating treatment-refusing patients. The notion expresses the uncomfortable tension between the perspectives involved: legal and clinical perspectives are sometimes at odds. Who, when, why, by what means, for how long, if ever, should one treat a patient over his or her objection?

The federal courts have recently provided three rather different legal answers to these questions. Chronologically, there was first the *Rennie* decision.[3] In that case, Judge Brotman found a qualified right to refuse treatment and established an elaborate, extrajudicial, quasijudicial process culminating in a review by an independent psychiatrist of contested decisions. Subsequently, in the *Rogers* decision, Judge Tauro found a right to refuse treatment which allowed only for very narrowly defined emergency treatment over the patient's objection and treatment authorized through the guardianship process.[4] Lastly, in *A. E. and R. R. v. Mitchell*, the court found no right to refuse treatment.[5] Lest that sound draconian, one should be aware that this last decision occurred in the context of a Utah statute which provided unusually specific commitment criteria: that the patient was incompetent to consent to treatment; and that hospitalization constituted the least restrictive treatment.[6]

We will consider some of the costs and benefits (those terms are used in their broad, nonmonetary sense) of each of these decisions. Then, we will suggest an additional mechanism for dealing with the compelling and (often) competing equities in the right-to-refuse treatment arena. First, however, one caveat is in order: we take it for granted that any system created to deal with the issue of treatment refusal will have advantages and disadvantages. That is, it is presently impossible (legally, technologically, and therapeutically) to maximize patients' rights and needs simultaneously. At best, all one can do is to strike a reasonable balance and to be clear about the values implicit in that balance. One might call this the "no free lunch" concept, as applied to treatment refusal.

As it occurred first, and because it represents a useful midposition, the *Rennie* decision is a good starting point. A number of benefits can be derived from its approach. First, the opinion deals explicitly with the problem of functionally incompetent patients as distinct from legally incompetent patients. For a patient to be declared legally incompetent, he or she has to be so adjudicated in a probate court proceeding. In contradistinction, many patients, for a variety of reasons including but not limited to psychosis, may be functionally incompetent for brief emergency situations. Second, *Rennie* allows for significant clinical discretion in determining what constitutes an emergency. Third, the decision keeps the locus of clinical decision making within the treating professions. It is the treatment professional, not lawyers or judges, who makes the ultimate treatment determination. Last, it places patient advocates (typically attorneys) in a position where they have immediate access to patients and can rapidly scrutinize the kind of on-the-spot decision making inherent in good clinical care.

Each of these benefits is tangible and significant; yet we believe that this system has some important costs as well. As noted earlier, what Judge Brotman has created is a system of extrajudicial and quasijudicial review. We believe that such a system is, for lack of a better word, bulky. What do we mean? First, as Judge Brotman noted in his chapter, he envisions a system in which it might well be appropriate for an attorney to aid the independent psychiatrist in the review process.[7] What concerns us is that such a system may tend to become adversarial, potentially to the patient's detriment. Second, even if the attorney were not aiding the independent psychiatrist, he or she would generally be the patient advocate. Again, there is a risk of the advocate, just by being present, fostering an atmosphere of suspicion. This may be particularly true when patients, because of their illness, are already paranoid, ambivalent, or negativistic. Lastly, such a system appears to ignore financial costs. Though it may be true that patients' rights and needs are enhanced by a such an elaborate review process, it may also be true that their rights and needs will be further enhanced if the same funds used to create the review process were spent instead for newer buildings, more clinicians, etc. Determining how best to utilize funds for patient care has generally been an administrative or clinical function. We believe that the cost of the *Rennie*-mandated review system is considerable and (sadly) insufficiently acknowledged by the court.

We confess to strong feelings about the *Rogers* decision for we believe that as originally constructed it embodied few benefits. One clear benefit, however, is that it vigorously protects the right of patients to refuse treatment. Judge Tauro stopped short of creating an absolute right by allowing for narrowly defined emergency treatments and treatment authorized by guardians.[8] He acknowledged, at least operationally, that some patients need to be treated even over their own objections.

What about the costs of the *Rogers* decision? First, with nonemergency patients, treatment may be significantly delayed, because the decision effectively segregated commitment and treatment. That is, a patient could be sufficiently ill to warrant hospitalization; but, paradoxically, not sufficiently ill to warrant treatment. Several commentators have termed the situation a commitment/treatment discontinuity.[9] For those patients who fall into this category, the slow guardianship process is apt to mean that treatment will be long delayed. Occasionally, if the family is willing and affluent and knows an able attorney, obtaining a guardianship may take a week or less. More typically however, it takes a month. We are aware of some cases where it has taken many months. Massachusetts presently does not have a public guardian's act to provide for a pool of public guardians. Nor does present state law circumscribe a guardian's liability; nor, better still, provide guardians with appropriate protection from liability. At bottom, though, our concern is that treatment delayed may be treatment denied. At least one study has specifically suggested that a long hospitalization tends to incur longer and more frequent hospitalizations.[10] Thus, we believe the cost of Tauro's construction is unacceptably high.

Another cost of the *Rogers* decision, as Dr. Gill points out, is the increasing use of seclusion and restraint.[11] These techniques have become more employed as pharmacotherapies have been restricted. There are undoubtedly times when seclusion by itself is an optimal treatment, but in the majority of cases it is probably more efficacious if employed concurrently with pharmacotherapy.[12] Again, we are concerned that the patient may be receiving unnecessary seclusion, ineffective seclusion, or both.

Third, we are concerned about the implementation of the *Rogers* decision. Since the case was filed, the Massachusetts Department of Mental Health has promulgated a series of regulations that mandate not only changes in patient treatment, but also significant changes in the documentation of that treatment. Some of these changes appear overdue to the most doubting eyes, while others appear needlessly formalistic and even downright wasteful of clinical, administrative, or clerical time.

One of us works with two full-time administrative assistants, one of whom spends nearly her entire time compiling information required by these regulations. The administrative costs of the decision are considerable; one needs to think critically whether such a deployment of those resources is sound. We believe that on balance *Rogers*' costs to the patients are too high.

The benefits of the *A. E. and R. R.* decision are clear: rapid access to treatment, even over the patient's objections, is guaranteed; and economic costs are minimized. Because the Utah statute provides that the treatment being offered or imposed is the least restrictive alternative, no detailed documentation is required. Unfortunately, the noneconomic costs of such a system are equally evident. It is surprising that the court appears to have assumed away the very issue it should have considered. On the face of it, the court's construction appeared reasonable. When examined more carefully however, the decision appears to hold that no further scrutiny (psychiatric, or legal) of the commitment decision is necessary. As the American Psychiatric Association has argued in its amicus brief, it may be true that patients who fit carefully constructed commitment criteria are functionally incompetent to consent to treatment, and therefore should be allowed to be treated (at least briefly) even over their objections. But many careful commentators believe that some additional examination is warranted. Thus, in our view the *A. E. and R. R.* decision appears to underprotect patients.

These three decisions leave one wondering whether a plan could be conceived by which patients' rights are well-protected, access to treatment is clear and also well-protected, and economic and administrative costs are minimized. We propose such a model system, not so much to suggest it is the optimal one, but to illustrate that it is possible to approach each of these criteria in a somewhat different manner. As an aside, it is important to note that the appellate decision in *Rogers* constructs a rather similar system.[13]

The trend of the law over the past decade, and the clear assumption of both *Rennie* and *Rogers*, is that patients should be assumed competent.[14] The presumption of competency should include the right to refuse treatment unless there is a compelling and countervailing state interest, or unless there is significant evidence that the patient in fact is not competent. Given the legal trend towards assuming a patient's competency, a model system should start with that premise. Thus, one should assume that a refusal of treatment should be honored, and that treating the patient over his or her objections should not be a routine matter.

How could such treatment proceed? One of us has proposed elsewhere a system in which, following a careful examination, the treating psychiatrist could fill out a formal declaration alleging five points about the patient's need for treatment: (1) that the patient has been carefully examined; (2) that at the time of the examination, the reason(s) for involuntary hospitalization continue (*i.e.*, civil commitment criteria are fulfilled); (3) that the patient is at present not capable of making an informed-consent decision (and it appears likely that the patient's incapacity to make such a decision will last a significant portion of the maximum allowable period of the civil commitment); (4) that pharmacotherapy is indicated; and (5) that the risk/benefit ratio of the proposed pharmacotherapy is such that a reasonable person would consent to a trial.[15] Clearly, the essence of this series of allegations is the third point: the patient after considered examination is not capable of making meaningful decisions about his or her treatment. One could then couple such a declaration with a provision that treatment via the declaration could only be for some brief, specified period—somewhere between three days and a week.

Let us then consider this proposal in the same fashion that we have considered the three decisions. What are the benefits of this plan? First, it seems to us that it explicitly focuses psychiatric attention upon the issue of the patient's competency to consent to treatment, and preserves the possibility of finding competency even when a patient has been involuntarily committed. It deals with the potential for insufficient review inherent in the *A. E. and R. R.* approach. Second, although it presupposes a rigorous, clinical evaluation, treatment can be initiated rapidly (even over the patient's objection) without the kind of delays built into the *Rogers* approach. Third, patients are afforded significant consideration of their competency and of their right to refuse treatment without the kind of cumbersome adversarial system intrinsic in the *Rennie* approach.

An illustration may make this process more understandable. When contested under the proposed model-declaration system, competency would have to be specifically adjudicated. Thus, the patient might say "I don't want to take this medication," and the treating psychiatrist might say, "We are going to give this medication to you anyway, because you fulfill the commitment requirement, the risk/benefit ratio is in favor of benefit, and you are presently not competent to refuse the medication; however, we can only treat you in this fashion for a week and we will be going to court with you at the end of that time." In order to continue treating the patient over his or her objections, the treaters (hospital, psychiatrist, state, etc.) would have to prevail in three allegations at the court hearing. That is, the treaters would have to establish that (1) the patient has a mental illness as defined by the state civil commitment statute; (2) the patient meets the specific criteria for commitment (generally, dangerousness or inability to care for oneself) under the state statute;

Legal Approaches

and (3) the patient does not have sufficient competence to consent to or refuse treatment. The notion that a patient's treatment request would be heeded once his or her competence is restored would be explicit in such a system.

This scenario illustrates another benefit of our proposal. That is, the patient's rights are carefully considered twice in relatively rapid succession, first by the treating psychiatrist and then, if contested, by the court.

What are the costs of this proposal? Although they may be somewhat less than those of the three federal court decisions, this approach too has its costs. First, it is possible, using this model, to override the patient's wishes. Thus, although carefully circumscribed temporally, this model would not protect the right to refuse treatment quite as carefully as did *Rogers* or *Rennie*. Second, one would have to demonstrate (if contested) incompetence in the formal context of a court hearing. Such hearings are characterized by a kind of administrative bulkiness and may be financially burdensome. However, if one were willing to tip the scales slightly further in the direction of treatment, one could envisage a system in which incompetence did not have to be adjudicated formally. In such a system, alleged incompetence could be affirmed by an independent psychiatrist (internal review), and treatment could then proceed.

As noted earlier, however, the point of this example is to illustrate that a variety of legal alternatives exist. Interestingly, Judge Coffin in the court of appeals' decision in *Rogers,* moves the treatment/rights pendulum in the treatment direction by allowing dangerous patients to be treated, even over their objections, in situations beyond the lower courts' narrowly defined emergencies.[16] That opinion will warrant careful critique, but until the appeals court holding is clear (it "affirmed in part, reversed in part, and vacated and remanded" the ruling of the lower court), that discussion must be held in abeyance.

Above all else, the various approaches taken by the different federal courts suggest that the competing equities in this arena are genuinely vexing. There are no ready solutions. In the end, all the alternatives trade some measure of legal protection of rights for some measure of protection of treatment access. Reasonable people can differ about precisely where the balance should lie.

We would like to offer one last point: it is important not to overreact as the courts attempt to fashion better solutions. We suspect that in the long run, a workable balance will be achieved. Given this perspective, we hope that by accepting the state's petition for *certiorari*, the Supreme Court is indicating its willingness to comprehensively review the present right-to-refuse treatment balance.[17] In the meantime, it is difficult for clinicians to see their patients "rotting with their rights on" and for attorneys to see their clients being treated over competent objections.[18]

NOTES

1. *Rogers v. Okin*, 478 F. Supp. 1342, 1367 (D. Mass. 1979).
2. Bazelon, D. L., *Institutionalization, Deinstitutionalization and the Adversary Process*, COLUMBIA LAW REVIEW 75(5):897, 907 (June 1975).
3. *Rennie v. Klein*, 476 F. Supp. 1294 (D.N.J. 1979).
4. *Rogers v. Okin, supra* note 1, at 1367.
5. *A. E. and R. R. v. Mitchell*, No. C-78-466 (D. Utah June 16, 1980) (under state's comprehensive civil commitment statute patients do not have a constitutional right to challenge treatment decisions through a due process hearing).
6. *Id.*
7. Brotman, S., chapter 3 this text.
8. *Rogers v. Okin, supra* note 1, at 1365.
9. Gutheil, T. G., Shapiro, R. and St. Clair, R. L., *Legal Guardianship in Drug Refusal: An Illusory Solution*, AMERICAN JOURNAL OF PSYCHIATRY 137(3): 347-52 (March 1980); Mills, M. J., *The Continuing Clinicolegal Conundrum of the Boston State Case*, MEDICOLEGAL NEWS 9(2):9-12, 18 (April 1981).
10. Gruenberg, E., *The Social Breakdown Syndrome—Some Origins*, AMERICAN JOURNAL OF PSYCHIATRY 123(12):1481-89 (June 1967).
11. Gill, M. J., chapter 6 this text.
12. Gutheil, T. G., *Restraint versus Treatment: Seclusion as Discussed in the Boston State Case*, AMERICAN JOURNAL OF PSYCHIATRY 137(6):718-19 (June 1980); Mattson, M. R. and Sacks, M. H., *Seclusion: Uses and Complications*, AMERICAN JOURNAL OF PSYCHIATRY 135(10):1210, 1212 (October 1978).
13. *Rogers v. Okin*, 634 F.2d 650 (1st Cir. 1980).
14. *Rennie v. Klein, supra* note 3; *Rogers v. Okin, supra* note 1.
15. Mills, M. J., *The Right of Involuntary Patients to Refuse Pharmacotherapy: What is Reasonable?* BULLETIN OF THE AMERICAN ACADEMY OF PSYCHIATRY AND LAW 8(3):313-34 (1980).
16. *Rogers v. Okin*, 634 F.2d 650 (1st Cir. 1980)
17. *Rogers v. Okin*, supra note 1, *cert. granted* 49 U.S.L.W. 3788 (April 20, 1981).
18. Appelbaum, P. S. and Gutheil, T. G., *The Boston State Case: "Involuntary Mind Control," the Constitution, and the "Right to Rot,"* AMERICAN JOURNAL OF PSYCHIATRY 137(6):720-23 (June 1980).

Discussion

Nathan T. Sidley, J.D., M.D., Moderator

MR. RICHARD DANARD (Professor of Law, Northeastern University Law School, Boston, Massachusetts): I wonder how much of what Dr. Gill was describing could be due to the trauma of being involved in a lawsuit?

DR. MICHAEL J. GILL (Conference Faculty): I do address the issue of being in the middle of a lawsuit and what the effect of that position is. I again would like to request the legal profession to find some way other than litigation to bring these matters to the attention of the courts. The *Rogers* case has had a profoundly harmful effect on many worthy individuals, especially our patients.

UNIDENTIFIED SPEAKER: Dr. Gill and Dr. Nelson seem to give the impression that the right to refuse treatment creates an adversarial situation. I suggest that many patients have always felt that an adversarial situation between staff and patients exists in institutions of confinement. I would like to ask Dr. Nelson how he believes that patients can be involved in their treatment plan if they don't have the right to refuse or to acquiesce in the psychiatric decision.

DR. SCOTT H. NELSON (Conference Faculty): Involvement in the treatment plan does not necessarily mean that the treatment team and the patient will agree on what ought to be done, although I think that in many instances agreement can be achieved. Patients do in fact agree that they need medication or that they need a certain kind of treatment approach.

MR. JOHN C. HOLME, JR. (Staff attorney, Advocates for Basic Legal Equality, Toledo, Ohio): I'm counsel for the plaintiff on a case just decided by the federal district court in Ohio about a qualified right to refuse treatment. I'd like to raise a question about the procedure for the patient's informed consent. In seeking to implement the court order, we had a hearing to determine what sort of due process we would use, and the hospital psychiatrist testified that in his opinion no patient in the hospital was competent to refuse treatment. He noted, for example, that he had patients with antisocial personalities who would not be competent to refuse. I would like to ask Dr. Mills how his proposal deals with such a biased view of competency.

DR. MARK J. MILLS (Conference Faculty): I hope relatively well. It seems to me that my proposed plan distinguishes specifically between the criteria for committability and the criteria for treatability, although I think they are roughly coincident, at least for psychotic patients. In the case of a patient with an antisocial personality disorder, it's conceivable that on the basis of mental illness and on the basis of dangerousness to others the person would be committable and yet on the basis of mental status examination would also be found to have the requisite capacity to consent. I think my proposed model deals adequately with that dilemma. But my model does not deal well with the traditional ethos of even well-intentioned psychiatry, which is a kind of paternalism that has gotten psychiatry into a great deal of trouble historically. On the other hand, I also think that much of that paternalism is genuinely well-intentioned, even though very often the mental health bar has assumed otherwise.

UNIDENTIFIED SPEAKER: What does the astute clinician do about the patient's concern about side effects from medication?

DR. THOMAS J. GUTHEIL (Conference Faculty): The problem of side effects has been treated as if it were some kind of fixed event and fixed quantity. In good treatment, one treats the side effects either with medication or a change of dosage. If a physician were actually ignoring the patient's complaint of side effects I would consider that to be bad treatment, which I certainly can't go on record as defending. Side effects of all medications—including aspirin, oxygen and water—are serious potential complicating factors in the treatment phenomenon.

UNIDENTIFIED SPEAKER: Dr. Gill, with all respect for the anger which I sensed in your communication, I wonder if that anger has helped you understand the anger that some patients and former patients feel for the way that they have been repressed or unfairly locked up?

DR. GILL: I come from a country with a long heritage of people being unfairly treated and dominated. Much of that history is quite recent, and I am familiar with it. With that heritage, I was very sensitive to individuals who were being mistreated by various elements of society and by themselves. And it was largely for that reason that I chose psychiatry as a profession. As a psychiatrist, I have worked in institutions in which individuals were subjected to various kinds of abuse from within themselves. Many patients who have mental illness have a great deal of self-inflicted pain. They look to institutions for relief from that pain, and we do the best we can to provide them with whatever relief is available. The *Rogers* case did not particularly help me in that regard. I don't think that one can really appreciate the dilemmas of patients when one is locked into an adversarial struggle, because one loses one's ability to care and to persevere. One loses one's patience, and one loses one's capacity for empathy in the heat of this kind of adversarial process. I do understand and appreciate the legal dilemma. But I also appreciate the dilemma of mentally ill people, and have spent long years trying to help.

DR. NATHAN T. SIDLEY (Moderator): It seems to me that you didn't respond to one aspect of this question, which was that mental patients, particularly those who are committed to a hospital, very often feel that they are unfairly and arbitrarily committed to the hospital. To what degree has your recent experience enabled you to sympathize with that kind of impression on the part of the patient?

DR. GILL: There's no question that patients, including those in institutions, are treated unfairly. It's not necessarily the responsibility of those who are working in the institutions to address that particular issue, because the individuals working in the institutions are doing the best they can under the conditions provided by the legislature and by our society to provide those treatments. They are often providing treatment with facilities and budgets which are inadequate to cope with the patient's difficulties.

DR. SIDLEY: I'm going to address a question to Dr. Nelson. Consider a hypothetical case in which a hospitalized mental patient is assigned to a clinician who: (a) is incompetent, (b) is alcoholic, (c) has so many patients that he really can't give any one of them enough time to do an adequate job, and (d) has prescribed a drug that the patient feels is likely to lead to more harm than good. If there is no right to refuse treatment, what sort of remedies can the patient use to try to improve that seemingly impossible situation?

DR. NELSON: I think you know that I would not defend a situation like that, Dr. Sidley. Hospitals do have physicians who are incompetent and alcoholic and who have a variety of problems that lead to inferior treatment. I think some of the things I have suggested, such as second opinions, the serious use of hiring standards, and review of a person's practice, will help patients who feel they get a raw deal in the hospital.

These are serious problems within our system, and I think that the problems involve residency training, the willingness of the profession to police itself, and the willingness of states to provide adequate treatment and to establish procedures to hold the system accountable. I do believe that many people have been helped in hospitals in spite of their resistance at the time. Some of the questions imply that people have been purposely mistreated, which I don't think is the case.

PAUL AUCOIN (Attorney, Murphey, Young and Smith, Columbus, Ohio): Dr. Gill, you expressed a great deal of resentment for the legal system in regard to your problems with the litigation in Massachusetts. I'm curious as to how much time your lawyer spent allaying your anxiety and that of your staff during the litigation.

DR. GILL: A great deal. But I think there was an enormous flood of anxiety, partly because we were confronted with a process with which we were quite unfamiliar, particularly depositions. It was very scary for a lot of the staff. The attorney general's office was very helpful in that regard, but despite their help the anxiety spilled over into all kinds of situations at the hospital, and staff felt themselves unable to carry out their responsibilities effectively.

ROBERT FRANK (Judge, District Court of Tulsa County, Tulsa, Oklahoma): Dr. Mills, when a court rules on questions involving the right to refuse treatment, to what extent can or should it look at the therapeutic efficiency that might be affected by its decision?

DR. MILLS: I think the court has to consider the particular technology being employed. A very intrusive treatment such as psychosurgery, or a somewhat less intrusive treatment like electroconvulsive therapy, clearly demands a particular kind of scrutiny and attention. My own sense is that neuroleptics have more risk associated with them than aspirin, but that they probably have fewer risks associated with them than psychosurgery by a very substantial margin. So I think it is important for the court to consider the cost/benefit ratio of the particular therapy.

MINNA J. KOTKIN (Attorney, New York Lawyers for the Public Interest, New York City): Considering the positions discussed today, do the panel members feel that they could serve as neutral decision-makers in any of the models that Judge Brotman proposed?

DR. NELSON: One might approach this question in terms of the model that's currently being used—the second opinion model. For example, if a surgeon who specializes in cardiac bypasses has been asked to give a second opinion on whether a patient should have a cardiac bypass, the surgeon's own capacity to do that operation might influence the opinion. It's difficult to be a clinician these days without having a bias that a particular medication is beneficial, especially if the clinician uses that medication. If somebody else is treating the patient, the physician has a somewhat increased objectivity. It should be possible to at least speak about the usefulness of medication, or the pros and cons for someone else's patient. Yet there's really no way to escape certain kinds of treatment

Discussion

biases, or even a bias in favor of treatment *per se,* although one can try to be objective. So all our great efforts to be objective must fall before this rather basic truth.

UNIDENTIFIED SPEAKER: Dr. Nelson, you seem to deny the right of the patient to bring this matter to court, and you insist on saying that these are medical/clinical decisions.

DR. NELSON: That's not true. The patient has always had the right to bring the issue to court in the standard malpractice/tort kind of action. All the things we've been talking about are batteries.

DR. LOREN H. ROTH (Conference Faculty): One point that you haven't discussed is that some patients who refuse treatment in mental institutions should be allowed to refuse. Sometimes the treatment is not clinically indicated. When this is the case there's something rotten, something wrong, and the patient does have a legitimate objection. But I don't think the first objection should be malpractice.

DR. NELSON: The malpractice remedy is available theoretically, but it's used so rarely that it's not much of a remedy. I'm a bit reluctant to give too much weight to it. Second, the thrust of my remarks earlier was that each alternative, whether *Rennie, Rogers, A. E. and R. R.* or *Mills,* has costs and benefits. There is no simple monolithic solution that's going to guarantee maximum rights and maximum benefits. I agree with Dr. Roth. Oftentimes the proper treatment is not adequate, not successful, and not appropriate. Patients ought to have the right to refuse that treatment providing they have the requisite competence.

UNIDENTIFIED SPEAKER: Several of us feel that our patients have a right to the adversarial process. Our question is whether or not it's a benefit to have that right, in terms of the patient's treatment. It really comes down to a matter of values and social policy. As a physician I have a lot of difficulty in approving an adversarial process that may lead a person to go without treatment. That's a value that I hold as a physician; I understand that people have different value sysems. The adversarial process may be necessary, and if that is so, my concern is that its negative effects be minimized so that people can get better.

DR. GILL: In my experience the introduction of the adversarial process really works against the most effective treatment. I know of many patients who were not medicated, and I myself have treated several without medication. My own profession would be likely to tell me that these patients should have been medicated if standard medical process were followed. The patients did not want to be on medication; they wanted to try psychotherapy and other forms of rehabilitation treatments without medication, and they were given that option. That's always been true in the institution in which I work.

Part IV

Commitment and Competency: Medical, Legal and Judicial Issues

10

Competence to Refuse Treatment

Robert Michels, M.D.

Competence is not a clinical, medical, or psychiatric concept. It does not derive from our understanding of health, sickness, treatment, or persons as patients. Rather, it relates to the world of law, to society's interest in deciding whether an individual should have certain rights (and obligations) relating to person, property, and relationships.

Many people in a variety of circumstances are generally regarded as incompetent to make many or most decisions in their lives. They include children under a certain age; the mentally retarded under a certain intelligence; persons who have diminished consciousness, for example, those in coma; and those who are delirious, demented or confused. Many other persons would generally be regarded as competent, even though most of their fellow citizens find their values and decisions in life to be foolish, deplorable, or disgusting. They would include criminals, derelicts, other social deviants, and members of some political or religious groups.

Psychiatrists treat a wide variety of patients. The great majority of these patients would seem to be as competent as most other citizens to make life decisions, and would share most of their values with their mentally healthy neighbors. However, some psychiatric patients share characteristics with children, the retarded, and the neurologically impaired—groups the law views as incompetent. Others seem similar to the socially deviant. This conflict between two views of the mentally ill is at the heart of many of our conflicts about their care.

The largest group of psychiatric patients, those who are manifestly competent, may occasionally refuse psychiatric treatment. The question of competence would seem no more relevant here than in any other episode of refusal of medical treatment. It may be raised, however, because of the social stigma attached to mental illness and the widespread assumption that such illness is associated with incompetence, or because of a general reluctance to assert other justifications for coerced therapy (*e.g.*, prevention of risk or nuisance to others, control of costs, aesthetic or moral values, paternalistic preference for health above liberty). By definition, however, there is no genuine question of competence here, but only the possibility of the abuse of competency evaluations.

When there is appropriate reason to question the competence of a psychiatric patient, the issue would seem to be a function of the decision confronting the patient. However, the question of competency is far more likely to be raised when there is a conflict between the choice selected by the patient and that deemed appropriate by his physician. In other words, competence to consent to treatment would seem to be identical with competence to refuse it, but in borderline cases few will question the competence of a consenting patient, while the same patient's refusal would quickly raise the issue. For example, consider the case of a psychotic Christian Scientist who, in his confusion, agreed to the doctor's prescription only to have his consent ruled invalid when his competence was questioned.

One might argue that this asymmetry in itself creates a subtle coercion toward compliance on the part of the patient, since he can avoid the humiliation of having his competence questioned by accepting the doctor's advice. This problem could be altered if the patient's competence were determined before he made his choice, and if he were not presented with the options unless he had been adjudged able to choose among them. Such an approach would seem to be more equitable and less coercive, but also more expensive, and probably impractical. It would also reveal the large number of socially approved decisions that are casually accepted although they are made by those who are not really competent to make them. In current practice, the question of a patient's competence usually does not arise in evaluating whether or not the patient is competent to consent or to refuse treatment, but rather as a step in resolving conflicts between prescribing physicians and their patients.

The most fundamental issue about competency and treatment resides in the fact that a patient's decision, like anyone else's, reflects his values as well as his competence. Mental illness may alter either or both of these factors. There is general agreement that regardless of the cause, an individual who is considered incompetent to make decisions about treatment should not be allowed to do so. The problem here is in constructing the appropriate standards and procedures. There is also general agreement that an individual who holds socially deviant values that are not related to his mental illness, but who otherwise is competent, should be allowed to act on those values even if they lead to a socially unpopular decision concerning treatment. An example would be a member of a religious group that refused all medication.

The toughest case is the mentally ill patient who is competent in the usual sense of the terms and who rejects treatment based upon socially deviant values that are a clear product of his mental illness. This can be seen in the paranoid patient who mistrusts the doctor and the treatment, but who has not lost the ability to test reality to the extent of forming delusions. On the one hand, if we do not allow this patient to refuse treatment, we are in the position of discriminating against one group of competent, yet socially deviant individuals, those whose deviance stems from mental illness. Further, we risk broadening the concept of mental illness to include many whose beliefs or behavior may be unpopular, a problem that has become a reality in some parts of the world. On the other hand, if we allow this patient to refuse treatment, we condemn a group of sick individuals to lives of misery, even though effective treatment may be known and available, because one of the symptoms of their illness is the rejection of treatment. How unfortunate if we could treat a disease that affects the liver, the spleen, or the part of the brain that controls movement, but could not intervene if the disease affected the part of the brain that controls thought and values.

I believe that we have escaped some of the most difficult aspects of this dilemma until now because of the inadequacy of our diagnostic methods and the inefficacy of our treatments. Many people have even questioned whether we are dealing with diseases in the usual sense at all and have viewed treatments as nonspecific attacks on the patient's mind, rather than specific interventions intended to treat mental illness. This problem, however, is rapidly being resolved and will soon succumb to the availability of specific effective treatments. As a result, we will soon have to face a fundamental conflict of values between our concern for health and the right to treatment and our concern for freedom and autonomy and the right to express unpopular views and behave in socially deviant ways.

Let us shift to the question of the standards and procedures to be used in evaluating competence to consent or to refuse treatment. As indicated earlier, there are no real clinical, medical, or psychiatric criteria available for this purpose. However, issues that seem relevant include:

1. The person's knowledge that he has a choice to make
2. The patient's ability to understand the available options, their advantages and disadvantages
3. The patient's cognitive capacity to consider the relevant factors
4. The absence of any interfering pathologic perception or belief, such as a delusion concerning the decision
5. The absence of any interfering emotional state, such as severe panic, depression, euphoria, or emotional instability
6. The absence of any interfering pathologic motivational pressure, such as irresistible rage

7. The absence of any interfering pathologic relationship, such as the conviction of helpless dependency on another person
8. An awareness of how others view the decision, the general social attitude toward the choices, and an understanding of his reason for deviating from that attitude if he does so

There are, however, several problems with such a series of tests. First, they would be time-consuming and difficult to apply in practice. Second, each of the evaluations involves judgments by the evaluator and many of them would have low reliability. Finally, and most significantly, a great many individuals socially judged competent would have difficulty passing the test.

What is the role of the psychiatrist? First, he has technical scientific expertise about the treatments, their effects and their risks, as well as about the patient's prognosis with and without them. Second, he is the patient's caretaker with responsibility for prescribing, treating, comforting, and protecting him. Third, the psychiatrist is regarded as the most capable person in assessing the patient's competence and in evaluating the various functions and capacities listed above. Problems may stem from the conflicts that can occur between these roles. The physician who devotes his time and energy to treating a patient may be biased in making a judgment about competence, if the result of that judgment may be to make the treatment more or less likely to be effective. One solution would be to have different psychiatrists for each function, but like many such solutions, this would involve increased expense, and probably a consequent decrease in the resources available for care and treatment.

This brings me to my final point, the psychiatrist's general perception of the whole question of competence and the right to refuse treatment. I will sidestep the legal, medical, and ethical issues, and talk about how it feels, aware that my feelings may be difficult to defend. The mentally ill are among the most abused of our citizens; they are often inadequately treated and often inhumanely cared for in terms of simple creature comforts. The limiting factors in their care and treatment are often money, trained personnel, and related resources. Concern with issues such as the right to refuse treatment are inherently morally appropriate and enhance the humanity and dignity of the mentally ill. They may, however, also have an opposite effect if they detract from the resources available for these persons' care and treatment. Unfortunately, this is the case today. Society's interest in patients' right to refuse treatment has not always been accompanied by willingness to make available to patients the most attractive treatment options.

Further, the cumbersome procedures associated with concerns over rights, when balanced neither with resources required to comply comfortably with the procedures, nor with resources necessary to provide the treatment, add up to a potent and convincing argument to psychiatric professionals to pursue other areas of endeavor. Regrettably, they are electing to do so in ever-increasing numbers.

The libertarian concerns of the mentally healthy are dramatized in conflicts over the rights of the mentally ill, although those rights are of far less concern to most mentally ill individuals than are their most basic needs for humane care and treatment. This is clearly a dangerous argument; it can be used to justify almost any infringement on the most basic rights of the mentally ill. At the same time, it would be ironic if society's concern with the right to refuse treatment became just another way in which the values of the mentally healthy majority were imposed on the mentally ill minority.

11

The *Rennie* Philosophy and Treatment in the Private Sector

Irwin N. Perr, M.D., J.D.

The *Rennie* case[1] has attracted much academic and judicial attention because it leads logically to the discussion of constitutional issues close to the hearts of legal philosophers. One encounters commentary about psychiatric therapy as cruel and unusual punishment, invasion of the right to bodily privacy, and interference with freedom of expression or with mental processes. Other issues deal with lack of both consent and of informed consent to bodily invasion, competency, dangerousness, and a multitude of due process issues. Mental health litigation usually has not involved discussion of specific psychiatric treatment other than in a brief, cursory fashion.

In the *Rennie* case there was attempted an in-depth review of the diagnosis and treatment of one patient; reference was also made to inappropriate treatment and management of other patients. *Donaldson v. O'Connor*,[2] *Rogers v. Okin*,[3] and other cases have also focused upon the inadequacies of specific psychiatric management or upon the physical abuse of individuals. Clearly, mistreatment of involuntarily hospitalized patients was a major element in the need of the courts to establish some legal principle upon which to intervene. Legal theories provided the justification for judicial intervention to correct abuses, sometimes actual and clearcut and sometimes vague or questionable.

The courts have acknowledged the now-widespread knowledge that the treatment of patients in the collapsing public mental health system has been superficial, inappropriate, and mechanical. Such treatment systems do not approach the level or standard of care known to the psychiatric profession at large. Public hospitals frequently have large numbers of untrained or poorly trained, uncertified psychiatrists. Many would be unqualified for appointment to hospitals in the private sector; many could not function as physicians if they did not work in public institutions. Psychiatrists themselves have been systematically excluded from the patient management process as a plethora of individuals have created a model based on sociology, economics, politics, or superficial and simplistic psychologic ideologies. Significant psychiatric illnesses, such as schizophrenia and major affective disorders, became "problems of living" to be treated with kindness and benevolent intervention. Patients were no longer patients; they metamorphosed into clients. As treatment programs became demedicalized, the courts and the attorneys increasingly became unknowing worshippers at the shrines of the church of clientology. Many psychiatrists reacted to this process by disappearing, qualitatively and quantitatively, from the public sector to the clean air and greener pastures of the private arena. The policy-makers were then left with the responsibility for reviewing mass treatment inadequacies in the undernourished system known euphemistically as "mental health" systems or "community mental health" programs. It is no wonder that the public mental health system has failed, occasioning this outcry for a "right to refuse" treatment.

The scrutiny of legal advocates and the publicity of treatment inadequacies in the public arena revealed the fact that many involuntary patients were indeed receiving little benefit from their loss of freedom. Various legal approaches have been directed to the problem of therapy deprivation. The courts themselves, however, were confused. They knew not what to direct, and they had no background upon which to establish standards. Such a judicial function was different from the traditional one of establishing a past fact by collating a myriad of testimony. The courts were now forced into futuristic judgments as to what might be good, selecting from conflicting sets of standards, and attempting to apply them to individuals in a prospective fashion.

For example, the *Wyatt* case,[4] in dealing with the inadequacy of treatment, directed attention at known but questionably significant defects.[5] Certainly a consideration of due process, the provision of a reasonable, livable environment, the establishment of written, individual treatment programs, and minimal staffing levels are all good. They are not, however, very meaningful in terms of the merits of a treatment program for a given psychotic patient. A benign environmental temperature—not too hot and not too cold—ample toilets and washbasins, and a large staff-patient ratio do not relate to the provision of a high level of psychiatric care. To the contrary, many people believe that psychiatric care itself has deteriorated amidst the flood of good intentions and legal interventions.

To use a comparable analogy, consider the well-intended and legally rational desegregation of school systems by busing. In many instances, the result has not been desegregation; it has been a more rigidly segregated school system combined with a loss of social integration. This was not anticipated in the original glow of righteousness and humanitarianism that were the substrata of the ensuing legal decisions and legislative directives. Sheepishly we ask, what went wrong?

The same question may be raised about public mental health systems. The more things improve, the worse they get, as often we have not anticipated the ripple effect of seemingly reasonable actions.

Returning to the issue of the adequacy of psychiatric treatment, one may ask, "How can such patient care be improved?" One answer is obvious, although it is rarely, if ever, considered and is seemingly not acceptable: the provision of well-trained, board-certified psychiatrists in sufficient numbers for public programs. This would not only be expensive in general, but would require much higher individual salaries for the appropriately qualified individuals. The public, however, especially in these days of tax revolts, does not seem willing to pay the price.

Other legal approaches theoretically might improve patient care. Malpractice litigation in individual cases might ameliorate occasional grossly negligent situations, but malpractice litigation *per se* has never been shown to be related to the quality of patient care and is ultimately quite costly. Similarly, civil rights suits such as the *Donaldson* case are not really relevant and may have an unwanted consequence of further frightening psychiatrists away from the public sector. Due process litigation will protect due process and patient "rights," but it has little relevance to treatment other than in delaying it.

PUBLIC V. PRIVATE PSYCHIATRIC CARE

The gap between private psychiatric treatment and public mental health programming grows. This is not the case in other areas of medicine, where the same principles of therapy apply to the rich and to the poor. The surgical removal of a cancer or the medical management of an ailing heart is theoretically the same for rich and for poor. Only in our psychiatric or "mental health" institutions is there an underclass specifically provided with an inferior and often shoddy standard of care.

Perhaps sensing this, the courts have placed a growing system of protections, rules, and procedures for patients in the mental health treatment system. As public programs wallow in the hopelessness of an anachronistic mental health model, the philosophies that work so poorly there are being forced upon the private sector. The predictable result is increased cost, inappropriate treatment, and extended chronicity for all. As I recently stated elsewhere, "Those who have brought us the dubious benefits of an egalitarian public health system would compound their sins by lowering the private system to that level...."[6]

Let us now turn our attention to the ripple effect of the *Rennie* decision. That case brought great policy changes to New Jersey. Judge Brotman, in his first ruling, found himself in the position of making a psychiatric diagnosis and prescribing treatment. Perhaps in awareness of the inappropriateness of having judges exchange their black judicial robes for the white coats of physicians, and in recognition of the Supreme Court's cautions in the *Parham*[7] case, he recommended a number of measures to resolve the problems of treatment of involuntary patients. A major recommendation was the provision of an independent psychiatrist to act in conjunction with a patient advocate. That patient advocate, of dubious professional qualification, is to be a trained attorney, psychologist, social worker, registered nurse, paralegal, or equivalent person (whatever that is) who must be given training in the effects of psychotropic medication. The advocate acts in a decision-making capacity about pharmacologic treatment. Judge Brotman's decision, a compromise alternative to dumping treatment problems on judges, is based on the hope that there is such a thing as an independent medical decision-maker.

These steps were taken in response to inadequate decision making by staff physicians in public psychiatric programs. The essence of the formula is that since we cannot trust the professional acumen of Doctor A, we will bring in a real expert, Psychiatrist B, who will supervise the treatment to be administered and who will place an imprimatur on the treatment to be recommended.

Medically, this system has certain inherent faults. It is slow. It allows decisions to be made by a person who often will have only a single contact with the patient and who will have no responsibility for the patient's care. It ignores both the flexibility required in ongoing treatment and the need to react constantly to changing circumstances. It implies merit in rigidly tying therapy programs to a given moment in time. Further, it demeans the position of Doctor A, who becomes the errand boy (or errand girl) of Psychiatrist B. The history of Mr. Rennie and the chaotic treatment administered to him while he was under court jurisdiction attests to the problems inherent in this type of approach.

In New Jersey advocacy has been extended to private hospitals, which have turned increasingly to the courts for guidance. Fear of litigation has become as potent as actual suit itself; the paralysis of the public sector has crept into the private psychiatric health delivery system. To exemplify this, I present two cases for your consideration.

Case Number One

Mrs. A., aged 55, was admitted for her fifth hospitalization to a private psychiatric hospital. Diagnosis was a manic episode in a woman with a clearcut manic-depressive illness, bipolar type. She was first hospitalized in 1945 and had been given electroshock therapy with a good remission, remaining well until 1965, when she was hospitalized again and treated with medication. Between 1972 and 1980 she was hospitalized twice, once at a public hospital, but the details are not known.

On January 1, 1980, she was again admitted for acute mania on the authority of a two-physician certificate and a judge's oral assent. Although hearings in New Jersey are supposed to be held within 20 days of admission, a judicial review ultimately took place 37 days later. In the interim, Mrs. A. was held on the intensive treatment evaluation unit and was frequently placed in seclusion because of violent aggressive outbursts during which she hit those in the immediate environment and burned herself with cigarettes. On January 6, she was given 12 mg. of Trilafon a day, and on January 7, 900 mg. of lithium a day was begun. On January 8, her Trilafon was increased to 24 mg. a day in liquid form. The lithium was discontinued because of her refusal to take the medication and her combativeness. She continued to take the Trilafon in liquid form. On January 18 she stopped all medication, and the staff did not treat her further because of the implications of the *Rennie* decision. She also suffered from chronic obstructive pulmonary disease with asthma and refused treatment for that condition. She remained untreated until February 6.

On February 6, the court authorized both commitment and treatment. Trilafon was again instituted at 24 mg. a day, as was lithium at 1200 mg. a day. This was increased to 1800 mg. a day on February 18. By March 3, Mrs. A. showed significant improvement, and she was discharged on March 17 on lithium 1800 mg. a day and Trilafon 45 mg. a day.

As a result of the delay in treatment, Mrs. A. spent three extra weeks on the evaluation unit, the most expensive ward (new admissions were ordinarily kept for one to two weeks on this unit). She was unmedicated for 19 days. Her husband was advised by the hospital to obtain legal assistance. The family also hired an outside psychiatrist following a recommendation by the hospital and approval by the public advocate.

The total cost of the hospitalization was $25,137. Extra hospital charges due to the delay in treatment were estimated at $11,550. Insurance covered 80 percent of the hospital charges and the family paid 20 percent. In addition, other known costs were $100 for the public advocate, $175 for the independent psychiatrist, and $742 for the family's attorney—raising the total known cost of the judicial process to $12,567. The hospital attorney did not attend the hearing.

This hospital now has a policy in cases of treatment refusal to consult with the family and to refer the family for outside legal advice. If the patient refuses medication and the patient is considered dangerous, the patient is referred to a public mental hospital.

Other "soft" costs such as the time involved in extensive family consultation and unusual administrative time are not included in the above estimate of costs relating to delay of treatment because of legal procedure.

CASE NUMBER TWO

Mr. B., a 48 year old professional man, was voluntarily admitted to another private hospital on January 1, 1980, in an agitated paranoid state. He was first hospitalized in 1964 at age 33 for a severe paranoid schizophrenic episode and had four hospitalizations between 1967 and 1973 totaling about three years. His illness resulted in the loss of an academic position and the breakup of his first marriage. He later moved to New Jersey where he remarried and established himself in a successful professional endeavor. Throughout the years, he was followed as a psychiatric outpatient and took such neuroleptic drugs as Mellaril, Taractan, Stelazine, Thorazine, and Moban. For many years he had a spastic torticollis with a slight but clearly visible twisting of the head. His family reported that this began in the 1960s and has been static since. He also had choreiform movements, particularly in his left arm. Other neuromuscular symptoms were periodically noted.

In the spring of 1979, Mr. B. stopped medication and had increasing symptoms over a five-month period. Because of his bizarre behavior, hostility, and confrontations with those with whom he worked, he was suspended from his position. He reported close friends to the bar association for various alleged delinquencies, wrote letters to local newspapers about the plots against him, accused several acquaintances of intercourse with his wife, whom he believed was pregnant by a close friend, and threatened numerous lawsuits. He also claimed that he was shot at and followed.

In the hospital he expressed ideas of persecution and harassment and was hypervigilant. He was noted to have tardive dyskinesia with torticollis as the most prominent symptom. Diagnosis was paranoid schizophrenia with schizoaffective features. Although hospitalized as a voluntary patient, he would take only Stelazine up to 20 mg. a day, and refused either an increase in Stelazine or other medication. Such treatments as lithium, electroshock therapy, and other medications were considered; he refused all. He also declined treatment for his bursitis and would not see an orthopedist called to evaluate him; this condition ultimately resolved spontaneously.

Mr. B. was kept on a closed unit where he was seen daily for individual psychotherapy, with slight but insignificant improvement. He refused medical evaluation, including an electroencephalogram and neurology consultation. Mr. B. was quite sophisticated about drug therapy and its benefits and risks, including tardive dyskinesia, and had read extensively about pharmacology. He felt that his life was threatened, that the staff was stealing from him, and that his food was being poisoned. He refused to eat in the hospital dining room.

The staff were unsure as to his committability and uncertain what to do if he requested his release. The staff also were quite upset about his not being treated and his continuing belligerence, threats, paranoid ideas, and verbal abuse. Initially he was not assaultive, but after two months he engaged in pushing episodes with nurses, and threatened a physician. The staff finally decided to have him committed.

Psychological testing on admission was limited because of his lack of cooperation and refusal to complete tests. He was noted to be of superior intelligence but in the throes of an acute and florid paranoid schizophrenic disorder. His associations were loose and his responses bizarre. He was considered not to be amenable to any form of psychotherapy.

The family (wife, sister, and brother-in-law) were quite upset by his refusal to be treated, his continuing accusations, and the overall stressful situation. They hired a prominent law firm for advice. The latter in turn employed an outside psychiatrist to act as a consultant in determining their own recommendations. The family, attorney, and psychiatrist met to review the situation in depth.

After 71 days, on March 11, 1980, a commitment hearing was held at the hospital. Mr. B. refused to see the psychiatrist hired by the family, and frequently interrupted the proceedings. The judge issued a commitment order but would not act on the hospital's request to treat him. Prior to the hearing, both the county attorney and an appointed legal advocate were brought into the case. Four attorneys—one for the patient, one for the county, and two for the family—attended the hearing. At later hearings, the hospital was represented. Two psychiatrists, including the medical director, testified on behalf of the hospital. The patient's neurologic condition and the difficulties in management were discussed in depth.

The judge found the patient to be committable in accord with legal criteria, but ordered a second hearing on March 30 to review the patient's competence to refuse treatment. At that hearing, a decision was again deferred to allow the original referring psychiatrist, whom the patient found tolerable and who was a friend of the patient, to consult with him. The third court hearing was held 96 days after admission, on April 16, 1980. The second and third hearings were held at the county seat, requiring special transportation arrangements for the patient. In the interim, Mr. B. was examined by a neurologist who felt that his neuromuscular symptoms were a manifestation of tardive dyskinesia.

At the second hearing, an "independent" psychiatrist brought in by the hospital testified in addition to the hospital staff psychiatrist and medical director. The hospital staff psychiatrist recommended lecithin, reserpine, and possibly lithium carbonate. The outside psychiatrist recommended Stelazine, lithium, and a cholinergic stimulant such as Choline or Deanol.

The judge finally authorized treatment on April 15, 1980. Mr. R. was treated with Navane and then with Stelazine, reserpine, and Artane. He improved rapidly and was discharged on May 9, 1980—121 days after admission.

The delay in treatment from the first hearing until April 15, 1980 was 35 days. Costs for this period were $6,400 for the hospital and $900 in psychiatrists' fees. Additional charges were $1,600 for the hospital attorney and $450 for the presence of the hospital psychiatrists at the various hearings. The independent psychiatrist brought in by the hospital charged $400 for his examination and appearance at the second court hearing. Transportation costs for the second and third hearings were $120. The fees for the public advocate, county adjuster, and patient's referring psychiatrist are not known. Nor, of course, are the indirect costs of the judge and his staff. Other costs were $8,800 for the attorneys representing the family and $1,235 for the psychiatrist consultant to the family. Thus, at a minimum, the increase of costs to the patient or his family due to the delay of approval for treatment was well over $19,000. The patient did not have hospital insurance. The above estimate also does not include loss of income for this additional period—a potentially significant amount of money.

Discussion

The application of the *Rennie* principles to private hospitals can be seen to have certain potential consequences for hospitals as well as for patients. Hospitals, fearful of lawsuits, have sought judicial approval for treatment. Patient treatment itself has been delayed significantly. In addition to the delay of psychiatric therapy, both case histories cited also represented situations where other significant medical modalities were not provided to the patient. In these cases, the lapses were not consequential; in other cases, such omission of medical care might have serious results. This focus on neuroleptic medication alone obscures the greater problem of total patient care—an obvious requirement if treatment is to be of acceptable medical quality.

In the two cases reviewed, the known additional costs to the two patients and their families from legal procedure were far in excess of

$30,000. The inefficiencies of judicial review in supervising medical treatment are exemplified by this remarkable waste of resources. This has not been considered in the litigation involving public hospitals, where the actual per diem costs, while not so high, are clearly significant and a public burden—particularly in view of possible prolonged time periods.

In the cases reviewed, the quality of physician care is not realistically at issue. The hospitals involved are established, prominent hospitals of known quality in the state. Similarly, the psychiatric staffs are well-trained and of a level not seen in public institutions. The therapies are generally appropriate, even when one acknowledges professional differences and preferences, and the programs reasonable. These are not cases of neglect or ineptness. The clinical status of the patients and the need for treatment are not subjects of doubt or disagreement.

Such cases do raise questions as to appropriate public policy. What should be public policy is open to legitimate question. The reason for presenting this material is to demonstrate the ripple effect of legal decisions such as that in the *Rennie* case. These cases illustrate how abuses of public patients have resulted in major legal changes that have spread to the private sector and that may harm private patients. Considering the fact that the average hospitalization insurance policy in New Jersey is for 30 days, another possible consequence must be considered—a resulting deprivation of treatment. Families of lesser resources or with different insurance policies may well face the fact that as a result of legal procedures designed to protect the rights of patients there may be minimal or no treatment while the patient is at a well-staffed and amply endowed nongovernmental psychiatric hospital, followed by transfer to an undernourished and inept public program. One must then question the ultimate benefit to the patient of such an exercise in legal protection.

How to balance therapeutic needs and legal rights remains a vexing problem. Before the courts cast public policy into a rigid new mold, they must carefully consider all possible consequences. Otherwise, the originally anticipated benefits will once more be dwarfed by unanticipated harms that will bedevil us all.

NOTES

1. *Rennie v. Klein*, 462 F. Supp. 1131 (D. N. J. 1978), 476 F. Supp. 1294 (D. N. J. 1979), 481 F. Supp. 552 (D. N. J. 1979).
2. *Donaldson v. O'Connor*, 493 F.2d 507 (5th Cir. 1974), *vacated and remanded*, 422 U.S. 563 (1975).
3. *Rogers v. Okin*, 478 F. Supp. 1342 (D.Mass. 1979), *aff'd in part, rev'd in part, vacated and remanded*, 634 F.2d 650 (1st Cir. 1980).

4. *Wyatt v. Stickney*, 325 F. Supp. 781 (M.D. Ala. 1971), 334 F. Supp. 1341 (M.D. Ala. 1971), *supplemented*, 344 F. Supp. 387 (M.D. Ala. 1972), *modified and remanded sub nom.*, *Wyatt v. Aderholt*, 503 F 2d 1305 (5th Cir. 1974). *See also Wyatt v. Stickney*, 344 F. Supp. 373 (M.D. Ala. 1972).
5. *Id.*, 334 F. Supp. at 1343.
6. Perr, E., *President's Message: Egalitarianism, Medical Care, and Mental Health*, BULLETIN OF THE AMERICAN ACADEMY OF PSYCHIATRY AND THE LAW, VII (4):iv–vii (1979) at v.
7. *Parham v. J. R.*, 442 U.S. 584 (1979), *reversing* 412 F. Supp. 112 (M.D.Ga. 1976).

12

Assumptions Underlying Competency, Commitment, and Treatment Decisions

William J. Curran, J.D., LL.M., S.M.Hyg.

As we examine the right to refuse treatment and argue in support of the court decisions in this area, we must realize that the concept of individual competency is the essential issue. This concept, briefly, recognizes the right of the individual to make his or her own decisions about care and treatment, and acknowledges that each person can make these decisions even if an outside observer feels that it is not in the person's best interest. It is important to note that those who support this concept consider most people, including those civilly committed to mental hospitals, to be competent to make most decisions. We would have a completely different discussion if examining these people resulted in declaring the great majority of them incompetent.

It is important to recognize that the legal argument in support of the right to refuse treatment does not require us to examine the past or present poor quality of treatment in the mental institutions. This examination would be beside the point. We are concerned with the recognition of a person's competency to make a decision. From this position, it is not relevant that the patient might make a poor decision that could result in remaining sick or becoming sicker. The point is that we must recognize the right of individuals to decide for themselves in all instances, and thus we characterize most people as being legally competent. It is only when we turn to the task of determining which individuals are incompetent to make treatment decisions that we get into trouble. If we consider the question simply as a legal issue, we can merely require that when patients cannot make a treatment decision, someone else must be empowered to make it for them. In the usual legal context, this entails appointment of a guardian.

What I've said up to this point explains the essence of the *Rogers v.*

Okin decision.[1] Under that ruling, patients are generally considered to be competent; if they refuse treatment, their refusal must be honored. Only in emergencies that involve the potential for immediate physical danger is the psychiatrist or state permitted to medicate over the patient's objections. Otherwise, the refusal must stand, and the state must go to court and seek the appointment of a guardian.

It is worth noting that one place at which *Rennie v. Klein*[2] departs from *Rogers v. Okin* is on this last point. The *Rennie* decision says that the appointment of a guardian by the court is perhaps not in the best interests of the individual, and suggests another alternative: the use of independent psychiatrists to make clinical judgments about the patient's best interests, and the use of clinical advocates.

Within either the *Rogers* concept of the court-appointed guardian, or the *Rennie* concept of a combination of independent clinical judgment and advocate support, there must be a standard upon which the surrogate decision maker can make a judgment. This standard is not clear in either opinion. The standard seems to be based upon either of two grounds. One is that the guardian or other agent makes the decision in the best interest of the patient; the other is that the agent tries to determine what the patient would do if competent—the idea of substituted judgment. The latter, I believe, is very difficult to apply by those who do not know the patient, since it requires the third person to decide as the patient would have decided, and not according to his or her judgment of what is in the "best interest" of the patient. This is an important point; although difficult to apply, the second model fully recognizes that the individual's wishes are preeminent.

The state of Massachusetts has adopted the concept of substituted judgment in the *Saikewicz* case,[3] and the District of Columbia has applied the same test in a mental health area in the *Boyd* decision.[4] I think the courts use this standard because it sounds less paternalistic or coercive than "acting in the best interest" of an incompetent person. Voltaire many years ago said that the greatest tyrant is the person who works in your best interest.

In both the Massachusetts and the New Jersey decisions, courts relied upon the concept of a constitutional right of privacy, essentially because the action of coercion was that of a state acting under law. Otherwise, I think the concept added nothing to the reasoning applied.

Notice that the rules for determination of competency do not depend upon the involuntariness of the patient's commitment. This status issue is not essential. It comes up only when one wants to keep the refusing patient in the institution long enough to allow some negotiation about treatment. It is not clear to me whether a distinction is required in this situation either. As mentioned in *Rogers*, if a voluntary patient refuses treatment, the hospital can discharge the patient. The law, however, also allows the institution to discharge at any time a committed individual it determines is capable of being released. So it seems to me that even in cases of involuntary commitment, the institution might still be able to release patients if they refused treatment and nothing else was available. There would not be time to negotiate. I believe there should be time for negotiation, and I think we must adjust our concept of commitment in order to provide for it.

Turning to the issues surrounding commitment, it seems to me that the law of commitment tends to support arguments *against* a general right to refuse treatment. Those who support involuntary commitment and reject a right of involuntarily committed patients to refuse treatment, argue that the law intends treatment. And commitment, we must recall, is the basic argument for earlier court discussions concerning the right to treatment.[5] The essential quality of the commitment order is its recognition of the patient's need for treatment. This assumption cannot be denied. Commitment assumes that the person is currently unable to make sound decisions about his or her need for psychiatric treatment *and* that it would be dangerous to the person or to others to allow him or her to remain in the community.

I would suggest that there is more support today for this assumption in the commitment laws of this country than there ever was in the past. Many years ago, when almost the only alternative in the area of psychiatric care was a large state hospital, patients were committed to such hospitals because that was all there was. Treatment was not so important as removing the individual from society. Since then, we have been steadily narrowing the concept of involuntary commitment, so that today it is applied only to the patient who has gone through whatever is available in the community, has utilized all forms of voluntary care and treatment, and for whom this system of care has been inadequate. This individual now needs some constraints, some pressure to move toward additional care and treatment in his or her best interest. If this historical view of involuntary commitment is correct, it is compatible with the view that persons committed today are generally not capable of making a decision about their treatment, which they are being committed to receive, and thus should not be permitted to argue that they have a right to refuse all forms of proffered treatment.

If we view commitment in this fashion, then it seems to me that we should utilize a very narrow legal definition of competency. Incompetence resulting from commitment should not deal with the broad nature of the person's capacity to control property, to have dealings with relatives, or to consider long-term treatment needs. It should concern only the situation at the time of the commitment, and should entail only a finding of whether or not the patient is competent to make clinical judgments in his or her own best interests. I'm not sure that this standard would satisfy the description of an emergency or crisis of a physical nature, like that suggested by Judge Tauro in *Rogers v. Okin*.[6] Many of the people who are committed are certainly in crisis, but they are in varied and sometimes multiple crises. They are in crises that may concern family or personal decisions, they may need more help and assistance than they can get in the community, or they may present a danger to themselves or to those around them due to a particular unresolved problem.

This narrower definition of competency for commitment, then, would suggest that during a time of crisis, such patients could be treated, even if they objected. One would hope the treatment would proceed with the patients' active participation and understanding. But, if not, they could still be forcibly treated to the extent that they would be able later to make judgments and to contribute to their further treatment. If the institution is operating on a short-term treatment basis, the patients should be ready to go back to the community at that point. At this stage there is no longer any need to force treatment upon them. If they have reached a point of balance where they are beginning to resist the treatment only when they are about to be released, they can be referred to a different milieu where mutual negotiation can take place. This approach avoids the problems of long-term commitment and the more custodial kind of care, and recognizes the patient's general competence.

This approach, however, also leaves us some serious issues to discuss. There are going to be people who need longer term care in the institutional setting. It may mean that we must move some people, if they are judged to be highly dangerous, into the criminal system. It may mean that some people will have to be in some other kind of civil custodial care program. Neither of these possibilities necessarily means that the dangerous patients will get forced treatment. The recent British Royal Commission Report on the medical and psychiatric treatment of prisoners came up with almost exactly the same concept as the *Rennie* court: it recommended the consultation of an outside, independent psychiatrist when a prisoner refuses treatment.

Considering both competency and commitment in relation to treatment, I feel that we must continue the movement toward individualized treatment orders. We need well-tailored programs that acknowledge and utilize the input of the patient. Mental health care should be delivered through negotiated treatment programs. We should avoid the situation in which one party produces a treatment program and orders the other to follow it. To accomplish this objective, I think patients need some power. The completely passive, or the completely naked individual, is rarely listened to. Patients need to be listened to, even if they're not speaking.

That may sound a little like "the sound of one hand clapping," but I do not think it is. There are many ways of considering and listening to patients' needs.

I am nonetheless concerned about court-supported efforts to grant patients total power to resist treatment. Such power leads to rigid confrontation and to long-term guardianships, neither of which is in the best interests of the patient. We need the use of independent psychiatrists who will look at the issue of the moment and not try to decide at a given time about the long-term needs of the patient. Long-term needs should always be negotiated and be reexamined as the patient progresses in treatment.

All of this discussion, however, is a hollow legal argument unless we look to improvements in the quality of the system, the quality of the people in it, and the quality of the methods of treatment. I believe that we must confine compulsory commitment to those patients determined to be dangerous to themselves or to others, that such commitment should be short-term, and that the system should always be moving toward greater and greater freedom for the patient. Thus, I do not favor total power over treatment decisions on either side. I believe that negotiation should be used to bring out the true reason for treatment, and the true reason for resistance.

Notes

1. *Rogers v. Okin*, 478 F. Supp. 1342 (D. Mass. 1979), *aff'd in part, rev'd in part, vacated and remanded*, 634 F.2d 650 (1st Cir. 1980).
2. *Rennie v. Klein*, 462 F. Supp. 1131 (D. N.J. 1978); 476 F. Supp. 1294 (D. N.J. 1979); 481 F. Supp. 552 (D. N.J. 1979).
3. *Superintendent of Belchertown State School v. Saikewicz*, 370 N.E.2d 417 (Mass. 1977).
4. *In re Boyd*, 403 A.2d 744 (D.C.App. 1979) (where mental patient, adjudicated incompetent, had while competent rejected psychotropic drugs on religious grounds, trial court in deciding whether to authorize nonconsensual drug treatment must use substituted judgment test to determine what the individual would decide).
5. *O'Connor v. Donaldson*, 422 U.S. 563 (1975); *Rouse v. Cameron*, 373 F.2d 451 (D.C. Cir. 1966).
6. *Rogers v. Okin, supra* note 1, at 1374 (emergency situation is defined as one where there is the occurrence or serious threat of extreme violence, personal injury, or attempted suicide). *See* Mass. Gen. Laws Ann. c. 123 § 21.

13

Commitment and Other Matters: Some Comments from the Bench

The Honorable Alfred L. Podolski

At the outset of my remarks I should note that I speak for myself and not for any court or for any other judge. The views I share with you are my own and are not to be taken in any sense as the law of this or of any other jurisdiction.

This is not to say that I do not have a keen interest in the questions surrounding competency and the treatment of incompetents. My interest in the subject predates the now-famous *Saikewicz* decision.[1] In the spring of 1977, I had occasion, during a visit to the Hampshire County Court, to learn of the growing concern by some members of the bar regarding the medical treatment of incompetent patients at state institutions. At that time, it was brought to my attention that attorney Paul Rogers was pursuing legal goals which would eventually bring *Saikewicz* before the probate courts of this state, and ultimately lead to a decision which would put Massachusetts at variance with the state of New Jersey, as the law of that state was expressed in the *Quinlan* case.[2]

Concern for incompetents and their treatment is a legitimate exercise of judicial authority by the probate and family courts of Massachusetts, and our Supreme Judicial Court has so held in numerous cases since *Saikewicz*. It was predictable that after *Saikewicz*, the courts of this state, absent a legislative incursion into the field, were to embark on a case-by-case common law approach to one of the last frontiers of discovery. How does one pass from this life to death with dignity and without unnecessary prolongation of life but having in mind the sanctity of all human life? Who is to make decisions in this area for those not competent to make those decisions for themselves?

As an aside, I believe that one of the best results of *Saikewicz*, intended or not, was the promotion of a serious and perpetual dialogue between medical and legal professionals. This conference is a prime example, but the same dialogue has occurred in legal and medical classrooms as well as in courtrooms and hospitals. We are talking and thinking about these questions, and that is important.

It is my task to discuss here the issues surrounding competency and the commitment of psychiatric patients from a judicial perspective. I begin with a review of the law.

Ways to Commit Incompetents

There are two ways to commit incompetents under the laws of Massachusetts. The first method is via chapter 123 of the Massachusetts General Laws, which is administered by the state's district courts. This chapter mandates that the department of mental health adopt regulations that establish procedures utilizing the "highest practicable professional standards" for the "reception, examination, treatment, restraint, transfer of mentally ill and mentally retarded persons in department facilities."[3] The statute provides for the transfer of persons by the department from one facility to another; periodic review, hearing, and discharge by the department of mental health of persons in the care of the department; hearings for commitment or retention of persons in a facility with a right to counsel; and the right to petition a district court for commitment and retention of persons considered dangerous by the superintendent of a facility (and others) with a guaranteed hearing thereon within 14 days.[4]

Under the statute, a district court judge may not commit or review commitment of a person in a facility *unless* the court finds after it conducts a hearing that (1) such person is mentally ill, and (2) the discharge of such person from a facility would create a likelihood of serious harm. A person committed under this statute may be held for six months, and thereafter persons may be held for one year with certain conditions. Intelligent waivers of hearings under this section are possible.[5]

The statute also provides that the appellate division of the district court may review matters of law arising in commitment proceedings or in competency to stand trial proceedings. On the written application of any person, a justice of the Superior Court, after notice, may hear allegations that a person is held in a mental health facility "who should no longer be retained."[6]

With proper legal safeguards, a superintendent of a state mental health facility may receive and retain a voluntary patient in need of care and treatment. The superintendent may also discharge a person voluntarily admitted, or may treat or discontinue treatment of such person as an outpatient.[7] After written notice, a person voluntarily admitted under this statute may leave a facility during normal working hours and on weekends. The superintendent, at his discretion, may require three days notice of withdrawal.[8]

Let me review the process for you. A duly licensed physician who, after examination, has reason to believe that failure to hospitalize a person would create a likelihood of serious harm *by reason of mental illness*, may restrain or authorize the restraint of the individual in question. The physician may also apply for the hospitalization of such a person, for a ten-day period, at a public or duly authorized private facility. If an examination of the person is not possible because of the emergency nature of the case or the unwillingness of the person to be examined, the physician may nonetheless apply for hospitalization. If a physician is not available in an emergency situation, a police officer may apply for a ten-day hospitalization at an appropriate facility.[9] If the applying physician has been specifically designated by the department of mental health to have the authority to admit a person to a specific facility, the individual may be admitted to the facility on reception if the application is made by a non–department designated physician. The person then must be given a psychiatric examination by a designated physician, who must find that failure to hospitalize such person would create a likelihood of serious harm by reason of mental illness, before the person is admitted for care and treatment.[10] No person can be admitted to a facility under this statute unless he or his legal representative is given an opportunity to apply for voluntary admission under §10(a), and no hospitalization can exceed ten days. Furthermore, if admitted, the person is automatically discharged from the facility at the end of ten days, unless the superintendent requests otherwise, or the person remains voluntarily committed.

The statute also provides that any person may make an application to a district court judge for a ten-day commitment of a mentally ill person.[11] After a hearing, the justice may issue a warrant for the apprehension and appearance of such person before the court. If a designated physician who has examined the person reports to the court that failure to hospitalize would create a likelihood of serious harm, the court may order the person committed to a facility for ten days.

The balance of the statute deals with transfers of dangerous persons, competence to stand trial, hospitalization of persons incompetent to stand trial, the periodic review of incompetence, hospitalization of mentally ill prisoners, the power of courts to have parties and witnesses examined by a department physician, extradition of escapees, and a plethora of laws dealing with alcoholic and drug addiction problems. Only the first 12 sections of chapter 123 bear on the subject of this discussion.

It is worth noting that in December 1979, District Court Chief Justice Samuel Zoll, with the help of an excellent committee of district court judges, published "Standards of Judicial Practice—Civil Commitment."[12]

The standards were designed to help district court justices and other district court personnel in the task of administering chapter 123. The standards incorporate two interesting extensions of chapter 123 by case law, namely, *Gallup v. Alden*[13] and *Worcester State Hospital v. Hagberg*.[14] The *Gallup* case, a decision of the appellate division of the district court, requires the trial judge to find that hospitalization is the least restrictive alternative for dealing with the threatened harm. The *Hagberg* case holds that the amount of proof required in commitment cases is the same as it is for criminal cases; that is, proof beyond a reasonable doubt.

The second method of commitment in Massachusetts occurs via the laws of guardianship, chapter 201.[15] The power to appoint guardians in this state is vested exclusively in the probate and family courts. The applicable provisions of this statute, and their judicial interpretation, require some analysis.

Section 6 of chapter 201 provides that a parent of a mentally ill person, two or more relatives or friends of such a person, a nonprofit corporation authorized to act as a guardian of such person, or the department of mental health may file a petition in the probate court asking to have a guardian appointed for an alleged incompetent. If after notice and hearing, the court finds that such a person "is incapable of taking care of himself by reason of mental illness," it is empowered to appoint a guardian to supervise all decisions concerning the ward's person and estate. Please note that thus far the section does not give the guardian authority to commit the ward to a mental hospital. Later on in the same section it is expressly stated that no guardian shall have the authority to cause to admit or commit such person to a mental health or retardation facility unless the court specifically finds the same to be in the best interests of such person and specifically authorizes such admission or commitment by its order or decree. This may be done only after a hearing (counsel for the ward, if necessary, is appointed) which the ward attends if possible.

Section 14 of chapter 201 contains most of the same provisions regarding the appointment of temporary guardians as §6 contains for the appointment of permanent guardians. Section 14 also contains essentially the same provisions regarding commitment power for temporary guardians as does §6, *i.e.*, commitment may not occur without notice, hearing, a finding of best interests, and specific authorization for commitment.

Two important cases interpreting these statutes were decided by the Massachusetts Supreme Judicial Court (SJC) in 1978 and 1979. The first of these cases was *Fazio v. Fazio*,[16] a case that was unusual in that it combined the appeals of a 30 year old man who had a permanent and temporary guardian appointed for him together with a separate support action between his mother and father. The 30 year old had been diagnosed by a psychiatrist some years prior to the case as having a definite mental illness—psychoneurosis and schizophrenic personality. At that time, around 1961-1962, the psychiatrist recommended that the man be treated in a hospital because he had a phobia and obsession concerning contamination. In 1965, the same psychiatrist gave the patient a certificate stating he was unable to work due to mental illness. In 1970, the psychiatrist diagnosed the young man as having a schizophrenic personality, an obsession about contamination, and a definite mental illness. At the hearing, the psychiatrist recommended that a guardian be appointed to take care of the young man and his belongings.

The SJC vacated the guardianship order, and held that a trial judge's findings must be twofold to support the appointment of a guardian: a person (1) must be incapable of taking care of himself, (2) by reason of his mental illness. In this case the trial judge's findings did not contain a finding that the proposed ward was incapable of taking care of himself by reason of mental illness, and thus the trial judge could not properly determine that the person was in need of a guardian. This decision did not hold that there was not enough evidence, only that the judge had not followed the statute.

In the *Fazio* case, the SJC cited but declined to apply the standard of proof beyond a reasonable doubt, which was adopted in the *Hagberg* case, because *Fazio* was *not* a commitment case. The court did, however, discuss the statutory phrase "incapable of taking care of himself by reason of mental illness," and interpreted it as encompassing a general inability on the part of an individual to manage his own personal and financial affairs, such inability being caused by mental illness.[17] The SJC, for the benefit of the trial court, added that the type of evidence necessary to support such a finding (besides evidence of mental illness) should consist of facts showing a proposed ward's inability to think or act for himself about matters concerning his health and safety and general welfare, or to make informed decisions as to his property or financial interests.[18] The same was said of findings under chapter 201, the guardianship statute. The court went on to say that there was little or no evidence of this type presented at the hearing in the instant case. Here again, on the due process question the SJC interpreted a statute by supplying what it lacked in order to pass constitutional muster.

In the case of *Doe v. Doe*,[19] the SJC decided that chapter 201 required a finding beyond a reasonable doubt that failure to commit would create a "likelihood of serious harm" as defined in Massachusetts General Laws ch. 123, §1. By reading in this requirement, the SJC was able to sustain the constitutionality of the statute, which, before it was amended in 1977, had permitted the guardian to commit the ward to a mental health facility without prior court approval.

Thus, the commitment of an individual to a mental health facility in

Massachusetts may be accomplished in somewhat dissimilar ways in the district court and in the probate and family court departments of the trial court. Each department, moreover, has been aided by at least two Supreme Judicial Court decisions interpreting the relevant statutes. In comparing the statutes and the cases, we see that in order to accomplish a commitment under either law, due process safeguards have been applied by the court to make the procedures approximately similar.

It would be perhaps unwise to leave the matter of commitments without looking at the increasing number of judicial decisions dealing with the medical treatment of incompetents who may or may not be residents at mental health facilities. The springboard for discussion of the medical treatment of incompetents was the *Saikewicz* case, and three related decisions: *Candura*,[20] which held that if the person was not incompetent there was no occasion for the appointment of a guardian; *Dinnerstein*,[21] a Massachusetts appeals court case, holding that, at least in the case of a patient with Alzheimer's disease, it was not necessary for the court to be consulted about every medical eventuality; and most recently, *In the Matter of Earle Spring*,[22] which seems to indicate that judicial intervention in the case of all terminally ill patients is not required. The *Spring* case recites 13 factors which bear on whether or not judicial intervention is warranted, upholds the "substituted judgment" test enunciated in *Saikewicz* and states that even judicial intervention does not provide a guarantee of immunity to the parties in a particular case. Given such cases, it was appropriate that *Rogers v. Okin*[23] be filed to determine the rights of mental patients vis-a-vis treatment. Another case considering the psychiatric treatment of a person who is not hospitalized was recently considered by the Massachusetts SJC. The case concerned the power of a guardian to consent to the forcible administration of antipsychotic medication without first having to seek court approval in a substituted judgment hearing.[24]

What does the future hold for this area of law? First, it appears that, at least in Massachusetts, there is a trend away from district court civil commitments and toward guardianship proceedings in the probate and family courts. In 1969, for example, there were 4,392 civil commitments and only 541 guardianships. In 1979, there were 2,226 civil commitments (a 49 percent decrease in ten years), while the number of guardianships had grown by 53 percent to 1,167. The reasons for this shift are unclear. It may be due, in part, to a greater reliance by members of the medical community (and their attorneys) on guardianship orders as a means of achieving legal protection. Perhaps this is because the guardianship process gives them a person, the guardian, to deal with, rather than a piece of paper which embodies a commitment order. The guardian may or may not be empowered to authorize treatment, but at least the issue can be discussed.

The continued emphasis on deinstitutionalization of the mentally ill will also affect these matters. More and more persons of borderline competence will be needing medical and psychiatric treatment at general hospitals, which may be unwilling to treat them without prior court authorization regarding the sufficiency of their consent to treatment. Except in the limited circumstances of dangerous persons (when civil commitment is sought), the probate and family courts will probably be the courts to which institutions will turn to seek guidance on this and similar questions.

I will conclude with a comment on the ability of the judiciary to handle such cases effectively. I do not think the present legal system can handle this onslaught of cases without assistance. The most significant problem facing us now, for example, is the unavailability of suitable persons to serve as guardians. This problem probably will be resolved through the use of corporate guardians, such as those already authorized by statute.[25] One such organization has already been formed in western Massachusetts, but a lack of funds is presently preventing it from operating. As the caseloads grow the resources of the courts will be strained. More justices, support personnel, and facilities will be needed. In these days of fiscal austerity, funding will be difficult to come by.

In all, this is probably one of the fastest developing and most rapidly changing areas of the law, with most of its development yet uncharted. It is a challenge to be a part of it, and conferences such as this make me sure that the medical and legal professions are willing to discuss solutions for problems.

NOTES

1. *Superintendent of Belchertown State School v. Saikewicz*, 370 N.E.2d 417 (Mass. 1977).
2. *In re Quinlan*, 355 A.2d 647 (N.J. 1976).
3. MASS. GEN. LAW ANN., c. 123, §2.
4. MASS. GEN. LAW ANN., c. 123, §§3–5, 7.
5. MASS. GEN. LAW ANN., c. 123, §8.
6. MASS. GEN. LAW ANN., c. 123, §9(6).
7. MASS. GEN. LAW ANN., c. 123, §10.
8. MASS. GEN. LAW ANN., c. 123, §11.
9. MASS. GEN. LAW ANN., c. 123, §12.
10. MASS. GEN. LAW ANN., c. 123, §11(6).
11. MASS. GEN. LAW ANN., c. 123, §12(e).
12. District Court Department of the Trial Court, Committee on Mental Health (Pub. #800–12–79–152427) (December 1979).
13. *Gallup v. Alden*, 57 Mass. App. Dec. 41 (1975).

14. *Superintendent of Worcester State Hospital v. Hagberg*, 372 N.E.2d 242 (Mass. 1978).
15. MASS. GEN. LAW ANN., c. 201, §6, 14.
16. *Fazio v. Fazio*, 378 N.E.2d 951 (Mass. 1978).
17. *Id.* at 956–57.
18. *Id.* at 957.
19. *Doe v. Doe*, 385 N.E.2d 995 (Mass. 1979).
20. *Lane v. Candura*, 376 N.E.2d 1232 (Mass. 1978).
21. *In re Dinnerstein*, 380 N.E.2d 134 (Mass. 1978).
22. *In re Spring*, 405 N.E.2d 115 (Mass. 1980).
23. *Rogers v. Okin*, 478 F. Supp. 1342 (D.Mass. 1979); *affirmed in part, reversed in part*, 634 F.2d 650 (1st Cir. 1980).
24. *In re Guardianship of Roe*, 421 N.E.2d 40 (Mass. 1981).
25. MASS. GEN. LAW ANN., c. 201, §§6, 6A.

14

Implementing the Right to Refuse Psychotropic Medication: Can the Judiciary Respond?

Jonathan Brant, J.D.

The constitutional right of involuntarily committed mental patients to refuse psychotropic medications, as expressed in *Rogers v. Okin*[1] and *Rennie v. Klein*,[2] draws heavily from earlier court decisions which recognized the right of competent adults to decide whether or not to accept prescribed medical treatment.[3] The notion of informed consent—that patients have a right to be informed of the implications and risks of medical procedures in order to decide whether to undergo them—is now a well-accepted and basic tenet of medical law.[4] As far as the law is concerned, the recognition of the right of incompetent patients, such as Karen Ann Quinlan[5] or Joseph Saikewicz,[6] to decline medical treatment is not much different from recognizing a similar right for involuntarily committed mental patients. The reasoning of some of the early right-to-refuse blood transfusion cases (that the refusal should be honored as long as the patient is competent, and even if the action seems odd or even bizarre)[7] is very similar to that which holds that mental patients, even if incompetent, retain the same right to refuse medical treatment that competent patients have. It does, however, present tremendous challenges for clinicians, and implementation of the constitutional principal poses several problems for both attorneys and physicians.

It seems obvious that the courts are not going to adopt the well-intentioned view of many clinicians that, since patients are committed because of the existence of a thought disorder, their refusals of treatment are *per se* incompetent and need not be adhered to.[8] In Massachusetts, and in many other states, commitment does not equal incompetency, and committed patients retain the same presumption of competency as is retained by other adults.[9] So the questions are really when and how can the rebuttable presumptions be overcome?

This is, of course, not to say that all committed patients are in fact competent to make all decisions, including judgments concerning their treatment and medication. Rather, patients are presumed competent, and that presumption can be removed only by a guardianship proceeding or when clinical judgment indicates the immediate need for treatment.[10] An obvious implication of *Rogers* and particularly *Roe* will be an increase in the number of court proceedings involving committed patients.[11] The practical effects of this new body of guardianship proceedings upon the court system are my principal concern here.

NEED FOR ATTORNEYS AND GUARDIANS

For the attorney representing a psychiatric patient, the greatest difficulty is establishing sufficient professional rapport with the client in order to provide adequate representation. To the patient involuntarily committed to the custodial care of the state and feeling entrapped by that milieu, the attorney may well appear to be simply another governmental person. To the delusional or paranoid patient, the attorney, rather than appearing to be his representative, may instead appear to be Richard Nixon, a Martian, or some sort of persecutor.

Rogers and *Roe* create a need for more legal services to be available for committed patients, since many will lack funds for an attorney. Legal services programs and the private bar will have to create and maintain a mental health bar to provide representation for patients.[12] Given the cost of such programs, this may be difficult, especially given the anticipated reduction of government financing of legal services.

In order to adequately represent the mental health client, attorneys must be trained to understand medical and psychiatric terms, and must be trained, through role playing and in other ways, to relate both to their patient-clients and to mental health professionals. One cannot talk about implementing the constitutional principles described in *Rennie* and *Rogers* without being concerned about the availability of trained and competent legal representation for both patients and institutions.

Second, and perhaps more important, *Rogers* and *Rennie* will require the increased availability of persons to serve as guardians for committed patients adjudicated incompetent. Presently, in Massachusetts, it is virtually impossible to find guardians for elderly or incompetent persons who require medical treatment. The task of being a guardian is onerous, since it involves making fundamental decisions for someone else, and there is no provision for compensation if the ward lacks funds.

Implementation of the District Court opinion in *Rogers* would have necessitated creation of a guardianship service, perhaps in conjunction with legal services.[13] Obviously, this service would have to recruit and train highly motivated persons, who would be willing to consider their wards' needs for treatment and be able to weigh fairly the asserted benefits of particular medications against potentially deleterious consequences. A promising development in this area is the idea of creating nonprofit guardianship programs which could act as guardian for several persons at a time.[14]

Role of Judicial Proceedings

The judicial proceeding could be successfully utilized to determine a patient's competency and a patient's need for psychotropic medication. In Massachusetts, such proceedings have been used to determine whether patients should receive medical treatments when the patient is incompetent or unable to consent.[15] The extension of the judicial role to that of the decision-maker for overcoming refusal to consent could be another matter.[16] However, experience in Massachusetts suggests that the courts can accept the additional caseload created by the need to obtain judicial approval in such cases. It is fair to say that judges, like the rest of us, do not volunteer for additional work, especially work which is difficult. Nonetheless, the probate court in Massachusetts has developed mechanisms such as 24-hour hot lines to respond to emergencies and to make judges available when required in medical treatment cases. Further, the powers of a guardian can be limited according to the patients' needs and shaped according to the patient's ability to handle certain aspects of his life but not others.[17] The courts, over time, can develop a body of case law to serve as precedent in guiding both mental health professionals and attorneys.[18]

Mental health professionals have less to fear from this process than they realize. They should not support the indiscriminate drugging of patients in public institutions. Both the medical and legal professions share a concern in learning about the long-term implications of psychotropic medication.[19] It does not help the discussion to minimize the implications of the side effects of these drugs.[20] The side effects are very real, as are the benefits.[21] The judiciary can decide these cases if the facts are properly presented in a court proceeding.[22]

The increased judicial involvement in the administration of medical treatment for involuntarily committed mental patients raises the question of the standard of proof which must be met before a guardian for a nonconsenting patient may be appointed. It would follow that the standard for overcoming nonconsent should be equal to that which must be satisfied before the patient was involuntarily committed in the first place.[23] This is because loss of the power to make treatment decisions constitutes a further loss of liberty.[24]

This latter point raises questions about the relationship between the original commitment proceeding and a subsequent guardianship proceeding or, more pejoratively, whether we are creating too much procedure. For example, in Massachusetts, commitment and competency determinations are made by different courts.[25] To make the process work more smoothly, issues of nonconsent should be brought before courts as soon as possible after a patient's hospitalization. If a patient has refused treatment at the time of commitment, and the institution believes that it can meet its burden of proof that the patient should be treated despite refusal, there is no reason why commitment and treatment cannot be determined in the same proceeding. While *Rennie, Rogers,* and *Roe* require increased judicial involvement there is no reason why the procedures cannot be streamlined and made simpler.

The assertion of a judicial role in the refusal of treatment subject area presents a threat to the assumptions of many mental health professionals. Whether the judicial involvement will prove beneficial in the long run will likely be a function of whether these expedited proceedings can be made to work. Thus, the bench and the bar have an obligation and a challenge before them.

NOTES

1. 478 F. Supp. 1342 (D. Mass. 1979) *aff'd in part, rev. in part,* 434 F.2d 650 (1st Cir. 1980), *cert. granted* 49 U.S.L.W. 3788 (April 20, 1981).
2. 462 F. Supp. 1131 (D. N.J. 1978); 476 F. Supp. 1294 (D. N.J. 1979).
3. *See, e.g., Satz v. Perlmutter* 362 So.2d 160 (Fla. App. 1978) *aff'd* 379 So. 2d 359 (Fla. 1980).
4. *See, e.g., Canterbury v. Spence,* 464 F.2d 772 (D.C. Cir. 1972) *cert. denied,* 409 U.S. 1064.
5. *In re Quinlan,* 355 A. 2d 647 (N.J. 1976), *cert. denied sub nom., Garger v. New Jersey,* 429 U.S. 922.
6. *Superintendent of Belchertown State School v. Saikewicz,* 370 N.E.2d 417 (Mass. 1977).
7. *In re Estate of Brooks,* 205 N.E.2d 435, 442 (Ill. 1965).
8. Appelbaum, P.S. and Gutheil, T.G., *"Rotting With Their Rights On:" Constitutional Theory and Clinical Reality in Drug Refusal by Psychiatric Patients,* BULLETIN OF THE AMERICAN ACADEMY OF PSYCHIATRY AND THE LAW 7:306, 313 (1979).
9. MASS. GEN. LAW ANN. c. 201 §12. *In re Roe, III,* 421 N.E.2d 40 (Mass. 1981).
10. *Rogers v. Okin, supra* note 1 at 660-61.
11. *Rogers* appears to allow guardians to overcome a patient's incompetent expression of nonconsent to antipsychotropic medication. In a more recent decision, the Massachusetts Supreme Judicial Court adds the requirement that a decision to overcome the express nonconsent of noninstitutionalized patients who are under guardianship must receive judicial approval. *In re Roe,*

III, supra note 9. Nonconsent can only be overcome by proof beyond a reasonable doubt in which the stated refusal to consent must be balanced along with the probable benefits and detriments likely to result from the treatment. *Id.*

The Supreme Judicial Court's requirement that courts make the ultimate decision to overcome refusal to consent is an extension of the principles first enunciated in *Superintendent of Belchertown State School v. Saikewicz, supra* note 6, and modified in *In re Spring*, 405 N.E.2d 115 (1980). See generally Brant, J., *Last Rights: An Analysis of Refusal and Withholding of Treatment Cases*, MISSOURI LAW REVIEW 46:337(1981).

12. See *The Attorneys Role at the Commitment Hearing: Guidelines and Practical Considerations: Guildelines for Defence Counsel in Commitment Cases*, MENTAL DISABILITY LAW REPORTER 2:427 (1978). See generally L. Kopolow and H. Bloom, eds., MENTAL HEALTH ADVOCACY: AN EMERGING FORCE IN CONSUMER'S RIGHTS (1977).
13. Again, the need for guardian services is somewhat initiated by the decision of the Court of Appeals which appears to allow less formal procedures to be followed, *Rogers v. Okin, supra* note 1; *Roe* of course, will increase the demands on judicial measures, *In re Roe, supra* note 9.
14. There are three nonprofit guardianship programs: Foundation for the Handicapped in Seattle; Association for the Help of Retarded Children, New York City; and Center for Guardianship Services, Amherst, Mass. GUARDIANSHIP NEWS, 1(1):7 (Dec. 1980).
15. See *Superintendent of Belchertown State School v. Saikewicz, supra* note 6, and *In re Spring, supra* note 11.
16. *In re Roe, III, supra* note 9.
17. *In re Bassett*, 385 N.E.2d 1024 (Mass. 1979).
18. See Baron, C.H., *Assuring "Detached but Passionate Investigation and Decision": The Role of Guardians Ad Litem in Saikewicz-Type Cases*, AMERICAN JOURNAL OF LAW & MEDICINE 4(2):111-30 (Summer 1978).
19. See generally, Task Force on Late Neurological Effects of Anti-Psychotic Drugs, *Tardive Dyskinesia: Summary of a Task Force Report of the American Psychiatric Association*, AMERICAN JOURNAL OF PSYCHIATRY 137:1163 (1980).
20. Appelbaum and Gutheil, *supra* note 8, at 307 (all drugs have side effects).
21. See *In re Roe, supra* note 9, at 58-59.
22. Baron, *supra* note 18.
23. The Supreme Judicial Court has so held requiring "proof beyond a reasonable doubt" before expressions of refusal to consent can be overcome on grounds of the patient's "dangerousness." *In re Roe, supra* note 9 at 60-61. This is the Massachusetts standard for civil commitment. *Superintendent of Worcester State Hospital v. Hagberg*, 372 N.E. 2d 242 (1978). The United States Supreme Court has declared the constitutional standard for commitment to be "clear and convincing evidence." *Addington v. Texas*, 441 U.S. 418 (1979).
24. *In re Roe, supra* note 9, at 60.
25. MASS. GEN. LAWS ANN., c. 123 §4 *et seq*. (West Supp. 1981) (commitment); MASS. GEN. LAWS ANN., c. 201 §6 *et seq*. (West Supp. 1981).

Discussion

Leonard H. Glantz, J.D., Moderator

DR. THOMAS J. GUTHEIL (Conference Faculty): When we consider that many attorneys, who are savvy about the law, refuse to become guardians, believing it too risky due to its undefined liability, how can we expect laymen to take the job? Family members can be sued as easily as anyone else.

MR. JONATHAN BRANT (Conference Faculty): While it is true that the role of the guardian is ill-defined, we must remember that lawyers are trained to be cautious. I think the liability is more theoretical than real, since it is hard to imagine who is going to sue a guardian, and on what grounds. This issue is similar to that of withholding treatment: if you are acting in a professionally competent fashion, conscientiously, and in the best interests of the ward, the chances of being sued successfully are quite slim. I think the reluctance to become a guardian stems from taking on the responsibility of someone else's life. That person's needs may be very clear, but the role of the guardian is very unclear. It is simply easier to say that you are too busy.

I will not suggest the creation of a bureaucracy to take away people's rights. Yet, since some people obviously need guardians, I think that providing a trained group of guardians is a good thing. Programs such as the Friends of Belchertown State School, where most of the guardians are parents, should be expanded. It is not surprising that attorney Paul Rogers has attempted to broaden into a statewide system the concept he helped to create at Belchertown.

UNIDENTIFIED SPEAKER: Mr. Brant, you spoke about negligence when answering the question on guardians' potential liability. In a recent case in my state, a hospital sued the guardian's estate for payment of a bill incurred by the ward which was not covered by insurance and which was in excess of the ward's estate. The local probate statute did not make the guardian's estate immune from such action. In guardianship cases, this problem seems a more likely issue than negligence. Does the Massachusetts statute address this issue?

MR. BRANT: Actually, I'm not sure. I suppose one could construct a contractual argument of the guardian standing in the place of the ward. But, that strikes me as bad law. Public policy should encourage people to become guardians. They should not incur personal liability for trying to help others.

DR. GUTHEIL: How do you understand Judge Tauro proposing guardianship as a solution to all of the cases where it would be appropriate?

MR. BRANT: A judge faces two questions in this area: defining the constitutional violation and then defining the remedy. In any institutional litigation, developing a remedy is usually the more difficult phase. Especially in light of the 1980 election, lawyers and others are debating the feasibility of federal courts' having a continuing involvement in running schools for the retarded through receivers, masters, and monitors. Judge Tauro might not have been looking at the practical issue of finding guardians. He looked at the state law, which provided for guardianship and for guardians to have designated authority including power to consent to medical treatment. He said, in effect, "This is the hook upon which to hang the hat." People are now saying that he is correct constitutionally, but that there are still practical problems to be answered.

UNIDENTIFIED SPEAKER: If a case arises in which it is determined that it would be appropriate to appoint a guardian for someone who is institutionalized, but no guardian is available, will a judge then order that a drug or treatment be given anyway?

JUSTICE ALFRED L. PODOLSKI (Conference Faculty): Assuming that there was a hearing, and that there was evidence a guardian was needed, and evidence concerning the need for treatment, I would say yes, the judge would order treatment.

DR. HUGH SMITH (Psychiatrist, Veteran's Administration Hospital, Boston, Massachusetts): Would you comment upon the involvement of the lawyer in the team-treatment process? The courtroom is a poor place for the lawyer to become involved in other than an adversarial manner. I have found that where the lawyer has been drawn into the process, the staff is far less anxious in dealing with the patient, and many of the legal complications are mitigated.

JUSTICE PODOLSKI: I know of a lawyer who insists on going into the operating room and observing the process in transplant cases, with, it seems, no objection by the surgeons. The more that both the lawyer and the judge are involved in the process, the more everyone is educated. However, the answer, as Professor Curran says, need not be a long-term guardianship. I think that no one has any objection to the short-term guardianship, but then, that is a question for this conference.

JUDGE MAURICE RICHARDSON (Massachusetts Trial Court, Dedham, Massachusetts): The role of the judge is in the initial commitment phase. The court appoints an attorney to represent the patient in every involuntary commitment case, and does seek an adversarial posture from the attorney. However, there does exist a great deal of room for negotiation between the hospital's attorney, the psychiatric staff, and the patient's attorney. A number of accommodations can be made at the hearings in order that the hospital may provide an extended treatment program for the patient.

There is the question of the patient who refuses treatment during the time the judge makes a determination on the evidence. Perhaps two percent of the public facility cases in Justice Podolski's court will require guardians. Why not invest the district court judge, when sitting in a hospital hearing, with probate authority for the limited issue of determining whether the patient should be treated against his will?

From my viewpoint, as a judge sitting in hearings at Medfield State Hospital in Massachusetts, *Rogers v. Okin* does not seem to have any great impact on the operation of the hospital or on the staff.

UNIDENTIFIED ATTORNEY: Relative to the issue of liability, the Massachusetts statute has been changed to require the guardian to agree to be bound personally for any death liability. Further, in the recent case of *Downs v. Sawtelle*,[1] the United States Court of Appeals for the First Circuit held that a guardian could be liable for the sterilization of a slightly retarded deaf woman from Maine. The state hospital's chief administrative officer, who was also the physician, was considered to have qualified immunity. Even though the guardian was acting in concert with these state agents, he could be held liable for a deprivation of the patient's civil rights because he was *not* a state agent. Although the jury eventually found that there was in fact no liability, the case still stands for the proposition that where a ward is being cared for in a state institution, the potential liability rests solely upon the guardian.

I think that trust is the important issue. There is distrust on the part of hospital management and staff towards advocates. Advocates should be more accepted, and there should be some "give" on the other side. While I was counsel to the department of mental health, we had a pilot program to train advocates to work for patients in pubic hospitals under the supervision of outside legal counsel. Only one facility was willing to accept these advocates, and the program was abandoned.

Discussion

Perhaps there is good reason to distrust the guardian. His only accountability is to the ward's estate. The guardian must report to the court on what he does with the ward and with the ward's estate. The probate court otherwise has no way of knowing what the guardian is doing. But I do not feel that we have looked into the reasons why the situation of distrust exists. Why didn't the medical profession do something about a bad situation which has required advocacy?

MR. WILLIAM J. CURRAN (Conference Faculty): It is a good thing to have fearful guardians. The tendency towards negligence on the part of a guardian is enormous, and I am greatly afraid of guardianship systems. I hope that Massachusetts will not convert its system for the medical care of the dying, those in great danger, mental patients, and the retarded, into guardianship proceedings. This would be totally ridiculous. Only a small group of these patients, perhaps one to two percent, require guardianship.

At the time of commitment a judge should have a concern for whether or not short-term forced treatment ought to be allowed, but he should not have the additional capacity to appoint a guardian. However, I would not object to his considering both issues at the same time. In the case of short-term treatment with provision for review, the judge can make a determination based upon the present evidence, realizing that the situation can, and often does, change over time.

As lawyers, we are concerned with building a guardianship system to respond to the requirements of the *Rogers* decision. However, that does not mean a system which will take over the rest of the system: any guardianship system should be limited in scope. So long as patients will be committed to hospitals for any length of time, they must themselves have a role in their treatment. I hope that advocacy can be made to work. Discussions such as this can help break down the distrust that exists, and make the system work so that we don't abandon all our problems to a guardianship system.

UNIDENTIFIED SPEAKER: Do you agree with the characterization of mental health personnel as distrustful of advocates?

DR. ROBERT MICHELS (Conference Faculty): The tension is clearly present, and there are two causes. The first is a feeling of dislike. Each side feels that the other is insensitive to its values. The physician feels that the patient's health comes before his rights, and the advocate feels the opposite. Each finds the other's view to be untenable. Second, there are scarce resources currently available for treatment, and an immense amount of time is required to incorporate the legal representative into the treatment process. No additional resources are made available to offset the costs of this requirement. An eight-hour hearing recently forced 50 patients to go without treatment because five doctors were involved in the hearing. This is a more powerful determinant of the unwelcome reception that the law receives than such "soft" issues as trust and liking.

UNIDENTIFIED SPEAKER: How many patients are not being seen because you are at this conference? Does that concern you as much?

DR. MICHELS: There is a risk that treatment resources will become poorly distributed because of the legal procedures involved in the assessment of treatment protocols. That potential is probably significantly greater than the amount of resources spent by people like me attending conferences like this—on a holiday, I might add.

MR. CURRAN: I would like to return to the issue of the doctor's trust and who is right. First, I think we must recognize that advocacy creates a problem in the state hospital. In a general hospital, the patients are competent, paying, and short-term. The give-and-take is very clear. It is not that way in a large state hospital. Traditionally, all action there was taken "in the patients' best interests." The patients seem to be in a cloud of commitment, closed off from any connection to the community. They are in the hands of a staff of caretakers and a few psychiatrists, and they are not short-term. The patient is in a *process* which is of a different style from the process of a general hospital. The difficulty for the advocate in this situation comes not so much from differences of opinion within the medical community as from the process itself.

DR. ROBERT A. FEIN (Assistant Psychiatrist, McLean Hospital, Belmont, Massachusetts): Traditionally, we had three methods of dealing with large numbers of our population. There were the almshouses, the mental institutions, and the prisons. We have done away with the first, are now in the process of eliminating the second, and are increasingly in danger of shifting people into the third. The courts are telling us to stop treating difficult persons, that a level of management is all that can be expected. There are thus enormous pressures on guardians to try to help, to take responsibility. But in the last year there has been a 100 percent increase in the number of men sent to maximum security prisons in Massachusetts. How can we be humane and preserve human rights when, in our concern, we actually increase the number of people sent to prison—including many whom we would have traditionally considered in need of help?

UNIDENTIFIED SPEAKER: Dr. Michels, you stated that it would be too expensive to require additional psychiatric evaluations in a competency assessment. What is your opinion on utilizing a system similar to the second opinion for Medicare clients as a means for preventing inappropriate or unnecessary treatment?

DR. MICHELS: I did not mean to say that it would be too expensive, but

Discussion

simply that expense would be a problem with such a system. My reading of the literature on the issue of second opinions in medical and surgical treatment is that it has generally been much less effective in diminishing inappropriate procedures and treatment than good peer review systems have been. Serious questions exist about the earlier reports of the immense successes of the second opinion surgical study that was done at Cornell Medical School.

I believe the question is really one of the distribution of a scarce resource—not money, but professional time. There are not enough trained mental health personnel even to begin to treat all the patients who need care. Any system that requires personnel to devote time and energy to activities other than care and treatment further diminishes the amount of professional time available for care and treatment. One of the costs of any system for evaluating competence is the time of trained personnel—both in terms of time being diverted from other purposes and in terms of someone paying for that time. In the real world, as new procedures for making such evaluations are created, the institutions that care for the patients involved generally do not get new personnel or budgets. The time of staff psychiatrists shifts towards administrative decisions concerning competency and commitment questions, and away from the evaluation of disease and the planning and conduct of treatment. It is important to note that as this shift occurs, the attractiveness of institutional psychiatry to new professionals decreases. The answer clearly is not to ignore the appropriate concern for an unbiased evaluation of competence. My final rhetorical plea is that we pay attention to these factors as we devise solutions.

UNIDENTIFIED FORMER PATIENT: Dr. Perr demonstrates the attitude mental patients constantly encounter: psychiatrists are superior, patients inferior; patients should obey whatever the psychiatrist says. We can match our stories with yours, but trading horror stories doesn't get us anywhere. The point is that *everything* is a cost to the patient who suffers from bad medical practice.

DR. IRWIN N. PERR (Conference Faculty): I have not discussed how to address these issues in either the private or public sector because of limited time. I do believe there are systems that could be applied. One, all hospitals should have competent psychiatrists on their staffs. Two, ombudsmen within hospitals would be quite helpful, if they are able to question anyone and go to higher administrative authority in effectively representing patients' rights and opinions.

UNIDENTIFIED SPEAKER: With different hearings and the establishment of some type of individualized program, would you advocate a mini-hearing for a patient who refuses to accept treatment? Where does your model begin to permit such hearings?

MR. CURRAN: Hearings under my model would be triggered in a way similar to that set out in *Rogers v. Okin*; that is, anytime the patient refuses, he or she should be listened to. I am disturbed that we could be treating many people who have just as much disregard for the treatment without saying so as those who actually refuse. Under any system, the patient's refusal should be listened to, one hopes without creating the idea that the patient must be discharged or that all power must go to one party or the other. A negotiated situation would seem most appropriate; I would not invoke a formal hearing immediately. Rather, I would try to see if time and participation by an advocate or other patient support mechanism works, and if it doesn't, then I would have a hearing.

DR. MICHAEL A. INGALL (Medical Director, Providence Mental Health Center, Providence, Rhode Island): I am a psychiatrist at a community mental health center. Why do we need commitment laws at all? The point has been made several times that involuntary patients who receive psychotropic medication and don't complain may be just as incompetent to weigh the risks and benefits of taking that medication as those who do object. If individuals were not taken through a commitment proceeding, but rather to a probate competency proceeding, it could be determined there whether or not they had the capacity to know whether they were in need of psychiatric hospitalization, and a guardian could then be appointed. The guardian could sign the ward into the hospital and could agree to treatment as deemed necessary by the guardian and treating psychiatrist.

JUSTICE PODOLSKI: In Massachusetts, from 1970 to 1979, the number of commitment proceedings initiated in the district courts decreased 50 percent, while guardianship proceedings have increased 50 percent. That indicates to me that the trend is going as you suggest.

DR. MICHELS: In the world today, a fair number of clearly competent people are committed because they pursue courses of action that society has a strong interest in preventing. The most common of these is suicidal action. By the usual criteria of competency, these people usually understand the journey they are embarking upon, they understand the options, and they have made a decision. For a variety of reasons the world doesn't like that decision, and so it chooses to prevent them from acting upon it. I do not believe commitment is equivalent to incompetence, but rather is equivalent to a decision to coerce somebody.

MR. JOHN CROSS (Department of Mental Health, Northampton, Massachusetts): I was concerned about two elements of Mr. Brant's

Discussion

presentation. The first element is the delay in treatment. For an individual about whom there is a question of competency, there is the initial district court commitment proceeding, which is followed by the probate court guardianship proceeding. These proceedings are prior to any treatment of a person who is in fact refusing medication. The second element is the lack of an effective way to find individuals to serve as guardians. Is this process in Massachusetts a very cumbersome one which results in individuals going without treatment?

MR. BRANT: I'm not sure. Are you, as you are the person who sees these patients? It's clear that a lot of court process is required, and it's clear that courts have tried, as Judge Podolski mentions, to cut the delay and to make the system work. But the process is cumbersome; it requires calling in experts, holding a hearing, and making the process adversarial. All that judges can do is speed up the calendar and make themselves available, which they have done. The bifurcation of hearings is sometimes a problem but it is not clear to me whether there is a gap between the two proceedings. That is why I ask you about your experience at Belchertown.

MR. CROSS: For the incompetent committed individual who is refusing treatment, that process is indeed "cumbersome." Incompetent individuals refusing treatment do languish without treatment. I do not think the existing probate court mechanism is geared toward expeditious scrutiny of the situation; it is a problem I find quite exasperating.

MR. CURRAN: I would agree. My concern with the direction in which we may be going in Massachusetts is with the idea of long-term guardians. The appointment of a guardian means the loss of the ward's freedom; the ward's rights are placed in the hands of another. If we have a presumption of competence, then we should let it rest there, and not allow an individual's competent choices to be replaced by those of a guardian. I am concerned that Jonathan Brant seemed to suggest the establishment of a new and cumbersome system calling for a corps of guardians, even corporate guardians, and large numbers of lawyers representing all these patients. We must realize that with such a system it is the patients who lose. They lose their freedom to the guardians and to the lawyers. If that is what we are creating, I am not sure we are doing what the law says we must. We should be listening to the patients and acknowledging their rights and feelings. If a patient objects to a suggested treatment, he or she should be negotiated with before another form of treatment or even the original treatment is performed. The intent of the law is not to give patients' rights to a guardian. If institutionalized patients cannot obtain enough power to carry out this negotiating process, then we may have to change the system. I submit that the first change would be, to the extent possible, to remove all the patients who are able to make those decisions from the hospitals to other situations where they'll have greater freedom to negotiate. It's very difficult to negotiate in a closed, dirty, ward at Boston State Hospital. I worry about the long-term problems of the institutionalized retarded, but I also worry about the mentally ill. The current system converts the mentally ill to people with long-term undetermined incapacity.

The recent *Spring*[2] case, which took a year to negotiate the court process, hardly provides a basis for confidence in the current system. However, I do not think that comparing these mental health issues to the situation in *Saikewicz*[3] or *Spring* is good, or that the comparisons are effective.

It seems to me that what the Massachusetts Supreme Judicial Court said in *Saikewicz*, and affirmed in *Spring*, is that the judge, not the guardian, makes the decision. Guardians should be appointed but the judge, who is neutral, decides whether treatment is or is not given. This is very different from guardianship in mental health where we talk about handing decision making to a guardian, not having a judge make decisions individually. To me, mental health is a different subject—both medically and legally—from that of decision making for the terminally ill incompetent patient.

Incidentally, I also think that there is not a straight line between the abortion decisions and the problem of refusing mental health treatment. The legal problem with abortion was that states were making the decision of the individual a criminal act. There was no doubt the decision-maker was competent. The law created a barrier of privacy around the person's decision to have an abortion, and the state's interests, at least for a period of time, were not strong enough to interfere with that decision-making process. It makes no sense to transfer this reasoning to the mentally ill, who are sick and who have frequently demonstrated an inability and incapacity to make the immediate decision for care.

DR. PERR: New Jersey and Massachusetts seem to differ in their speed of addressing these decisions, although for acute physical emergencies the New Jersey court system does act extremely rapidly and prompt decisions can be obtained.

One thing we will all agree upon is that too often patients' best interests are injured. For example, recently I saw a patient in a state institution with a physical, not mental, illness. This woman had been in the hospital for 35 years, was both mentally retarded and paranoid, and she developed cancer of the breast. This was discovered during an annual physical in March. She rejected a biopsy. An attorney appointed on her behalf contacted me, and I saw her in October of that year. By February of the following year the situation had not been resolved. This woman suffered for eleven months from a known carcinoma of the breast which was

Discussion

highly treatable and which carries a high rate of five-year cure. Yet, because she refused the treatment, nothing was done; I find this unconscionable.

UNIDENTIFIED SPEAKER: I have a few concerns relative to the joining of commitment and guardianship proceedings. First, a family member frequently is responsible for committing a patient to a hospital. If that family member were appointed guardian, he or she could then consent to successive commitments; this could lead to a conflict of interest. Second, there are entirely different standards in commitment hearings and competency or guardianship proceedings. Combining them would be confusing to courts, to attorneys, and to medical experts. Third, if expert witnesses were from the institution where the patient would be hospitalized they could have a vested interest in having the patient declared incompetent so that the patient could not object to medication or other forms of treatment.

DR. JEFFREY GELLER (University of Massachusetts, Department of Psychiatry, Northampton State Hospital, Northampton, Massachusetts): After hearing Judge Podolski's remarks I must wonder if our area and Boston are really part of the same Commonwealth. My question is for the Judge and for Mr. Brant. The tone of many questions and of some presentations portrays the psychiatrist as someone who wants to lock up the patient or put a needle in his or her behind. The lawyers are arguing vehemently to get the patient out of the institution, and the ex-patients are cheering on the sidelines. In my experience, frequently the psychiatrist is the advocate of the patients' views and interests. But how does the psychiatrist deal with a legal system that seems to violate patients' rights?

For example, there are guardians *ad litem* whose written report to the judge consists solely of the psychiatrist's remarks, and contains no indication that anyone else was consulted. Other examples are an assigned defense attorney supposedly acting in the patient's best interests, who often hospitalizes the patient over psychiatric objections, and a probate court judge who will grant a full guardianship for the same patient for whom he recently denied a limited guardianship. Such people are probably not the judges and lawyers who attend conferences such as this—how do we deal with them?

MR. BRANT: Your comment is essentially, "It all sounds terrific, but out in the field it doesn't work." When I proposed training lawyers as guardians, I was very serious, and I think that the judiciary should be educated about these issues as well. All we can do is try to set up systems that work and are that concerned with patient's rights. Much planning and management are needed to create and maintain a system that has the possibility of being fair.

MR. ROBERT LEVY (Director, Mental Patients Rights Project, New York Civil Liberties Union, New York, New York): In my opinion, we need a more critical examination of the principles involved in diagnosing mental illness. For example, in response to the civil commitment question, Dr. Michels said that one of the reasons that we need civil commitment is that society has an interest in regulating self-destructive behavior. Yet people who engage in self-destructive behavior such as cigarette smoking are not considered mentally ill and are not being committed by the state. Psychiatry has not yet determined where to draw the line: some psychiatrists say sleeping in the streets is self-destructive, others say stabbing oneself is self-destructive. Psychiatry is not reliable enough to justify disparate treatment of people who engage in similar conduct. A system of commitment should not be founded upon a term subject to such diverse definitions.

DR. MICHELS: I agree that there is a potential continuum between smoking and trying to commit suicide. The existence of such a continuum, however, does not make it inappropriate to make distinctions for social purposes. Society has tolerated smoking and things of that degree of risk to life, but has acted when there is a clear intent to take one's own life. Society, but perhaps not the American Civil Liberties Union, believes that such people should be incarcerated to prevent their acting on such intentions.

Furthermore, the issue of diagnosis is not necessarily relevant, since it is the person's intent and the probability of action that leads to commitment, not the nature of the diagnosis. There is no diagnosis that indicates commitment. In fact, because of the nature of psychiatric illness, the diagnosis on the date of admission and the diagnosis on the date of discharge are often the same. Finally, I was always under the impression that the power to commit was vested in the courts, and that they were the ones that made the decision.

I did not understand a few things that Professor Curran said. First, he suggested that individual plans should be developed, that such an approach requires the participation of the patient, and that it is very important to listen to the patient. Later, however, he said that confrontation was not in the best interests of patients. Doesn't the refusal of medication by an institutionalized patient result in a confrontational situation?

MR. CURRAN: It's not easy to respond to your question; it is a dilemma for me as well. I tried to juxtapose the two different, almost polar, positions that one can take on these issues. One position favors competency and individual decision making almost to the point of self-destructiveness. The other position favors the traditional mental health

Discussion

system and the power of psychiatrists to make decisions. I was trying to suggest that total confrontation—the situation where only one or the other party would win—is not in anyone's interest. Rather, we need a system where refusals are listened to and where patients who refuse are helped by some clinical advocacy. The treatment refusals of psychiatric patients ought not to impede communication, but ought to be a means of continuing the negotiations. There should be a process rather than a contest.

Notes

1. *Downs v. Sawtelle*, 574 F.2d 1 (1st Cir.) *cert. denied* 439 U.S. 910 (1978).
2. *In re Spring*, 405 N.E.2d 115 (Mass. 1980).
3. *Superintendent of Belchertown State School v. Saikewicz*, 370 N.E.2d 417 (Mass. 1977).

Part V

Treatment Decisions: Values in Conflict

15

Refusing Treatment: The Patient's View

Judi Chamberlin

My name is Judi Chamberlin, and fourteen years ago I was a hospitalized mental patient. Originally, I was a voluntary patient, but later I was committed against my will to a state hospital. I was given various psychiatric drugs, initially voluntarily, but later against my will. I also, at times, took drugs "voluntarily," but under coercion. During this period I was diagnosed as a "chronic schizophrenic." For the past nine years I have been active in the psychiatric inmates' "mental patients" liberation movement, a federation of locally organized groups of former "mental patients." We use the term "mental patient" in quotation marks to indicate our nonacceptance of the medical model. Alternatively, we call ourselves former psychiatric inmates.[1] I am the author of *On Our Own: Patient Controlled Alternatives to the Mental Health System*.

The Ex-inmates' Movement

The ex-inmates movement is about ten years old. It is composed of independent groups of former patients in many cities of the United States, as well as groups in other parts of the world. The groups are linked through the publication *Madness Network News* and the annual Conference on Human Rights and Psychiatric Oppression. The Mental Patients' Liberation Front (MPLF) in Boston is one of the oldest groups. It was started in 1971 by a small group of dissatisfied ex-patients. Our goals include changing laws and public attitudes, providing advocacy for current patients, and promoting self-help and mutual support.

THE RIGHT TO REFUSE TREATMENT AND THE EX-PATIENTS' MOVEMENT

When lawyers and mental health professionals were busy congratulating themselves about the development of the concept of the right to treatment, we in the ex-inmates' movement were already talking about a right to *refuse* treatment. We knew that, as patients, our main problem was not in getting "treatment," but in maintaining our right to reject those kinds of treatment we believed were harmful, unnecessary, or undesirable. The concept of a right to refuse treatment, and the legal cases that have been started in an attempt to win recognition of that right, are a result of closer contact between various legal advocates and the ex-patients' movement. For example, in the Boston State Hospital case (*Rogers v. Okin*), many of the patients who became plaintiffs in the suit were members of a weekly patients' rights group at the hospital in which members of MPLF met with interested patients to discuss what rights patients had, what rights we believe patients should have, and how patients could work to implement these rights.

PATIENTS' PERCEPTIONS OF "TREATMENT"

A majority of people in mental institutions are there against their will, regardless of whether or not they are technically classified as "voluntary" patients.[2] This means there is a sharp differentiation between people in hospitals for physical illnesses and mental patients. Although general hospital patients are probably not happy about being ill and being hospitalized, they tend to be in agreement with their doctors that there is an illness and that the doctor has some curative or palliative techniques. In contrast, mental patients tend to be hospitalized because their behavior has brought them into conflict with their family, their friends or acquaintances, or the community in general. Mental patients are commonly brought to the hospital by the person(s) with whom they have been in conflict. While the "other" may agree with the doctor that there is an illness, and that the doctor has some curative or palliative techniques that should be utilized, the "patient" often does not agree with that assessment.[3] It is against this background that it is necessary to look at the right to refuse treatment.

Patients commonly experience psychiatric "treatment" (incarceration, administration of psychiatric drugs, electroshock, behavior modification, and psychotherapy) as intrusions into their lives. Mental health professionals may talk of a "therapeutic alliance," but patients are often justifiably wary of establishing such an alliance with a person whom they see as responsible for depriving them of their liberty and preventing them

The Patient's View

from acting as they wish. In addition, patients are commonly mystified about both "illness" and "treatment." It is common for mental health professionals to ascribe whatever elements of the patient's behavior they are attempting to change to his or her "illness," and to attribute improvements (or perceived improvements) to prescribed "treatments." Many patients have had the experience of complaining about unpleasant physical effects of psychiatric drugs (such as blurred vision, muscular stiffness, tremors, sleep disturbances, and restlessness) and being told that these effects are not caused by the drugs, but by the "illness." This is mystifying because the patients' accurate perceptions are being denied. Further, many patients who have decided to "cheek" or "palm" their pills have been described as improved by professionals who believed that the drugs were, in fact, being ingested.

Another factor leading to refusal of psychiatric drugs is tardive dyskinesia. Mental health professionals frequently say that tardive dyskinesia is a reasonable price to pay for the control of "schizophrenic symptoms"; however, it is the patient, not the professional, who must cope with being transformed into a grimacing puppet. If, indeed, the tradeoff is reasonable, it is the patient who must make the choice.

Some patients consider themselves to be in emotional distress; others are reasonably satisfied with their lives. Once subjected to "treatment," however, both groups are required to see themselves as "sick" and "treatment" as helpful. Patients who persist in calling mental hospitals prisons and the people who work in them jailers are commonly considered by mental health professionals to be displaying "symptoms" requiring further "treatment."

Historical Background of Psychiatric Institutions

Although they are both called by the name "hospital," institutions for the care of people with physical illnesses developed from a root considerably different from those for people with so-called "mental diseases." Historically, the "mental hospital" developed from the poorhouse, the place where societal undesirables were confined "for their own good."[4] Society's role was presumed to be a benevolent one; people so "treated" had no right to resist or object. As the "hospital" supplanted the poorhouse, the development of a theory of "illness" (rather than the earlier theory of unworthiness or sinfulness) made no change in the underlying power relationship. Those defined as "ill" were either to passively accept their fate, or be forced to accept it. This naturally led to the development of various methods of "treatment" based upon control—everything from high walls and remote locations to straitjackets and various stupefying agents. Thorazine fulfills the same function as shackles, which are an unpleasant reminder of an unacknowledged reality. (Of course, similar devices now euphemistically known as "physical restraints" continue to be used.)

Legal Rights and the Mental Patient

The whole concept of "patients' rights" denotes an acceptance of a special, lesser set of rights. If patients in fact had all the legal and constitutional rights of other citizens they could not be held or "treated" against their will in the absence of lawbreaking behavior. By receiving the designation of "mentally ill," a person loses control over his or her life, including such basic choices as a place to live, the choice of one's associates, the manner in which one spends his or her days, and so forth. This loss of power occurs not only when patients are institutionalized, but in so-called "community facilities," which have just as much potential to abuse individual rights as do large institutions. Deinstitutionalization changes the locations where psychiatric "treatments" are given, but the underlying power relationships remain the same. People designated as "mentally ill" lose their right to do many things that non-mentally ill people do routinely.

For example, it is not uncommon for adult residents of "community facilities" to be forbidden to drink alcholic beverages or engage in consensual sexual relations. At the same time, residents of mental institutions and community facilities are routinely required to ingest chemicals even though many of them find the physical and psychological effects undesirable. Common complaints about psychiatric drugs include feelings of lethargy, restlessness, and, as many patients describe it, feeling like a zombie. What we in the ex-patients' movement describe as the struggle to control our own lives involves challenging the ability of mental health professionals to exercise this degree of control in the name of "treatment."

Patients and former patients, by themselves or with the aid of legal or paralegal advocates, have begun to examine all these processes: commitment, legal rights within institutions, legal rights in "community facilities," and the right to control one's own body and what goes into it; and we have begun to propose changes. The right to refuse treatment, from the patients' point of view, is the key right. Only if the right to refuse is guaranteed does the individual become an agent who can negotiate with others the terms under which they are to interact. This is not to say that all patients would always refuse treatment. But, with their right to do so protected, they will be far better able to take a meaningful part in deciding

The Patient's View

what treatments to accept. A patient who perceives the effect of a specific treatment as helpful will be free to accept it; a patient who feels it is not helpful will be able to reject it, and rightly so.

This right is preserved, at least in theory, in the general health care system (which is not to deny numerous flagrant abuses). At least in theory, the medical patient is free to choose whether to become or remain a patient. The medical system becomes more overtly coercive, however, when payment is provided not by the individual receiving the treatment, but by various public benefit programs.

The mental health system, however, is coercive whether public or private, because all "mental patients" are presumed by treaters and the staff alike to be unaware of their own needs and unable to provide for them, and because they are almost always brought to treatment situations by others. In fact, the articulation by patients of their wants and needs (when that articulation differs from the treater's definition) is commonly denied, ignored, or interpreted to mean the opposite.[5] Without the right to refuse treatment, mental patients will continue to be powerless actors.

WHY THE RIGHT TO REFUSE TREATMENT CREATES CONTROVERSY

The legal rights of mental patients cannot be discussed without looking at questions of power and powerlessness. It is for this reason that the ex-patients' movement sees this as essentially a political struggle. At the same time, we do not deny that people can suffer great emotional pain, and we seek ways to help people survive this pain without losing their basic rights and dignity. This has involved the development of self-help alternatives (which fall outside the scope of this discussion). Given a system in which people did not lose their rights by accepting psychiatric treatment, we believe some people would continue to seek out mental health professionals for specific treatments, while others would participate in self-help and other nonpsychiatric alternatives.[6]

Any great social change in which a group formerly perceived by the larger society as unable to speak for itself begins to do so, is going to create a certain amount of upheaval. This has certainly happened with regard to blacks and women, and is happening now with disabled people and mental patients. Groups which begin to speak for themselves often speak truths which their benefactors do not want to hear. It caused great discomfort to liberal whites when blacks took over control of civil rights organizations; the net result for the black cause, however, has been positive. Similarly, disabled people are resisting their image as smiling poster children or as saintly, uncomplaining, desexualized adults.

People who have undergone emotional crises are beginning to speak up about *their own* perceptions of mental health professionals and their "treatments," and, not surprisingly, these differ from what professionals have assured themselves and the public that patients think.[7] Most mental health professionals consider themselves benevolent people and their patients as needy and helpless. Slavemasters thought the same about their relationship to their slaves; men have seen themselves as benefactors of women; white people saw themselves bringing "civilization" to people of color; people from developed nations have maintained these attitudes toward those they have called "primitive."

As members of these groups assert control over their own individual lives, and over their collective destinies, those whose power and control are threatened will object, will proclaim their own goodness and the dreadful results of the powerless obtaining power, and will sometimes fight to maintain control. The right to refuse "treatment" is one part of this vast process in which the goals are autonomy, freedom, and human dignity.

NOTES

1. Continuing news of the ex-inmates' movement may be found in MADNESS NETWORK NEWS (P.O. Box 684, San Francisco, CA 94101).
2. A study done at Northampton (Massachusetts) State Hospital by Western Massachusetts Legal Services in 1974 found that more than half of newly admitted patients holding so-called "voluntary" status were in the institution against their will.
3. This argument is a brief summary of Thomas Szasz's thoughts; *see* his MYTH OF MENTAL ILLNESS and MANUFACTOR OF MADNESS, among many other works.
4. *See* DAVID J. ROTHMAN, THE DISCOVERY OF THE ASYLUM (Little, Brown & Co., Boston) (1971).
5. *See, e.g.,* PHILIP MARGOLIS, PATIENT POWER (Charles C. Thomas, Springfield, Ill.) (1973), in which Margolis quotes an anonymous patient's complaints against her hospitalization and "treatment" and interprets them to mean that she wants such "treatment" to continue. While mental health professionals frequently "interpret" patient complaints to "really mean" approval, they do not similarly "interpret" verbal expressions of approval as their opposite.
6. For a full discussion of such alternatives, *see* Judi CHAMBERLIN, ON OUR OWN: PATIENT-CONTROLLED ALTERNATIVES TO THE MENTAL HEALTH SYSTEM (McGraw-Hill, New York) (1979).
7. *See, e.g.,* PAUL GOTKIN, JANET GOTKIN, TOO MUCH ANGER, TOO MANY TEARS (Quadrangle, New York) (1975).

16

The New Federal Role in Treatment Rights

Louis E. Kopolow, M.D.

The federal government's role in treatment rights has been slow to develop and is limited in scope. Historically, mental health has been a responsibility of the states, but recently the federal government has begun to provide community mental health services, funding for nursing home care, and special programs for the chronically mentally ill. With increasing federal involvement has come increasing demand for accountability by service providers and the advancement of quality care programs.

The initial involvement of the federal government in treatment rights occurred in the judicial system, invoked by litigants in the federal courts. Crucial cases have included the *Donaldson v. O'Connor*[1] decision concerning the treatment rights of involuntarily committed mental patients, the *Wyatt v. Stickney*[2] decision concerning the treatment rights of the mentally retarded and the involuntarily committed, and the *Parham*[3] decision concerning the rights of juveniles.

In addition to these court cases, a number of significant actions occurred in the federal executive and legislative branches. These include publication of the Skilled Nursing Facility Guidelines concerning the rights of individuals in nursing homes and of the report of the National Commission for the Protection of Human Subjects on research involving mentally disabled institutionalized persons. Several bills have passed Congress dealing with the rights of handicapped individuals and the role of the Justice Department in pursuit of the protection of such citizens. Most recently Congress passed P.L. 96-398, the Mental Health Systems Act.[4]

The Mental Health Systems Act outlines a new federal-state-local partnership for the provision of services and the protection of patient rights. Rights issues are scattered throughout the Act, but four areas deserve special attention:

1) the allotment of states to improve the administration of state mental health programs
2) the content of state mental health programs
3) the Mental Health Bill of Rights
4) grants for the protection and advocacy of mentally ill individuals

The first two sections place the responsibility for the rights-related activities in the mental health departments of the various states. Section 107, for example, makes available 15 million dollars for

> the purpose of assisting State mental health authorities to improve the administration of State mental health programs and to carry out their activities under this chapter relating to (1) planning and program design, (2) data collection, (3) data analysis, (4) research, (5) evaluation, (6) setting and enforcing regulatory and other standards, and ... [most important for this discussion], (8) establishing, expanding, or operating mental health patients' rights protection programs.[5]

The two sections most crucial to patient rights and advocacy are §501 and §502. While leaving implementation activities to the states, these sections set broad guidelines for individual action. The Mental Health Bill of Rights[6] evolved from, among other sources, the activities of the President's Commission on Mental Health.[7] The report of this commission states:

> The protection of human rights and the guarantee of freedom of choice are among the most basic principles of society. Mental health programs and services must not disregard these values. Each client or patient must have the maximum possible opportunity to choose the unique combination of services and objectives appropriate to his or her needs. This must include the option of preferring no services as well as the option of selecting particular services in preference to others.[8]

The rights that were included in the legislation include the following:

1) the right to appropriate treatment and related services in the least restrictive setting
2) the right to an individualized treatment plan
3) the right to participate actively in one's own treatment
4) the right to refuse treatment
5) the right not to participate in experimentation
6) the right to freedom from restraint or seclusion
7) the right to a humane treatment environment
8) the right to confidentiality of one's mental health care records
9) the right to access to one's mental health care records

10) the right to converse with others in a treatment facility to which one has been admitted, and reasonable access to telephone, mail, and visitors
11) the right to be informed of one's rights
12) the right to assert grievances with respect to one's rights, and to have those grievances considered in a fair, timely, and impartial grievance procedure
13) the right to access to a rights protection service within the facility or state mental health system, or to an independent advocate
14) the right to exercise one's rights without reprisal, including denial of any appropriate available treatment
15) the right to referral to other providers of mental health services upon discharge

It must be noted that the rights listed in this section are introduced by the statement that they represent the "sense of Congress," but what this assertion means in terms of the implementation of these rights is presently unclear.

The section which has particular relevance to treatment rights evolved from the activities of the President's Commission on Mental Health. It states that:

> The secretary may make grants to any public or nonprofit private entity for projects to protect and advocate the rights of mentally ill individuals if the entity
>
> (A) has the authority and ability to pursue legal, administrative, and other appropriate remedies to ensure the protection of the rights of mentally ill individuals, and
>
> (B) is independent of any entity which provides treatment or services to mentally ill individuals.[9]

Crucial questions raised by this section include how independence will be defined, how many awards will be made for each state, and what the minimum criteria for state advocacy programs will be. The most crucial issue, of course, will be whether any funds at all will be appropriated for this purpose.

This legislation signifies the federal government's recognition that patient rights must be protected, and that there is a need for patient advocacy. The role of advocacy is to help patients know and assert their rights, acquire their entitlement, and make their wishes known. No statement of high principles or broadly gauged policy about patient rights, however, can be implemented unless there is a dependable structure for advocacy that can translate legally stated rights into living reality for mentally ill people. While much discussion has occurred about advocacy, there has been little clarification of what it is, why there is a need, who the advocates are, and how they function.

What Is Advocacy?

Advocacy means coming to the aid of and speaking on behalf of another. It also connotes the promotion and support of a cause. Advocates take their mandate from the expressed wishes of the clients. Advocates believe their primary role is helping another person obtain what he or she wants. Their secondary goal is to empower clients in situations in which the clients traditionally have been powerless and to encourage them to speak and act for themselves.

Why Advocacy?

There are many reasons why advocates are necessary for present, former, and potential clients of the mental health services delivery system. The first and most crucial is the vulnerability of mentally ill individuals. While many groups are neglected or underrepresented in their relationship with various institutions and organizations, the mentally ill as a group are the most underrepresented. Many of us have experienced a sense of vulnerability, frustration, and helplessness in dealing with various complex situations. Think back to the last time you as a consumer had a question or a complaint in some area with which you had very little experience. The situation might have involved talking with a contractor about a leak in your roof, to a plumber about repairing a faucet, or to a mechanic about some frightening sound your car was making. In such situations, all you usually know is that something is wrong; you do not know the appropriate questions to ask or how to assess the quality of the work that is performed. If you think that you have been ripped off, you are usually just out of luck.

Now, suppose instead that your helplessness had to do with your need to pull yourself together, with your ability to function in your home or workplace. If you understand what that would be like, you have an idea of what it means to be a mental health services consumer. In addition to experiencing extreme vulnerability, these patients also suffer from special problems. One of these is the handicap of the illness itself, which makes it difficult for them to articulate their needs effectively. A far greater problem is the stigma attached to mental health patients, which leads others to underrate patients' ability to function outside a controlled environment and to make decisions for themselves.

A second stigma-related problem is the tendency of mental health care providers to interpret every client statement or request as being significant beyond the statement; for example, requests for aspirin for headache are interpreted as arising from a need for attention, or requests to leave the facility are interpreted as resistance to treatment. A third stigma-related problem is the low priority generally given to a patient's concerns, simply because the individual is a patient. Far too often the wishes of mental health clients are denigrated, ignored, or treated as the ramblings of children who do not know what is good for them.

Another problem of the mentally ill patient is the difficulty of maneuvering through the complex support system which has been created for handicapped persons, but for which few roadmaps have been developed. In addition to the need for advocacy, there is a need for the change agent, monitoring force, or watchdog to help create more responsive mental health services. Historically, these services have been conservative and slow to change.

Who Are the Advocates?

Advocacy functions are not limited to any one profession or group. Advocates may be lawyers, who obtain their skills through legal training, or former patients, who gain first-hand experience as recipients of mental health services and who are linked by a network of ex-patient organizations. Advocates may be families, concerned about the needs of loved ones, mental health providers, who are willing to hear a patient out and to advocate for appropriate and responsive services, or just concerned citizens. There are also a number of groups concerned about advocacy for mentally ill individuals. Some of these are well-known, such as the Mental Health Association. Others only recently entered the arena; they include the National Alliance for the Mentally Ill and the Mental Health Advocates Coalition. While the various advocacy forces differ in strategy, ideology, and style, all share certain characteristics. These include "feistyness," willingness to fight for an issue and take risks, persistence, refusal to accept defeat, and willingness to rock the boat if that is what is necessary to assure their clients' rights and entitlements.

How Advocates Function

Although mental health advocacy can be characterized by an attitude of "we do whatever is needed to get the job done," a more specific analysis identifies four functional strategies: rights protection, legal advocacy, services, and systems advocacy.

Rights protection advocacy is performed on-site by persons who educate clients and staff concerning rights issues and who investigate complaints of rights violations. These advocates are usually employees of the facility or service system, but they may also be volunteers or persons paid from some other source, such as a public defender's office. Such advocates should be able to negotiate with the system to direct attention to patient grievances. If these efforts do not result in resolution acceptable to the client, the rights protection advocate needs to be able to refer the complaint either upward in the system, or outside the system, such as to a legal advocate.

Legal advocacy is undertaken by attorneys, sometimes with the assistance of paraprofessionals. Legal advocates represent individual clients or classes of clients, and have the authority to pursue formal legal remedies. When litigation is not used, the threat that it could occur can increase the advocate's bargaining power. Legal advocacy cannot be characterized solely by the use of litigation, however. Lawyers or paraprofessionals also represent clients at administrative hearings and perform other functions such as lobbying, public education, and services advocacy.

Services advocacy refers to the assistance of clients who reside in the community and who need various services or entitlements (such as Social Security benefits, rehabilitation, or social services) but who encounter bureaucratic obstacles to obtaining them. This form of advocacy may be performed by volunteers, professionals, ex-patients, or others. For example, services advocates may be trained volunteers who work with chronically mentally ill persons prior to their discharge from hospitals, and who serve as supportive friends. Such advocates may help their clients to learn about the community, to gain access to services, and to cut red tape. Services advocates may also work in community mental health centers, in ex-patient groups, or in social, legal, and other community agencies. The crux of services advocacy is knowing how to obtain the services or entitlements which the clients need.

A resource manager may perform some of the work of services advocates, by identifying needed services and bringing them to the attention of the service system decision-makers. The two functions are not interchangeable, however. Services advocates, especially those functioning outside the service system, may still be needed to advocate vigorously for the development of needed or requested services.

Systems advocacy entails activities designed to bring about systemwide policy changes, through litigation, legislation, or administrative action. The means used are various and include strategies to capture public attention, such as confrontation, demonstrations, and media events: class action litigation; lobbying for and writing reform legislation; formulating administrative regulations; and pressuring for reallocation of funds.

These activities are not mutually exclusive and distinct. At this time, advocacy is a practice in flux, characterized by a sense of innovation and change which defies categorization. Sometimes this quality helps to promote the goals of client protection, empowerment, and systems improvement. Often, however, the pursuit of such goals is fraught with obstacles.

Obstacles to Effective Advocacy

As a new enterprise, the field of mental health advocacy is charged with the energy and idealism of a new cadre of personnel. It is filled with untapped opportunities, and beset by growing pains. However, many obstacles block advocates as they address their clients' concerns. Any initiative may be generated with good intentions, positive motivation, and ideology, but ultimately effort can be sustained only if there are sufficient resources to support it. Despite the importance of advocacy, this area has been underfunded and given low priority by the federal government, the state mental health department, and private foundations and organizations.

Another obstacle has been the resistance of some mental health personnel, who fear advocacy as a threat to their autonomy. While many mental health professionals yearn for the halcyon days before federal regulations and judicial scrutiny of mental health practices, such days never really existed. Mental health care has always been a public enterprise with significant governmental input.

Under the influence of many forces, the doctor-patient relationship has changed into a relationship that includes the provider, the consumer, third party payor, the judiciary, governmental regulators, and licensing boards. The advocate is not a new force, but aids the client in assuring that his voice will be heard adequately in a crowded and complicated situation.

Advocates also share the difficulties experienced by ex-patients in performing independent advocacy or assisting other advocate groups. Ex-patient organizations are a rich source of information and advice, but their lack of funding and administrative experience has prevented them from making their resources widely available. Despite these difficulties, ex-patient groups have sustained networks among themselves, printed newsletters, held meetings, and provided effective representation to many groups. They persist in their battle for patients' rights, a battle they often wage at great personal cost and sacrifice.

Another potential problem should be mentioned. As advocacy grows and utilizes more public funding, the demand for articulated standards and for accountability mechanisms will become more insistent. The

Mental Health Systems Act, which should support a nationwide system of individual advocacy programs, would undoubtedly lead to the development of specifications regarding qualifications of personnel, methods of operation, and expected outcomes of advocacy activities. At this point, research on the characteristics of effective advocacy is still in a rudimentary stage.

The advocacy movement has continued its activities despite formidable difficulties created by inadequate and unstable funding, short staffing, and uncertain public support. Advocacy programs have addressed critical patient needs and demonstrated solid achievement in meeting those needs. The role of the federal government will be to encourage the recognition and protection of the rights of citizens vis-à-vis the mental health care system.

The advocacy role will require courage in the face of the opposition, persistence in dealing with obstruction, and tolerance in working with suspicious clients and hostile staff. Advocates will at times feel isolated and frustrated, but will be sustained in their work by the recognition that without their efforts many of their clients' concerns, fears, and wishes would go unheard or unresolved. The immediate goal of an advocate is to assure patients' rights, but the long-term mission is to act as a change agent in creating a more responsive mental health system.

The advocate is guided by a willingness to look past the patienthood of mental health consumers to the personhood. That this is real, even in the most unattractive, recalcitrant of patients, is best communicated by a poem which has become a favorite around the National Institute of Mental Health. It was found with the belongings of an elderly woman who died in the geriatric ward of a hospital near Dundee, Scotland:

LOOK CLOSER SEE ME*

What do you see nurses, what do you see?
Are you thinking when you are looking at
  me—
A crabby old woman, not very wise,
Uncertain of habit, with far-away eyes,
Who dribbles her food and makes no reply
When you say in a loud voice—"I do wish
  you'd try."

---

*Poem courtesy of the Peninsula Hospital Center, Far Rockaway, New York, and Greater New York Hospital Association.

Who seems not to notice the things that
  you do,
And forever is losing a stocking or shoe,
Who unresisting or not, lets you do as you
  will,
With bathing and feeding the long day to
  fill.
Is that what you are thinking—is that
  what you see?
Then open your eyes, nurse, you're not
  looking at me.
I'll tell you who I am as I sit here so still;
As I do at your bidding, as I eat at your
  will,
I'm a small child of ten with a father and
  mother,
Brothers and sisters, who love one another,
A young girl of sixteen with wings on her feet,
Dreaming that soon now a lover she'll
  meet;
A bride soon at twenty—my heart gives a
  leap,
Remembering the vows that I promised to
  keep;
At twenty-five now I have young of my
  own,
Who need me to build a secure, happy
  home;
A woman of thirty, my young now grow
  fast,
Bound to each other with ties that should
  last;
At forty, my young sons have grown and
  are gone,
But my man's beside me to see I don't
  mourn.
At fifty, once more babies play round my
  knee.
Again we know children, my loved one and
  me.
Dark days are upon me, my husband is dead,
I look at the future, I shudder with dread,
For my young are all rearing young of
  their own.

And I think of the years and the love that
I've known.
I'm an old woman now and nature is
cruel—
'Tis her jest to make old age look like a fool.
The body it crumbles, grace and vigor
depart,
There is now a stone where I once had a
heart;
But inside this old carcass a young girl still
dwells,
And now and again my battered heart
swells,
I remember the joys, I remember the pain,
And I'm loving and living life over again.
I think of the years all too few—gone too
fast,
And accept the stark fact that nothing can
last,
So open your eyes, nurses, open and see
Not a crabby old woman, look closer see
me!

Notes

1. *Donaldson v. O'Connor*, 493 F.2d 507 (5th. Cir. 1974), *vac. and remanded, sub nom. O'Connor v. Donaldson*, 422 U.S. 563 (1975), *rev'd and remanded*, 519 F.2d 59 (5th Cir. 1975).
2. *Wyatt v. Stickney*, 325 F. Supp. 781 (M.D. Ala. 1971), *supplemented*, 334 F. Supp. 1341 (M.D. Ala. 1971), *supplemented* 344 F. Supp. 373, and 344 F. Supp 387 (M.D. Ala. 1972) *aff'd in part, remanded in part and rev'd in part sub nom. Wyatt v. Aderholt*, 503 F.2d 1305 (5th Cir. 1974).
3. *Parham v. J. R.*, 422 U.S. 584 (1979).
4. Mental Health Systems Act, Pub. L. 96-398, Oct. 7, 1980, 94 Stat. 1564, *codified at* 42 U.S.C.A. §9401 *et seq*.
5. 42 U.S.C.A. §9423(a).
6. 42 U.S.C.A. §9501.
7. 1980 U.S. Code Cong. and Ad. News, v. 4 at 3372, 3394-3405.
8. President's Commission on Mental Health, Report to the President, (Government Printing Office, Washington, D.C.) (April 1978).
9. 42 U.S.C.A. §9502(a) (1) (A), (B).

17

What We Do and Do Not Know About Treatment Refusals in Mental Institutions

Loren H. Roth, M.D., M.P.H. and
Paul S. Appelbaum, M.D.

Although some persons maintain that "ignorance is bliss," it would seem preferable to know more, rather than less, when discussing the rights of involuntarily committed psychiatric patients to refuse treatment. Like other controversial topics in the law-psychiatry area, such as the prediction of dangerousness or the determination of criminal responsibility, the topic of treatment refusals poses issues that touch upon both important societal *values* and certain *facts* pertaining to the effects of treatment interventions in psychiatry. Thus, while this text is named *Refusing Treatment in Mental Health Institutions: Values in Conflict*, it might equally well have been named *Refusing Treatment in Mental Institutions: Facts in Conflict*.

Some brief comments about "values" and the right to refuse are in order. As others have noted, the question of whether committed psychiatric patients should or should not be permitted to refuse treatment is heavily value-laden. The right to refuse controversy has been fueled by civil libertarian concerns about preserving the values of human autonomy, equality, and individualism—values about which none of us ought be indifferent. Some committed patients manifestly wish to chart their own course, to weigh for themselves the risks and benefits that they perceive in being treated with antipsychotic medications. As citizens, we can all be sympathetic to patients wanting to make this kind of decision, especially since, as has been amply demonstrated over the last decade, both the benefits and the risks for patients receiving antipsychotic medication may be considerable.

But there are other values and issues at stake in the right to refuse controversy. The treatment needs of hospitalized patients must certainly be considered, especially the treatment needs of those who (at least from the perspective of an outside observer) appear unable to make treatment decisions. Society too has its concerns. Society has a stake in the well-being of committed hospitalized mental patients, and in whether such patients, either treated or untreated, pose a present or future danger to themselves or others—including other hospitalized patients. Value preferences, implicit in concepts such as individualism, paternalism, "doing good," or "preventing harm," must also be considered when thinking about the right to refuse. This chapter will *not*, however, focus on these value issues, at least at their more abstract level. Instead, we will summarize and comment on some of the facts (or the absence of facts) relevant to the understanding of how these value concerns might best be isolated and addressed in thinking about the right to refuse.

VALUES AND FACTS

Questions of law and values become more precise (if not always easier to decide) when the underlying facts themselves become clear.[2] Thus, in constitutional and other litigation, a trial court typically summarizes the "facts" in a case before proceeding to its conclusions of law. Problems in law and ethics are compounded, however, when the facts are insufficiently attended to or not clear or when some of the more pertinent facts are absent altogether. Some of the most important "facts" we would like to know about treatment refusals in mental institutions are at present unknown, poorly studied, or mired in controversy. When the facts become clearer, we might have a more meaningful debate about the values involved.

It is also important to note that in formulating legal opinions, the courts are increasingly citing and discussing empirical, social science, and other scientific data relevant to the legal questions before them.[2] An example of this can be seen in a case in which the United States Supreme Court relied heavily on social science data in justifying its conclusion that criminal juries must contain at least six members. After consulting empirical social science data on the subject, the Court had substantial doubts about "the reliability and appropriate representation of panels smaller than six" jurors.[3]

While the phenomenon of the courts relying upon, or consulting, social science data for judicial decision making has not gone uncriticized, this approach to litigation will probably continue. For example, in recent leading mental health law cases, such as *Addington v. Texas*[4] and *Parham v. J.R.*,[5] the opinions of the Supreme Court contained citations to articles from the professional scientific literature relevant to both the stigma of mental illness and the treatment needs of mentally ill persons. In *Addington v. Texas*, the Court wrote, "it is not true that the release of a genuinely mentally ill person is no worse for the individual than the failure to convict the guilty. One who is suffering from a debilitating mental illness and is in need of treatment is neither wholly at liberty nor free of stigma."[6] In making this point, the Court cited studies published in the psychiatric literature.[7]

More directly relevant to our concerns here are the extensive discussions of both the potential benefits and the side effects of antipsychotic drugs in the briefs submitted by the parties, by the amici, and by the courts themselves. The court opinions suggest that the risk/benefit ratio for the patients receiving antipsychotic drugs is at issue, not merely whether patients abstractly have a right to give informed consent to medication.

Any doubts about this point have been removed by the decision of the United States Court of Appeals for the First Circuit in *Rogers v. Okin*.[8] The court explicitly stated that its opinion applied only to the use of "antipsychotic" drugs, since other

> 'psychotropic drugs,' which may include antidepressants and lithium, ... as far as the record shows do not have as substantial a potential for serious side effects as do the antipsychotics.... Accordingly, we interpret the district court's use of the term 'psychotropic drugs' to mean antipsychotic drugs.'[9]

If it were only abstract values at stake in the *Rogers* decision, then the patient's right to refuse treatment and to give informed consent to medication should include *all* medication. Ironically, other psychotropic drugs such as lithium and antidepressants do have potentially serious side effects when misused.

In sum, the right to refuse cases have litigated not only values, but also a host of pragmatic, poorly understood issues about the utility and effects of the involuntary administration of antipsychotic drugs.

We now turn to some of the important areas where, we believe, the scientific data most relevant to the right to refuse controversy fail to provide clear guidance for the courts as they wrestle with this problem. The purpose of this brief review of the empirical literature is to indicate where particularly relevant studies are or are not available, and to indicate where future research is needed.

The eight areas we will highlight concern: (1) outcomes of mental health commitment; (2) benefits for patients of receiving antipsychotic drugs, both acutely and chronically; (3) benefits for patients consequent to receiving *involuntarily* administered medication; (4) side effects of antipsychotic drugs, and whether those side effects may be prevented through careful drug administration; (5) assessments of hospitalized patients' competency to consent or refuse; (6) outcomes of giving the right to refuse to hospitalized committed patients; (7) patient satisfaction with psychiatric hospitalization; and (8) the effect of providing due process protections for the patient, including the provision of advocacy service and legal counsel.

Outcome of Commitment

It is somewhat surprising that after more than 100 years of experience with mental health commitment, the effect of commitment upon patient outcome—postcommitment functioning, participation in subsequent treatment, satisfaction with hospitalization—has been sparsely documented. There is a particular lack of controlled or descriptive studies that compare involuntarily committed to voluntarily admitted patients, or to those not hospitalized at all.

Recently, however, a few studies have suggested the value of brief periods of involuntary commitment for patients, although these studies are not uniform in their findings.[10] A substantial proportion of patients (about two-thirds) continue to participate voluntarily in treatment following a period of involuntary commitment. In general, the studies conclude that most patients appear to be helped, rather than harmed, by involuntary commitment.

Furthermore, the course of involuntary commitment in the modern era is fairly brief. In one recent study, 67 percent of involuntary patients were discharged with 38 days.[11] Another study found that 63 percent of the involuntary patients were discharged in less than three months.[12] These studies do not, however, clearly indicate which types of patient are helped or hurt by commitment, particularly whether it is patients who are dangerous to themselves or others, or those who have been committed on more paternalistic grounds.[13] Additionally, the studies fail to detail the type of treatment that the patients received in the hospital and whether, once hospitalized, treatment was subsequently administered to the patients over their objections. Clearly, some patients are not helped by commitment; instead they choose to escape from the hospital.[14] In sum, there are at present limited data concerning the effects of involuntary commitment. Considering that some 80,000 persons are committed each year, the paucity of studies in this area is regrettable.

Benefits for Patients of Receiving Antipsychotic Drugs

There is little doubt that the administration of antipsychotic drugs to acutely psychotic schizophrenic patients is helpful. This was established by the 1964 NIMH collaborative study,[15] and subsequently confirmed by other studies.[16] In the NIMH collaborative study, 75 percent of patients treated with antipsychotic drugs showed marked to moderate degrees of improvement within six weeks after being hospitalized, while only 23 percent of the placebo group were rated as showing marked or moderate improvement.[17]

Antipsychotic medication administered to acutely ill patients is most helpful in decreasing patient agitation, hallucinations, combativeness, sleep disturbance, tension, and paranoid behavior. Symptoms less likely to respond to such treatment are impaired judgment, lack of insight, depression, withdrawal, and poor motivation.[18] There is, furthermore, some evidence that early drug treatment (possibly by decreasing the patient's length of stay in the hospital and promoting "avoidance of . . . social disarticulation and institutionalization") results in benefits for the patients that may persist up to five years after release.[19]

Even in this area, however, some studies permit lingering doubts. Eminent researchers have reported that in intensive milieus, such as well-run research wards, it is possible to treat at least some patients with acute schizophrenia without medication, apparently not to their long-term detriment.[20] The typical state mental institution is, of course, hardly comparable to the treatment milieu of the well-staffed research ward, and it is very unlikely that public mental institutions will ever enjoy the comparative wealth of resources that permits the treatment of acute schizophrenia without drugs. Furthermore, as every clinician and most patients and their families know, the pain of psychosis is considerable. There is no clearcut reason to prolong psychosis more than necessary if it is the patient's welfare—and not only his or her rights—that is at stake.

For a significant number of chronically ill and stabilized schizophrenic patients, however, the value of receiving antipsychotic drugs is less clear. For discharged patients, the chronic administration of antipsychotic drugs prevents relapse and recrudescence of the more florid manifestations of illness. The rate of relapse for discharged schizophrenic patients receiving drugs is decreased by about one-half to two-thirds compared to the rate of relapse for patients on placebo.[21] Some researchers, however, have noted that patients on placebo who do not relapse seem to function as well in the community as some patients taking drugs. Nonetheless, the primary benefit of maintenance drug therapy appears to be the prevention of relapse.[22] Thus, for at least some, albeit a minority of stabilized patients, no clearcut benefit may accrue from continuing to take antipsychotic drugs.

Other recent studies show that significant numbers of discharged patients (approximately 50 percent) relapse over a two-year period, despite taking antipsychotic medication.[23] These studies show no significant difference in outcome between patients taking oral medication (fluphenazine hydrochloride, oral *Prolixin*) versus those taking intramuscular medication (fluphenazine decanoate, *Prolixin Decanoate*), thus confirming that for patients on drugs, relapse is not a simple matter of noncompliance.

When considering the question of whether a particular patient should take medication, the conclusion of the recent Tardive Dyskinesia Task Force Report from the American Psychiatric Association, based on a review of the relevant studies is frustrating:

> [U]nfortunately, clinically useful guidelines concerning the probable requirement for sustained drug treatment are not yet firmly established, although it is likely that factors predicting a generally favorable prognosis in psychotic illnesses . . . may also predict greater tolerance of *removal* of an antipsychotic drug.[24]

The relevancy of the above studies to the right to refuse controversy needs some explanation. These studies stand for the proposition that some patients, at least those who are more chronically ill, should have a "clinical," if not a legal, right to refuse continuing treatment with medication. For this minority of more chronically ill or stabilized patients, the risk/benefit ratio of continuing drug treatment may not be favorable.[25] This proposition, however, does not solve the problem of the committed patient's right to refuse antipsychotic medication, for the studies cited concerning the chronic administration of drugs are *outpatient*, not inpatient, studies.

We would hope and expect that if medication were not clinically indicated for the hospitalized patient, that is, if taking medication did not increase the likelihood that the patient would improve or be able to be discharged, then hospital physicians would not recommend it, and certainly would not insist that the patient take it. The above studies do, however, suggest that some psychiatric patients are correct when they assert that antipsychotic drugs are not consistently helpful for them, that their experience with the drugs has not been a positive one, and that they do not wish to take the drugs. If we had more extensive data about which hospitalized patients continue to require drugs, we would be better able to evaluate the claims of both physicians and patients about the necessity or lack of necessity for continued drug administration.

BENEFITS FOR PATIENTS CONSEQUENT TO RECEIVING MEDICATION INVOLUNTARILY

This issue is not exactly the same as that previously discussed. The studies mentioned above have clearly established the usefulness of antipsychotic medications administered both acutely and chronically for a significant number of patients with schizophrenia. But, it is frequently not recognized or admitted that these studies do not bear directly on the point most relevant to the controversy about the patient's right to refuse. For even if it is known that drug treatment is beneficial for most schizophrenic patients, the question is whether these same benefits accrue when (or if) patients are forced to take medication. For example, in the *Rogers* case, the plaintiffs argued that the cooperation of the patient is necessary for medication to be effective, and that patient attitudes are highly determinative concerning the outcome of treatment with antipsychotic medication.[26] While this assertion is certainly true concerning psychotherapy, or the utilization of supportive and other psychosocial treatments in psychiatry, it is hardly clear concerning medication. Instead, it is because medication can be used successfully without the patient's consent, at least to alleviate the more florid symptoms, that the controversy about the "right to refuse" has become so prominent.

Sadly, however, no satisfactory research or controlled data exist about this issue. Some research has shown that a patient's subjective response to a test dose of an antipsychotic drug may be a useful predictor of the patient's short-term symptomatic outcome following drug administration,[27] but this research was conducted with consenting, not refusing, patients. It is the experience of virtually all clinicians that giving medication involuntarily or quasi-involuntarily (for example, giving medication intramuscularly to acutely disturbed and psychotic patients) is extremely effective over the short run.[28] The effects of giving medication involuntarily in the acute situation compare favorably with the effects of giving medication voluntarily or by mouth. That is why it is used, and some credence must be given to clinical experience.

However, the impact of forced medication, whether on one or several occasions, on the *patient's long-term course* is presently quite unclear. For most committed patients, involuntary medication is used only occasionally, and then usually only for a brief period of time. After a period of brief involuntary administration of medication, patients frequently come to accept medication and to take it "willingly"—at least as "willingly" as is possible when the patient is still "committed" to the hospital. As studies about the outcome of commitment also show, at least some of these involuntarily treated patients subsequently take medication voluntarily once discharged. The impact of giving medication involuntarily on the patient-doctor relationship, and how this affects the treatment alliance over the long term, to our knowledge, has not been systematically studied.

Side Effects of Antipsychotic Drugs

Tardive dyskinesia is a condition characterized by involuntary muscle movements, especially those of the face, mouth, and limbs, and seems to result from treatment with antipsychotic drugs.[29] There has been considerable disagreement about the frequency with which tardive dyskinesia occurs, and its severity and seriousness for the patient when it does occur. The best data on this subject indicate that the syndrome occurs in approximately 10 to 20 percent of cases of antipsychotic drug administration, and that it is occasionally, though not very frequently, a serious and profoundly incapacitating side effect of medication.[30]

The time course over which tardive dyskinesia develops, however, is relevant to the right to refuse controversy. Few cases of tardive dyskinesia have been reported to occur as a result of less than three months of drug administration. More typically, tardive dyskinesia is not seen or reported until after antipsychotic drugs have been administered to a patient for more than two years. Considerably more study is needed about the causes and typical manifestations of tardive dyskinesia. But the low probability that it will result from the initial phases of drug treatment would seem to justify, in terms of the risk/benefit ratio of treatment, involuntary medication for most patients in the acute phases of illness.

Of course, many hospitalized patients have had considerable exposure to antipsychotic drugs during prior hospitalizations. The risks of drug administration accumulate over time, and are dependent at least in part upon the total dosage of drugs taken. If more chronic administration of the drug is at issue, or if the patient manifests signs of tardive dyskinesia, the possibility of this side effect does become a potent argument in favor of affording patients the right to refuse antipsychotic medication.

In this latter situation of more chronic drug administration, the pertinent question becomes: who should weigh the risks and benefits for the patient—the physician or the patient? Physicians view the possibility of the patient's relapse as a very serious setback, especially when the patient's history shows that the failure to take drugs has been associated with relapse. It is perhaps understandable that physicians view the possibility of relapse as more serious for the patient than the problem of tardive dyskinesia, especially when the patient does not currently manifest the syndrome, or manifests it only to a very minor degree. Assuming the risk of tardive dyskinesia is great, or that it has already been diagnosed, we believe that there is a strong argument that patients should be permitted to make this treatment decision, if they are able to weight the risks and benefits. For it is the patient, not the physician, who will experience both the benefits and the side effects of continued drug administration.

Another problem with tardive dyskinesia concerns the issue of prevention. Guidelines are now available concerning the proper administration of antipsychotic drugs. These guidelines indicate the need for continuing and sequential monitoring of a patient's responses to the drug, including testing for the presence of disorders of movement to detect the early signs of any disorder.[31] By stopping administration of the medication or reducing dosage, tardive dyskinesia may be prevented, even if it is not always successfully treated once it develops. The extent to which tardive dyskinesia is preventable through careful drug management, however, requires more study. If prevention were possible, the argument against the propriety of involuntary administration of antipyschotic drugs, at least for short periods of time, would be weakened.

Tardive dyskinesia is not the only side effect of antipsychotic medication cited by the proponents of the right to refuse. Extrapyramidal symptoms, especially akathisia (motor restlessness, muscular quivering), along with depression, sedation, and difficulty in concentrating, are frequently cited as serious concomitants of neuroleptic administration.[32] Although there are some data on the incidence of extrapyramidal symptoms,[33] much of the research predates the introduction of the newer, more potent neuroleptics and the widespread use of higher dosages of the drugs.

Data on the incidence of all types of side effects, and on how well they can be controlled by reducing dosages or utilizing antiparkinsonian medication, would be highly relevant to the risk/benefit assessment. Attention to the subjective effects of the drugs on patients' moods, emotions, cognitions, and perceptions (speculation about which played an important role in the First Amendment arguments in the district court decision in *Rogers*) would be particularly important. Despite the need for further research, it should not be forgotten that as far as the therapeutic effects of the medications are concerned, there is good evidence for their essentially normalizing effect on many aspects of cognition.[35]

THE VAGARIES OF COMPETENCY

Neither of the two leading cases concerning the right to refuse, *Rennie v. Klein*[36] or *Rogers v. Okin*,[37] affords patients an "absolute right" to refuse antipsychotic medication. Inevitably, the "incompetency exception" to informed consent can and will be invoked when patients refuse treatment and it seems advisable that they nevertheless be treated. Through judicial proceedings or other proceedings established by the courts, patients can be found incompetent to make decisions about their treatment and then be medicated involuntarily. Empirically, the problem is that at present we simply have no idea what proportion of hospitalized committed patients are or will be found to be legally incompetent.

The plaintiffs in right to refuse litigation essentially argued that only a very small percentage of patients are unable to assess for themselves the risks and benefits of medication. In *Rogers*, the district court opinion specifically notes that:

[t]he weight of evidence persuades this court that, although committed mental patients do suffer at least some impairment of their relationship [sic] to reality, most are able to appreciate the benefits, risks, and discomfort that may reasonably be expected from receiving psychotropic medication.[38]

Unfortunately, Judge Tauro's assertion cannot be supported by available studies or data. The judge may be right or he may be wrong, but this issue has simply not been studied sufficiently. There are few references in the literature to the possible prevalence of factual, if not legal, incompetency among committed patients. The references suggest that one-half to two-thirds of committed patients may not be able to make treatment decisions.[39] But these are only assertions, not systematic data, and they are not clearly relevant to the problem of medication refusals. One recent study comes to the conclusion that psychotic patients do not have the capacity to evaluate the risks and benefits of medication.[40] Other well-known psychopharmacologists have concluded that, at least as outpatients, most patients are able to give informed consent for the administration of antipsychotics.[41] The prevalence of "incompetency" among hospitalized committed patients needs more study.

It should be noted that this entire issue of competency, like the issue of patients' right to refuse, is extremely value-laden. The percentages of patients that can make, or will be found incompetent to make, treatment decisions depend heavily upon the standard of competency used to assess this matter. In a recent review of the literature, we summarized and discussed four standards for the assessment of competency that may be applied to treatment refusals.[42] These standards turn on whether the patient: (1) evidences a choice, (2) understands the relevant issues, (3) manipulates information rationally, and/or (4) appreciates the relevance of the information to his or her situation. Depending upon the choice of standard to be used for evaluation of competency to refuse medication, there will be wide variation in the percentages of patients who will or will not be permitted to refuse medication in the hospital because they are "incompetent." Further studies are needed to delineate the reliability and validity of these competency standards and the results of applying these different standards to the population of committed psychiatric patients.

Outcome When Patients Are Given the Right to Refuse

Except for the work of Appelbaum and Gutheil,[43] the question of the outcome of recognizing a right to refuse is virtually unstudied. If the findings of the district court in *Rogers*—that granting patients the right to refuse medication in nonemergency circumstances had little impact upon the hospital milieu or upon patient treatment—were correct, then affording patients the right to refuse might pose few problems. But there is much to suggest that this "finding of facts" was mistaken. In fact, the ruling of the Court of Appeals in *Rogers* noted: "[I]t does appear that the district court may have overlooked or misconstrued evidence of specific acts of violence occurring as a result of defendants' difficulty in applying the court's standard."[44] In a paper on the clinical effects of *Rogers*, Gill has summarized many detrimental outcomes of affording patients the right to refuse.[45] He reports that 89 of the 159 patients who persistently refused treatment during a two-year period, "deteriorated." These 89 patients

> were subjected to the terrors and harshness of their psychotic inner lives for long periods of time. Many times these patients deteriorated into states of physical emergency in which they resorted to physical assault on others or on themselves or became self-destructive through refusal of food to such a degree that it endangered their physical health.

Dr. Gill also noted that because of escalating violence, general disturbances, and tension, the unit found itself unable to care for and/or to contain some patients. After the litigation was commenced, the transfer of patients to a maximum security hospital escalated from about one transfer per year to about six or seven per year.[46] In considering these reports, however, it is important to realize that *Rogers* engendered bitter feelings at the hospital, and it has been difficult to separate the impact of the fact of litigation from outcomes directly attributable to the court's ruling that patients had the right to refuse treatment.

What has happened in the hospitals most directly affected by *Rogers* and *Rennie*, will, however, not answer the important question: what impact will the right to refuse have on mental health institutions and patients throughout the country? The New York State experience concerning the right to refuse is illustrative. During the mid-1970s, a New York State mental health regulation granted patients the right to refuse treatment, to have their objection reviewed by the "head of service," and then to appeal the result of this review to the director of the facility. This regulation resulted in only a very small number of appeals. In studying the implementation of this right to refuse regulation, Weinstein found that over a one-year period, only five patients (considerably less than one percent of all patients) made appeals to the director. In all five cases the director supported the doctor's wishes to medicate the patient.[47] In part, so few appeals may have been made because, as demonstrated in a later study by Johnson and Weinstein, psychiatric residents at the hospital were not knowledgeable about the regulation granting patients a qualified right to refuse.[48] About 20% of the residents responding to a questionnaire did not know that the regulation existed, and 75 percent had never seen a copy of it. Sixty-one percent did not know of the appeal procedure whereby patients could implement their right of refusal. If hospital staff did not know about patients' rights of refusal, it certainly is possible that patients did not know.

At present, it is quite unclear what impact the right to refuse doctrine might have on the typical hospital milieu—where patients are adequately informed of their rights, where staff is knowledgeable about patients' rights and respects them, or where advocacy systems exist and permit other knowledgeable persons to effectuate the patients' rights to refuse. The only relevant study in this area was conducted in a Massachusetts mental hospital that anticipated the decision in *Rogers*.[49] The study found that of the 23 patients who refused medication over a three-month period, five were persistent refusers. These five patients refused medications over a substantial period of time in a manner that significantly interfered with the hospital's ability to treat them. For these patients, the act of refusal resulted in serious clinical consequences for the patients and consternation to the patients' physicians.[50]

PATIENT SATISFACTION WITH COMMITMENT

While this topic relates in part to information we have previously discussed concerning the outcome for committed patients, it is worth special emphasis. One reason for the prominence afforded the right to refuse over the past decade is that a productive alliance has been forged between some angry, disaffected patients and ex-patients, who view themselves as inmates or ex-inmates, and legal services attorneys with a special interest in mental health law, who are vigorous proponents of the patients' right to refuse. One of these ex-patients, Judi Chamberlin, has written a provocative and interesting book about her experiences.[51] Yet, despite the cogency of such arguments, we simply have no idea how representative these views are. Very few studies touch upon this issue. Gove reports that, although committed patients were generally hospitalized against their will, once discharged "with the advantage of hindsight they tended to have a positive attitude toward their hospitalization."[52] Gove's study is partly supported by Weinstein's recent review of quantitative research concerning patients' attitudes about mental hospitalization. Reviewing 38 studies, Weinstein found that 78.9 percent of patients espoused favorable attitudes toward their hospitalization.[53] Unfortunately, the majority of inpatient studies reviewed by Weinstein (25 of 27) did not include the variable "voluntary" versus "involuntary" admission. Most clinicians know at least some formerly committed patients who say "thank you," even if others admitted say " ---- you," once discharged.[54] It would clearly be helpful to have more data on this important issue.

The Effect of Providing Due Process
Protection for the Patient

One outcome of the right to refuse controversy will be to increase the variety and volume of due process protections provided to patients, including the provision of advocacy services and legal counsel, to adjudicate patient competency or to check on the accuracy of physicians' judgments that involuntary treatment is truly needed. The procedural complexities involved in treating patients with medication will increase, much as have the procedural complexities necessary to commit patients to hospitals.[55] But, while much has been written about the legal, moral, and programmatic issues involved in providing due process and advocacy protections for patients,[56] the impact of providing due process and advocacy protections in terms of *long-term* patient outcome, has been studied hardly at all. Instead, there has been a long-standing, often heated debate between psychiatrists, lawyers, and advocates about whether providing due process hearings and/or advocacy is helpful or harmful for the patient.[57] While a few recent papers have begun to address the issue of the therapeutic or countertherapeutic elements of providing due process for the patient,[58] this is another area with virtually no data. Systematic studies, concerning the impact of providing due process protections and advocacy services for the patient, upon patient morale, the doctor-patient relationship, and patient outcome (defined both subjectively and objectively) are needed.

The effect of increased due process procedures on the functioning of the hospital staff, and thus indirectly on the care of patients, needs to be explored and documented. Similarly, research is needed to determine: whether excessive staff time will be diverted to legal hearings, as suggested in the recent Supreme Court decision in *Parham*,[59] whether the delay involved will redound to the detriment of effective treatment,[60] and whether the ethical standards of the treatment staff, and therefore their morale, will be compromised.[61]

Conclusion

We hope that this chapter has raised more questions than it has answered. Rather than focusing on mental health law relevant to commitment and informed consent, or solely on clinical issues, we have tried to identify a number of areas where the results of available empirical data might help us to think more critically about the right to refuse question. We recognize that empirical data relevant to the issues we have discussed will not untie the Gordian knot. However, were we to know more empirically, the value questions that underlie the right to refuse controversy might then come into clearer focus.

We have attempted to comment "objectively" on the above-mentioned empirical studies, at least as "objectively" as might be expected considering that we are physicians committed to the view that patients' rights and treatment needs must both be taken into account. We should, therefore, state our own point of view about the right to refuse controversy, so that our objectivity (or lack of it) can be assessed.

As we have previously written, we believe that something seems wrong about severing the decision to provide necessary treatment to the patient once hospitalized from the decision to commit the patient to the hospital in the first place.[62] We further believe that few persons—patients, their families, physicians, judges, or ordinary citizens—will, over the long run, tolerate a situation in which a substantial number of committed patients remain untreated either because the patients refuse the necessary treatment or because physicians believe themselves powerless to act. We thus believe that, over the next decade, and consistent with the ruling of the court of appeals in *Rogers*, a number of procedural and definitional changes will occur in commitment laws and the administrative regulations implementing them. These changes will permit the continued involuntary treatment of patients with medication, when and if, in the judgment of physicians responsible for their care, patients require the medication. The constitutionality of commitment laws that take this approach will be upheld. For example, a federal district court recently ruled that since committed patients in Utah had been found irrational and unable to make a treatment decision at the time of commitment, they were not permitted to refuse medication in the hospital.[63]

Increasingly, however, the empirical literature suggests that the risk/benefit ratio for the patients receiving antipsychotic drugs is more clearly favorable for short-term than long-term treatment. One likely effect of the right to refuse treatment controversy will therefore be to shorten the time during which forced medication will be permitted. Procedural safeguards and reviews must also be instituted to ensure that involuntary treatment with medication is truly beneficial for the committed patient, especially when it is maintenance treatment and not acute treatment that is being contemplated.

We hope, however, the right to refuse controversy will stimulate additional research, so that within a decade or so we will be better able to confront the important and complex issues of values underlying this topic.

Notes

1. Yesley, M. S., *The Ethics Advisory Board and the "Right to Know,"* HASTINGS CENTER REPORT 10(5):5-9 (1980).
2. *See*, Tanke, E. D. and Tanke, T. J., *Getting Off a Slippery Slope: Social Science in the Judicial Process*, AMERICAN PSYCHOLOGIST 34:1130-38 (1979); Loftus, E. and Monahan, J., *Trial by Data: Psychological Research as Legal Evidence*, AMERICAN PSYCHOLOGIST 35:270-83 (1980); Steadman, H. J., *The Use of Social Science in Forensic Psychiatry*, INTERNATIONAL JOURNAL OF LAW & PSYCHIATRY 2:519-31 (1979).
3. *Ballew v. Georgia*, 435 U.S. 223, 239 (1978).
4. *Addington v. Texas*, 441 U.S. 418 (1979) (the Court rejected the "beyond a reasonable doubt"standard of proof as required for mental health commitment in favor of the lesser standard of "clear and convincing").
5. *Parham v. J.R.*, 442 U.S. 584 (1979).
6. *Addington v. Texas*, supra note 4.
7. *Id.*, citing Chodoff, P., *The Case for Involuntary Hospitalization of the Mentally Ill*, AMERICAN JOURNAL OF PSYCHIATRY 133:496-501 (1976); Schwartz, C. C., et al., e.g., *Psychiatric Labeling and the Rehabilitation of the Mental Patient: Implications of Research Findings for Mental Health Policy*, ARCHIVES OF GENERAL PSYCHIATRY 31:329-34 (1974).
8. *Rogers v. Okin*, 634 F.2d 650 (1st Cir. 1980).
9. *Id.* at 653, n.1.
10. Zwerling, I., et al., *A Comparison of Voluntary and Involuntary Patients in a State Hospital*, AMERICAN JOURNAL OF ORTHOPSYCHIATRY 45:81-87 (1975); Spensley, J. et al. *Involuntary Hospitalization: What for and How Long?* AMERICAN JOURNAL OF PSYCHIATRY 131:219-22 (1974); Sata, L. S. and Goldenberg, E. E., *A Study of Involuntary Patients in Seattle*, HOSPITAL & COMMUNITY PSYCHIATRY 28:834-37 (1977); Ginzburg, H. M., et al., A Followup Study of Involuntary Commitments, (presented at the annual meeting of the American Psychiatric Association, Toronto) (May 1977); Peele, R., et al., *Involuntary Hospitalization and Treatability: Observations from the District of Columbia Experience*, CATHOLIC UNIVERSITY OF AMERICA LAW REVIEW 23:744 (1974).
11. Gove, W. R. and Fain, T., *A Comparison of Voluntary and Committed Psychiatric Patients*, ARCHIVES OF GENERAL PSYCHIATRY 34:669-76 (1977).
12. Tomelleri, C. J., et al., *Who are the "Committed"?* JOURNAL OF NERVOUS AND MENTAL DISEASE 165:288-93 (1977).
13. Roth, L. H., *A Commitment Law for Patients, Doctors, and Lawyers*, AMERICAN JOURNAL OF PSYCHIATRY 136(9):1121-27 (September 1979).
14. Zwerling, *supra* note 10.
15. National Institute of Mental Health Psychopharmacology Service Center Collaborative Study Group [hereinafter cited as NIMH], *Phenothiazine Treatment in Acute Schizophrenia*, ARCHIVES OF GENERAL PSYCHIATRY 10:246-61 (1964).
16. *See, e.g.*, W. S. APPELTON, J. M. DAVIS, PRACTICAL CLINICAL PSYCHOPHARMACOLOGY (Williams & Wilkins, Baltimore) (1980).
17. NIMH, *supra* note 15.

18. Kessler, K. A. and Waletzky, J. P., *Clinical Use of the Antipsychotics*, AMERICAN JOURNAL OF PSYCHIATRY 138(2):202–09 (February 1981).
19. See Appleton, *supra* note 16, and May, P.R.A. et al., *Schizophrenia—A Follow-up Study of Results of Treatment, II, Hospital Stay over Two to Five Years*, ARCHIVES OF GENERAL PSYCHIATRY 33:481–86 (1976).
20. Carpenter, W. T. et al., *The Treatment of Acute Schizophrenia Without Drugs: An Investigation of Some Current Assumptions*, AMERICAN JOURNAL OF PSYCHIATRY 134(1):14–20 (January 1977).
21. See Hogarty, G. E. and Ulrich, R. F., *Temporal Effects of Drug and Placebo in Delaying Relapse in Schizophrenic Outpatients*, ARCHIVES OF GENERAL PSYCHIATRY 34(3):297–301 (March 1977); Tardive Dyskinesia Task Force Report 18, American Psychiatric Association (December 1979) [hereinafter cited as T.D. Task Force].
22. Gardos, G. and Cole, J. O., *Maintenance Antipsychotic Therapy: Is the Cure Worse than the Disease?* AMERICAN JOURNAL OF PSYCHIATRY 133(1):32–36 (January 1976); and Kessler, *supra* note 18.
23. Hogarty, G. E., et al., *Fluphenazine and Social Therapy in the After-Care of Schizophrenic Patients*, ARCHIVES OF GENERAL PSYCHIATRY 36:1283–94 (1979).
24. T.D. Task Force, *supra* note 21 at 109.
25. *Id.*
26. *Rogers v. Okin*, 478 F. Supp. 1342 (D.Mass. 1979).
27. Van Putten, T. and May P. R. A., *Subjective Response as a Predictor of Outcome in Pharmacotherapy*, ARCHIVES OF GENERAL PSYCHIATRY 35:477–80 (1978).
28. Donlon, P. T., et al., *Overview: Efficacy and Safety of the Rapid Neuroleptization Method with Injectable Haloperidol*, AMERICAN JOURNAL OF PSYCHIATRY 136(3):273–78 (March 1979).
29. See T.D. Task Force, *supra* note 21.
30. *Id.*
31. *Id.*
32. Brief Amicus Curiae, Mental Health Association, Civil Liberties Union of Massachusetts, Mental Patients' Liberation Front, *Okin v. Rogers*, (1st Cir. December 8, 1977) reprinted in MENTAL DISABILITY LAW REPORTER 2:43 (1977).
33. Ayd, F. J., *A Survey of Drug-Induced Extrapyramidal Reactions*, JOURNAL OF THE AMERICAN MEDICAL ASSOCIATION 175(12):1054–60 (March 25, 1961).
34. *Rogers v. Okin*, *supra* note 26 at 1366–67.
35. Spohn H. E., et al., *Phenothiazine Effects on Psychological and Psycho-Physiological Dysfunction in Chronic Schizophrenics*, ARCHIVES OF GENERAL PSYCHIATRY 34(6):633–44 (June 1977); Hymowitz, P. and Spohn, H. E., *The Effects of Antipsychotic Medication on the Linguistic Ability of Schizophrenics*, JOURNAL OF NERVOUS AND MENTAL DISEASE 168:287–96 (1980): Meadow, A., et al., *Effects of Phenothiazines on Anxiety and Cognition in Schizophrenia*, DISEASE OF THE NERVOUS SYSTEM 36(4):203–08 (April 1975).
36. *Rennie v. Klein*, 476 F. Supp. 1294 (D.N.J. 1979).
37. *Rogers v. Okin*, supra note 26.
38. *Id.* at 1361.
39. Contemporary Studies Project, *Facts and Fallacies about Iowa Civil Commit-*

ment, IOWA LAW REVIEW 55(4):895-980 (April 1970) at 918; Deposition of Dr. Israel Zwerling in *Wyatt v. Stickney.* In B. J. Ennis and P. R. Friedman, eds., LEGAL RIGHTS OF THE MENTALLY HANDICAPPED, vol. 1, (Practicing Law Institute, Mental Health Law Project, New York) (1974) at 512.
40. Grossman, L. and Summers, F., *A Study of the Capacity of Schizophrenic Patients to Give Informed Consent,* HOSPITAL & COMMUNITY PSYCHIATRY 31(3):205-06 (March 1980).
41. Sovner R., et al., *Tardive Dyskinesia and Informed Consent,* PSYCHOSOMATICS 19(3):172-77 (March 1978).
42. Appelbaum, P. S. and Roth, L. H., *Competency to Consent to Research: A Psychiatric Overview,* ARCHIVES OF GENERAL PSYCHIATRY (forthcoming, 1982).
43. Appelbaum, P. S. and Gutheil, T. G., *Drug Refusal: A Study of Psychiatric Inpatients,* AMERICAN JOURNAL OF PSYCHIATRY 137(3):340-46 (March 1980).
44. *Rogers v. Okin, supra* note 8 at 655.
45. Gill, M. J., The Boston State Hospital Case: Its Impact on State Hospital Patients (Presented at the annual meeting of the American Psychiatric Association, San Francisco) (May 6, 1980). *Also see* chapter 6 this text.
46. *Id.*
47. Weinstein, H. C., *The Right to Refuse Treatment,* BULLETIN OF THE AMERICAN ACADEMY OF PSYCHIATRY AND THE LAW 5(4):425-37 (December 1977).
48. Johnson, R. E. and Weinstein, H. C., *Right To Refuse Treatment: The Knowledge Gap,* JOURNAL OF PSYCHIATRY AND LAW 7(4):457-61 (Winter 1979).
49. Appelbaum, Gutheil, *supra* note 43.
50. Appelbaum, P. S. and Gutheil, T. G., *"Rotting with their Rights On": Constitutional Theory and Clinical Reality in Drug Refusal by Psychiatric Patients,* BULLETIN OF THE AMERICAN ACADEMY OF PSYCHIATRY AND THE LAW 7(3):306-15 (September 1979).
51. J. CHAMBERLIN, ON OUR OWN: PATIENT-CONTROLLED ALTERNATIVES TO THE MENTAL HEALTH SYSTEM (McGraw-Hill, New York) (1978).
52. Gove, *supra* note 11.
53. Weinstein, R. M., *Patient Attitudes Toward Mental Hospitalization: A Review of Quantitative Research,* JOURNAL OF HEALTH & SOCIAL BEHAVIOR 20: 237-58 (September 1979).
54. A. A. STONE, MENTAL HEALTH AND LAW: A SYSTEM IN TRANSITION (National Institute of Mental Health, Rockville, Md.) (1975).
55. Roth, L. H., *Mental Health Commitment: The State of the Debate, 1980,* HOSPITAL & COMMUNITY PSYCHIATRY 31(6):385-96 (June 1980).
56. *See Developments in the Law—Civil Commitment of the Mentally Ill,* HARVARD LAW REVIEW 87(6):1190-1406 (April 1974); L. E. Kopolow, H. Bloom, eds., MENTAL HEALTH ADVOCACY: AN EMERGING FORCE IN CONSUMERS' RIGHTS (National Institute of Mental Health, Rockville, Md.) (1977); *see* issues of ADVOCACY NOW, THE JOURNAL OF PATIENT RIGHTS & MENTAL HEALTH ADVOCACY, 1978-81 (San Fernando Valley Community Mental Health Centers, Inc., Van Nuys, Calif.).
57. *See* Stone, A. A., *The Myth of Advocacy,* HOSPITAL & COMMUNITY PSYCHIATRY 30(12):819-22 (December 1979); Coffman, R., *Some Comments on Dr. Stone's*

Views on Advocacy, HOSPITAL & COMMUNITY PSYCHIATRY 31(4):275 (April 1980).
58. Ensminger, J. J. and Liguori, T. D., *The Therapeutic Significance of the Civil Commitment Hearing: An Unexplored Potential*, JOURNAL OF PSYCHIATRY AND LAW 6(1):5–44 (Spring 1978); Eisenberg, G. C., Barnes, B. M., Gutheil, T. G., *Involuntary Commitment and the Treatment Process: A Clinical Perspective*, BULLETIN OF THE AMERICAN ACADEMY OF PSYCHIATRY AND THE LAW.
59. *Parham v. J.R., supra* note 5 at 608, n.16 ("the judicial model of fact finding for all constitutionally protected interests, regardless of their nature, can turn rational decision making into an unmanageable enterprise").
60. Gutheil, T. G., Shapiro, R. and St. Clair, R. L., *Legal Guardianship in Drug Refusal: An Illusory Solution*, AMERICAN JOURNAL OF PSYCHIATRY 137(3): 347–52 (March 1980).
61. Gutheil, T. G. and Appelbaum, P. S., *Substituted Judgment and the Physician's Ethical Dilemma: With Special Reference to the Problem of the Psychiatric Patient*, JOURNAL OF CLINICAL PSYCHIATRY 41(9):303–05 (September 1980).
62. *See* Roth, *supra* note 13; Appelbaum, *supra* note 49, and Gutheil and Appelbaum, *supra* note 60.
63. *A.E. and R.R. v. Mitchell*, No.C78-466 (D.Utah, June 16, 1980); *see* Appelbaum, P. S., *A.E. and R.R.: Utah's Compromise on the Right to Refuse Treatment*, HOSPITAL & COMMUNITY PSYCHIATRY 32:167–168, 1981.

Discussion

Richard I. Shader, M.D., Moderator

UNIDENTIFIED SPEAKER: Dr. Gutheil reported that at the Massachusetts Mental Health Center, in 80 percent of the cases where the doctors approached the patient and sought his cooperation, the patient agreed to take the medication. From the psychiatric point of view, does that mean that there may be some benefits to the right to refuse treatment?

Ms. JUDI CHAMBERLIN (Conference Faculty): We can't know whether that means that 80 percent of the patients voluntarily took medications, in much the same way that we can't know how many of the "voluntary" patients are in hospitals against their will. There is a coercive atmosphere surrounding the decision, with an authority figure asking the patient to accept treatment and consequences to giving a "right" or "wrong" answer.

DR. LAUREN H. ROTH (Conference Faculty): Although that report is encouraging, it would be sad if it takes a legal decision to get doctors talking to their patients. I don't know if this shows anything new; considering what I know of Dr. Gutheil and the type of training that the doctors at Mass. Mental have, I am sure that most of these doctors always discuss these things with their patients. The real question is what are you going to do at a hospital like mine, with 1500 patients and three doctors? The doctors just won't talk to the patients.

Ms. ARLENE SENN (Coalition to Stop Institutional Violence): Could you comment on guardianship being used to obtain forced treatment?

Ms. CHAMBERLIN: It is misleading to see guardianship as some sort of positive development that will sidestep the whole right to refuse controversy. Guardianship can be as oppressive as the current mental health system.

The California system has been viewed as a model for the rest of the country, but I don't see it in any way as an improvement on patients' rights. The people in the ex-patient movement in California view being declared incompetent and given a guardian in the same way they view being forcibly committed or forcibly drugged.

Thinking that someone is incapable of managing his own affairs is similar to thinking that someone needs treatment or needs to be committed but is incapable of recognizing that. These are assumptions, equally capable of a great deal of abuse, and may bring about a loss of individual freedom.

DR. ROTH: Guardianship is a rip-off, and corporate guardianship is an even bigger rip-off. I predict that in an impersonal bureaucracy which doesn't know the patients, inexperienced and somewhat idealistic doctors will pass in and out in six months and go into private practice, and the guardianship records will be lost by the agency. I base this prediction on data which I have and on studies made by others. We must think of something better.

MR. DAVID OAKES: There's a group of us here who are ex-patients, and a lot of us have experienced forcible drugging and treatment. It's really torture. My question is directed to Judi Chamberlin. How can people here, in a practical way, not just agree with us but help the struggle for patients' rights?

MS. CHAMBERLIN: Mental health professionals can help by recognizing the legitimacy of ex-patient organizations. Professionals can enable us to meet and talk with patients in the facilities, and encourage the participation of ex-patients in ward conferences, and make the existence of ex-patient groups known to patients in case they decide to become involved in them. Professionals and others also can help by recognizing one very real difference between ex-patients and mental health professionals—that of finances—and contribute to some of our organizations.

MR. JOHN C. HOLME, JR. (Staff Attorney, Advocates for Basic Legal Equality, Toledo, Ohio): Dr. Roth, in your talk you refer to a number of facts, some of which we already know, and some of which we don't know. One fact that hasn't yet been mentioned is the risk of sudden death, either as a side effect or from an overdose of medications. In a recent federal court decision in Ohio the court followed the *Rennie* case, basically saying that patients have a qualified right to refuse medication. In a procedural hearing we received testimony about a death that had occurred at one state hospital, where the Coroner's report showed that the patient had received an overdose of trilafon. He was prescribed 90 to 94 mg when the manufacturer's recommended limit is 64 mg per day. There was also a problem of polypharmacy in the case, because he was also prescribed 400 to 800 mg/day of mellaril. Given the kind of risk we are dealing with in the real world in state hospitals, wouldn't you agree that there is a need for the independent psychiatrist that Judge Brotman brought into the *Rennie* case?

DR. ROTH: There is some debate in the medical literature about the existence of a sudden death phenomenon with antipsychotic drugs. But among the risks that are listed in textbooks is sudden death associated with phenothiazines. I don't know if the actual level of risk of sudden death or its cause has yet been determined. I do know that some of those conditions can be complicated. If there is polypharmacy, synergism, or interactive effects of combined drugs such as alcohol and antipsychotic drugs, that might increase the risk. In a normal person without other medicines the level of antipsychotic drugs that one could take without dying is really quite high. Sudden death is possible but extremely unlikely from pure overdosages of antipsychotic drugs. Of course, even medicine has side effects of risks if used inappropriately.

I have no problem with the independent psychiatrist, and in some ways it is a great idea. But if we are striving for medical competency, wouldn't it be better to have the first psychiatrist competent? There's nothing wrong with second opinions or 12 opinions, but I think there is something wrong in a system built on the assumption of medical incompetency. If the entire system we are designing is a fail-safe system for incompetent psychiatrists, my first notion is fire the incompetent psychiatrists and start over.

MR. HOLME: We're dealing with the real world where these deaths do occur, and we have to design a system that is going to minimize that risk.

DR. ROTH: I agree with that, but then we have to ask whether the system we design does minimize the risk. One of the things that has bothered me is that I can do anything to patients. There's no way you can protect patients from me. I am alone with the patient in the room, even if the patient has an advocate. The fact is, at some level you must trust me or get rid of me. Because—

UNIDENTIFIED SPEAKER: People have died here in Massachusetts as a result of your drugs.

DR. ROTH: Can I finish my statement? The problem, obviously, is that if the patient has a stiff neck or a fever, and I fail to investigate it, the patient could have an untreated medical illness which I would be ignoring. If I write the wrong order, there is a chance that it will be executed whether it's right or wrong. I think I'm trying to say the same thing that the patients do: ultimately, unless I know what I'm doing, no one can protect the patient from me.

Ms. CHAMBERLIN: Dr. Roth, perhaps you are stating your opinion in a misleading way. The way you're saying this is really due to your personality type. We think you're telling the truth when you say that you have full power over us and that there's nothing we can do. Maybe it's funny, but unfortunately we can't take it as funny. We believe it because that's how we've been disciplined to think. If this is your personality type, please don't force it on my friends—they tend to think you're telling the truth.

DR. ROTH: Let me try once more to explain what I mean. Doctors and patients meet and talk, and doctors write words on charts. We all work by what I call the "policeman at the elbow" model. By that I mean there is not a policeman on my left elbow checking everything I do, and even if the policeman were there he wouldn't know what I was doing. He would have to have his own psychiatrist. His own psychiatrist is on my right elbow. Or, to use Dr. Kopolow's analogy, when you turn your car in to the auto mechanic to see how well it's working, how do you know what that mechanic does on your car unless you're standing there every single minute and there's another auto mechanic watching the first auto mechanic? The point I'm making is that unless there is another psychiatrist with me every moment in every day, it's very difficult as a practical matter for somebody to check up on exactly what I do. That's all I'm saying. When I say I have all that power, that doesn't mean I like to exercise power or I'm seeking power. I'm saying that as a matter of fact doctors do have power. I am saying the very thing that ex-patients have said.

Ms. CHAMBERLIN: I'd just like to make a comment about the original question. The fact that patients do live in the real world has not been addressed enough here. Patients do die in institutions from overdoses of drugs, mistreatment, and being beaten. These all are real world facts that these very abstract conferences never come to grips with. In an investigation in California of more than 400 patient deaths many of them were found to be due to possibly improper prescribing practices, and many were due to—and I'm going to quote the exact legal terms—"death at the hand of another, other than by accident, where there were no indictments and certainly no prosecutions or convictions." These are real world facts that all of us have to grapple with. It may be presumed a benevolent system, but it's not a benevolent system.

UNIDENTIFIED SPEAKER: If you're not there on the wards, you don't see what really happens between patients, aides, and nurses. I remember one nurse who spoke at Senator Backman's hearing who said, "What are you supposed to do when patients run up and down the hall exposing themselves?" Maybe the reason why they're exposing themselves is anger at the people who have deprived them of their manhood and who are incapable of treating anybody decently or humanely. The patients have been robbed of their respect. If you, Dr. Roth, really mean what you say—that you are for us—then it might be a good idea if you were to hear both sides of the story. There are a lot of things that you don't see, and frankly, I think you'd do a lot more good if you started checking into it. No one ought to be a psychiatrist until he himself is incarcerated in the system as a patient.

DR. ROTH: I think that there are tremendous problems in the quality of care and in the competence of physicians and the other persons who work in public systems. I don't mean to stigmatize these people that work there, but their competence has been a problem. I agree completely with Judge Brotman, who described the shocking conditions he has found, and I agree with the former patients. The quality of care in many mental health systems is not good; it is very poor. The problem is that the same thing exists in all of our public institutions. I worked as a prison doctor for two years, and I was happy to leave, I'll tell you that. I've also had some experience working in large institutions—they are not pleasant for the people who are in them.

UNIDENTIFIED SPEAKER: What, then, is your position on forced treatment of the patients in such institutions?

DR. ROTH: I have the same position that I had an hour ago. My position is that committed patients should eventually be treated, involuntarily if necessary. When the committed patient refuses medication, my first response is not to give medication. I've waited two weeks, three weeks, a month. I've had many discussions with patients. In the great majority of cases, we're able to work out alternative treatment plans. I still subscribe to the idea that commitment is an abridgement of the patient's liberty. And if the patient is not treated in the hospital, commitment is a bigger rip-off than if the patient is treated. Therefore, if we're going to have a commitment system patients should be treated forcibly.

MR. RICHARD COLE (Conference Faculty): An important issue is the failure of the profession to set standards and to follow them. I would direct the attention of the people who have some power within the profession to force the profession to set some standards, to have those standards implemented, and to have the individuals who are not following those standards disciplined seriously. Until the day when the medical standards that are in the literature are followed, there will continue to be lawsuit after lawsuit.

DR. RICHARD I. SHADER (Moderator): Standards are essential in any profession. One of the difficulties in this complex society is that when we begin to set standards, we have an advocacy group on the other side which cries restraint of trade. This has happened, for example, when the profession has tried to have minimal criteria for excellence and competence that can be applied for obtaining hospital privileges.

MR. COLE: I know that there is a great deal of resistance. But in talking to both doctors and lawyers around the country, I have learned that too often the doctors are not following or reading the recent advances in the literature, so that they are overprescribing.

DR. SHADER: No question about it.

MR. COLE: Okay, but the practice continues. As long as the medical profession allows such physicians to practice in state institutions, patients will continue to be resentful.

DR. SHADER: I don't disagree. But I think it is not a problem of continuing education and keeping up with developments as much as it may be the level of education to begin with and setting adequate standards before receiving the public trust to practice. Every effort to do that has been opposed on the grounds of restraint of trade. I think this is a problem that advocacy groups have to come to terms with; they should not focus only on the right to refuse treatment.

MR. COLE: The people who feel strongly enough about setting standards do some fighting also.

MR. GEORGE UNIT: My name is George Unit and I'm a former psychiatric prisoner. I was subjected to forced drugging and persuaded to have shock treatment. I thought I would come to this conference and find that things had changed, that there is a little more hope from the system, but I find a lot of the things I'm hearing are still very threatening. People can still call me ill because of my thoughts or my ideas. And because of their power to label me and to incarcerate me, they believe they also have the right to treat me. I want to tell you that you don't have an obligation to seek out alien thoughts and to correct them and to treat them. We've had enough of the treatment, the asylum, the places of sanctuary. We've had enough torture. People are being killed by your techniques. We have to live in fear, and I'm sure that someday you people will be accountable for what you've done to those who did try to trust you, who put hope in your profession, and found out that psychiatry is not a helping profession. It is a disabling profession which puts its practitioners above other people and above the law.

DR. ROTH: To be frank, I don't know how to answer you. You see me

Discussion

differently than I see myself. I do see myself as trying to help people, and it is true that occasionally I do treat people forcibly with medication. I certainly don't feel that people should be treated with electroconvulsive treatment prior to a court hearing, but I also do believe that electroconvulsive treatment is helpful for some persons. And I believe that there are some ex-patients who share this point of view. But they will not be the people who had electroconvulsive treatment forced on them. I'm not surprised that many people who were treated involuntarily are resentful of it.

I'm an advocate of patients' reading their records, and I've talked with many ex-patients about their feelings about being in the hospital. What many of them say repeatedly is that, first of all, they hated being in seclusion. Seclusion really sticks in their craw. Some patients, who are what I would call manic, find seclusion restful and perhaps supportive. But the majority of patients are not manic, and they find seclusion to be a very distasteful and degrading procedure. There are other people who remember being put on the floor, held down, and given medication, and they found that degrading. I don't think I'd like to be treated involuntarily with medication. I too, would find it degrading.

But we do see some people, whom we feel are quite ill and unable to control their behavior, for whom the medications could be helpful. There's a famous psychiatrist named Fritz Redlich who has said that psychiatry is a low technology area. He meant that what you as patients have to confront, and what we as professionals have to admit, is that we don't always have the right treatment for the right patient. And that we're a long way from a complete understanding of the patients we treat and of the causes of the problems we treat.

Now your response to that may be that we're no good, that we're terrible people. Unfortunately, however, this has been the history of medicine in all different areas. In medical school we were taught that until the antibiotics, doctors had about as much chance of hurting people as helping people. For 200 years doctors bled people without helping them, probably hurting them, but that was the state of the art. And just as you want us to respect you as people, which is the message I always get from patients or ex-patients, you ought to respect my feelings too.

DR. SHADER: I think the point has been very clearly made that there is a compromise of your dignity, sense of integrity, and self-esteem, and that there is considerable pain and terror in having anything forced on you, even if others believe that the forced treatment is in your own behalf. That has been communicated by a number of people here, and I would hope that those of you who did not understand this before have indeed gotten that message. It is my hope that we can try next to find some areas where we can work together, rather than trying to work in an adversarial way.

UNIDENTIFIED SPEAKER: What right do psychiatrists have to play God and tell me what is good for me? This is what you don't want to see. Maybe you can't communicate with patients. Perhaps they cannot take care of themselves, but why don't patients have a right to be themselves and live life the way they see fit? They're not hurting you.

DR. SHADER: Just as I have respected your right to state your position, several times, I had also hoped that you would respect my right to express my own. I am disappointed that I have not heard today from the individuals who advocate the right to refuse treatment, either from the patient's point of view or from the federal point of view, that there must then be alternative treatments if there is a right to refuse medication. We must have alternative treatment so that those who need help can find sanctuary or some other form of solace, if that is what they need, or some capacity to have the terror, the disorganization, and the pain that is associated with serious illness treated. Patient advocate groups should also advocate research, so that there can be efforts to find less coercive forms of treatment and to demonstrate the efficacy of such treatments. If it is not equally part of the patients' bill of rights that one can advocate experimentation to find better treatments, we will remain stuck.

UNIDENTIFIED SPEAKER: The doctor claimed that there has been a long history of medical malpractice in other centuries. But if treatments today are still primitive, people should have the right to refuse them, especially when the doctors themselves know very little about the treatment's clinical efficacy.

In psychiatry there is a long history of torturing mental patients, of locking them into chairs, of dunking them, and currently, of drugging people to death. We have plenty of reasons not to trust psychiatry. I think it's wrong to put psychiatry and medicine into the same role. There's always been the element of the witch hunt in psychiatry, and I don't think that element has disappeared. I think Dr. Roth's cavalier attitude when he said that he can do whatever he wants to a patient alone in a room has the element of a witch hunt.

DR. SHADER: I'd like to allow the members of the panel to make any concluding remarks they want to make, and then we must draw the discussion to a close.

MS. CHAMBERLIN: It is very important for legal professionals, mental health professionals, and all interested people to be willing to recognize the anger that patients have. We very often hear, "Well, you're not willing to discuss it calmly, therefore we can't discuss it." The anger is real, and it is unpleasant to face. It is much easier to sit and be calm and have quiet discourse, in which nobody ever raises a voice or interrupts anybody else.

Discussion

But the anger is real, and it comes from people's experiences as patients—what's happening to them, what happened to us, and what happened to me. Unpleasant as it may be to deal with that anger, we have to deal with it if there is to be any communication. The anger can't just be whisked out of the system.

DR. ROTH: I agree with Ms. Chamberlin about the anger, and I'm certain that's what you experience. When I lose control of myself or my life it makes me angry too. I agree with some of the remarks made about aspects of the history of psychiatry. We don't know enough to know exactly what we're doing at all times. Medicine has always been an empirical science. If I give a patient medication which helps the patient, then I want to continue to give the medication, especially if the patient feels that I'm helping him. If the patient later feels that I am not helping and there is no reason to continue, we stop.

I'm going to try one more time to explain the comment that is seemingly misunderstood. Maybe it's my failure in communication. When I said that I can do whatever I want with a patient in a room, I didn't mean that I want power or that I want to abuse patients. I meant the very same thing that Ms. Chamberlin was talking about. Patients are vulnerable, and unless somebody is with me at all times, no one really knows what goes on in a room between me and a patient. When the doctor and the patient are together, no one is looking over the doctor's shoulder, and therefore you have to depend on the doctor's basic goodwill and feel that you can trust the doctor. Perhaps there are some psychiatrists you can't trust. However, no one can police the doctor. No matter how many mechanisms are put in place to control my behavior, at some point in going about my business I'm probably going to talk to patients while I'm alone. I can say nice things, I can say mean things. I will work to improve the standards of care in my profession and to get rid of the doctors who practice incompetently.

Selected Bibliography

Appelbaum, P. S., *A.E.&R.R.: Utah's Compromise on the Right to Refuse Treatment*, HOSPITAL & COMMUNITY PSYCHIATRY 32(3):167-68 (March 1981).

Appelbaum, P. S., *Civil Litigation and Mental Health: Section 1983*, HOSPITAL & COMMUNITY PSYCHIATRY 32(5):305-6 (May 1981).

Armstrong, B., *The Mental Health Lobby and How It Grew*, HOSPTIAL & COMMUNITY PSYCHIATRY 31(9):599-605 (September 1980).

Bernstein, B. E. and Weiner, M. F., *The Many Faces of Competence*, TEXAS MEDICINE 76(11):54-57 (November 1980).

Bloom, J. D., Shore, J. H. and Treleaven, J., *Oregon's Civil Commitment Statute: Stone's "Thank-You Theory"—A Judicial Survey*, BULLETIN OF THE AMERICAN ACADEMY OF PSYCHIATRY AND THE LAW 7(4):381-89 (1979).

Brakel, S. J., *Legal Aid in Mental Hospitals*, AMERICAN BAR FOUNDATION RESEARCH JOURNAL 1981(1):21-94 (Winter 1981).

Brakel, S. J., Schwartz, S. J. and Fleischner, R. D., *Legal Advocacy for Persons Confined in Mental Hospitals*, MENTAL DISABILITY LAW REPORTER 5(4):274-280 (July/August 1981).

Brooks, A. D., *The Constitutional Right to Refuse Antipsychotic Medications*, BULLETIN OF THE AMERICAN ACADEMY OF PSYCHIATRY AND THE LAW 8(2):179-221 (1980).

Byrne, G., *Wyatt v. Stickney: Retrospect and Prospect*, HOSPITAL & COMMUNITY PSYCHIATRY 32(2):123-26 (February 1981).

Carroll, M. A., *The Right to Treatment and Involuntary Commitment*, JOURNAL OF MEDICINE AND PHILOSOPHY 5(4):278-91 (December 1980).

Cole, R. W., *Rogers v. Okin: A Lawsuit to Guarantee Patients' Right to Refuse Anti-Psychotic Medication*, THE AMERICAN JOURNAL OF FORENSIC PSYCHIATRY 1(3):104-73 (July 1979).

Decker, F. H., *Changes in the Legal Status of Mental Patients as Waivers of a Constitutional Right: The Problem of Consent*, JOURNAL OF PSYCHIATRY AND LAW 8(1):31-58 (Spring 1980).

Dickey, W., *Incompetency and the Nondangerous Mentally Ill Client*, CRIMINAL LAW BULLETIN 16(1):22-40 (January-February 1980).

Compiled from the collection of the Sagall Library of LAW, MEDICINE & HEALTH CARE, American Society of Law & Medicine, 765 Commonwealth Avenue, 16th Floor, Boston, Massachusetts 02215.

Selected Bibliography

Esposito, V. M., *The Constitutional Right to Treatment Services for the Noncommitted Mentally Disabled*, UNIVERSITY OF SAN FRANCISCO LAW REVIEW 14(4):675 (Spring 1980).

Freedman, J., *Psychotropic Drugs and the Right to Refuse Treatment*, HOSPITAL AND COMMUNITY PSYCHIATRY 32(10):732-33 (October 1981).

Gutheil, T. G., *Restraint versus Treatment: Seclusion as Discussed in the Boston State Hospital Case*, AMERICAN JOURNAL OF PSYCHIATRY 137(6):718-719 (June 1980).

Gutheil, T. G. and Appelbaum, P. S., *The Patient Always Pays: Reflection on the Boston State Case and the Right to Rot*, MAN AND MEDICINE 5(1):3-11 (1980).

Gutheil, T. G., Shapiro, K. and St. Clair, R. L., *Legal Guardianship in Drug Refusal: An Illusory Solution*, AMERICAN JOURNAL OF PSYCHIATRY 137(3):347-52 (March 1980).

Johnson, R. E. and Weinstein, H. C., *Right to Refuse Treatment: The Knowledge Gap*, JOURNAL OF PSYCHIATRY AND LAW 7(4):457-61 (Winter 1979).

Masten, F., *Criticisms of the Mental Health System: The Need for Ex-inmates to Organize*, ADVOCACY NOW 2(2):65-66 (June 1980).

Matthews, D. B., *The Right to Refuse Psychiatric Medication*, MEDICOLEGAL NEWS 8(2):4 (April 1980).

Michels, R., *The Right to Refuse Treatment: Ethical Issues*, HOSPITAL & COMMUNITY PSYCHIATRY 32(4):251-55 (April 1981).

Miller, R. D., *Confidentiality or Communication in the Treatment of the Mentally Ill*, BULLETIN OF THE AMERICAN ACADEMY OF PSYCHIATRY AND THE LAW 9(1):54-59 (1981).

Mills, M. J., *The Continuing Clinicolegal Conundrum of the Boston State Hospital Case*, MEDICOLEGAL NEWS 9(2):9-12 (April 1981).

Mitchell, A. M., *Involuntary Guardianship For Incompetents: A Strategy for Legal Services Advocates*, CLEARINGHOUSE REVIEW 12(8):451-68 (December 1978).

Mitchell, A. M., *The Object of our Wisdom and our Coercion: Involuntary Guardianship for Incompetents*, SOUTHERN CALIFORNIA LAW REVIEW 52(5):1405-52 (July 1979).

Moriarty, E. M., *Guardianships of Mentally-Ill Persons: Recent Developments Reviewed*, BOSTON BAR JOURNAL 24(2):10-14 (February 1980).

Paull, D., *The Creation of an Ombudsman: The Guardianship and Advocacy Commission*, DEPAUL LAW REVIEW 29(2):475-92 (Winter 1980).

Rhoden, N., *The Right to Refuse Psychotropic Drugs*, HARVARD CIVIL RIGHTS–CIVIL LIBERTIES LAW REVIEW 15(2):363-414 (Fall 1980).

Roth, L. H., *A Commitment Law for Patients, Doctors and Lawyers*, AMERICAN JOURNAL OF PSYCHIATRY 136(9):1121-1127 (September 1979).

Roth, L. H., *Mental Health Commitment: The State of the Debate, 1980*, HOSPITAL & COMMUNITY PSYCHIATRY 31(6):385-396 (June 1980).

Scallet, L. J., *Mental Health Law and Public Policy*, HOSPITAL & COMMUNITY PSYCHIATRY 31(9):614-17 (September 1980).

Shavill, N. L., *Patients' Rights vs. Patients' Needs: The Right of the Mentally Ill to Refuse Treatment in Colorado*, DENVER LAW JOURNAL 58(3):567-608 (1981).

Sherrin, J. J. and Abrams S., *Equal Protection Challenges to Consent Judgment in the Right-to-Treatment Litigation: Are the States Getting More Than They Bargain For?*, ALBANY LAW REVIEW, 45(3):613–42 (Spring 1981).

Shindal, J. A. and Snyder, M. E., *Legal Restraints on Restraint*, AMERICAN JOURNAL OF NURSING 81(2):393–94 (February 1981).

Slovenko, R., *On the Legal Aspects of Tardive Dyskinesia*, JOURNAL OF PSYCHIATRY AND LAW 7(3):295–332 (Fall 1979).

Soskis, D. A. and Jaffee, R. L., *Communicating with Patients About Antipsychotic Drugs*, COMPREHENSIVE PSYCHIATRY 20(2):126–31 (March/April 1979).

Symonds, E., *Mental Patients' Rights to Refuse Drugs: Involuntary Medication as Cruel and Unusual Punishment*, HASTINGS CONSTITUTIONAL LAW QUARTERLY 7(3):579–632 (Spring 1980).

Tanay, E., *The Right To Refuse Treatment and the Abolition of Involuntary Hospitalization of the Mentally Ill*, BULLETIN OF THE AMERICAN ACADEMY OF PSYCHIATRY AND THE LAW 8(1):1–14 (1980).

Tancredi, L. R., *The Right to Refuse Psychiatric Treatment: Some Legal and Ethical Considerations*, JOURNAL OF HEALTH POLITICS, POLICY AND LAW 5(3):514–22 (Fall 1980).

Tancredi, L. R., *The Rights of Mental Patients: Weighing the Interests*, JOURNAL OF HEALTH POLITICS, POLICY, AND THE LAW 5(2):199–204 (Summer 1980).

Wesson, M., *Substituted Judgment: The Parens Patriae Justification for Involuntary Treatment of the Mentally Ill*, JOURNAL OF PSYCHIATRY AND LAW 8(2):147–65 (Summer 1980).

After A Decade of L-P-S—Uncertain Times in Mental Health Law, A Conceptual Reexamination of California Law Relating to the Civil Commitment of the Mentally Ill with Recommendations for Change, California Department of Mental Health (February 1981).

The Forcible Medication of Involuntarily Committed Mental Patients with Antipsychotic Drugs—Rogers v. Okin, GEORGIA LAW REVIEW 15(3):739–62 (Spring 1981).

Mental Health Law Project, Revision of Civil Commitment Laws, CLEARINGHOUSE REVIEW 15(1):59–62 (May 1981).

Table of Cases

Addington v. Texas, 50, 145, 180, 181
A. E. and R. R. v. Mitchell, 100, 103, 104, 111, 192
Alden, Gallup v., 138

Ballew v. Georgia, 180

Candura, Lane v., 68, 140
Canterbery v. Spence, 143
Cobbs v. Grant, 68

Davis v. Hubbard, 31
Dilgard, Erikson v., 70
Doe v. Doe, 139
Donaldson v. O'Connor, 63, 77, 120, 122, 132, 169
Downs v. Sawtelle, 150

Erikson v. Dilgard, 70

Fazio v. Fazio, 138-39

Gallup v. Alden, 138
Georgia, Ballew v., 180
Goedecke v. State Dept. of Institutions, 31
Grant, Cobbs v., 68

Hagberg, Worcester State Hospital v., 138, 139, 145
Hubbard, Davis v., 31

Indiana, Jackson v., 46
In re Application of President and Directors of Georgetown College, 67
In re Bassett, 145

In re Boyd, 131
In re Estate of Brooks, 146
In re Guardianship of Norman Loring III, 69
In re Karen Quinlan, 135, 143
In re Matter of Earle Spring, 140, 144, 145, 156
In re Matter of Guardianship of Richard Roe III, 56-57, 69, 140, 144, 145, 146
In re Mental Health of K.K.B., 31
In re Roger S., 53
In re Shirley Dinnerstein, 140

Jacobson v. Massachusetts, 24
Jackson v. Indiana, 46
J. R., Parham v., 27, 52, 53, 74, 77, 123, 169, 180, 191

Klein, Rennie v., 20, 23, 24, 27, 28, 29, 31-41, 45, 46, 49, 50, 51-52, 53, 54, 63, 74, 76, 88, 92, 100, 101-2, 103, 104-5, 111, 120, 122-23, 127, 128, 131, 133, 143, 144, 146, 187, 189, 198

Lane v. Candura, 68, 140

Massachusetts, Jacobson v., 24
Mitchell, A. E. and R. R. v., 100, 103, 104, 111, 192

O'Connor, Donaldson v., 63, 77, 120, 122, 132, 169
Okin, Rogers v., 20, 23, 25, 26-27, 31, 49, 50, 52-54, 57, 59-62, 63-65, 70, 74, 75, 76, 77, 78, 81, 82-86, 88, 95, 100, 102-3, 103, 104-5, 107, 109, 111, 120,

130-31, 131, 133, 140, 143, 144, 146, 150, 151, 154, 164, 181, 185, 187-89, 192
Olmstead v. United States, 67

Parham v. J. R., 27, 52, 53, 74, 77, 123, 169, 180, 191
Perlmutter, Satz v., 143

Rennie v. Klein, 20, 23, 24, 27, 28, 29, 31-41, 45, 46, 49, 50, 51-52, 53, 54, 63, 74, 76, 88, 92, 100, 101-2, 103, 104-5, 111, 120, 122-23, 127, 128, 131, 133, 143, 144, 146, 187, 189, 198
Rogers v. Okin, 20, 23, 25, 26-27, 31, 49, 50, 52-54, 57, 59-62, 63-65, 70, 74, 75, 76, 77, 78, 81, 82-86, 88, 95, 100, 102-3, 103, 104-5, 107, 109, 111, 120, 130-31, 131, 133, 140, 143, 144, 146, 150, 151, 154, 164, 181, 185, 187-89, 192

Saikewicz, Superintendent of Belchertown State School v., 69, 131, 135, 140, 143, 145, 156
Satz v. Perlmutter, 143
Sawtelle, Downs v., 150
Schloendorff v. Society of New York Hospital, 21
Society of New York Hospital, Schloendorff v., 21
Spence, Canterbery v., 143
State Dept. of Institutions, Goedecke v., 31
Stickney, Wyatt v., 121, 169
Superintendent of Belchertown State School v. Saikewicz, 69, 131, 135, 140, 143, 145, 156

Texas, Addington v., 50, 145, 180, 181

United States, Olmstead v., 67

Wyatt v. Stickney, 121, 169
Worcester State Hospital v. Hagberg, 138, 139, 145

Index

American Orthopsychiatric Association, 77
American Psychiatric Association, 19, 49, 50, 51, 52, 76, 77, 103, 184
Ancora Psychiatric Hospital, 33, 37, 38, 39

Bleuler, Eugene, 4
Bleuler, Manfred, 15-16
Boston State Hospital, 52, 54, 56, 59, 60, 62, 63, 64, 65, 66, 75, 76, 81, 83, 84-87, 164
Bowes, H. A., 11
Brandeis, Justice Louis, 67
Bridgewater State Hospital, 86
Brotman, Stanley, 23, 24, 27, 28, 40, 44, 51, 100, 123, 201
Burger, Chief Justice Warren, 63, 67

Cardozo, Benjamin, 21
chlorpromazine, 9, 10-11, 11
Cole, Richard, 97
commitment
—generally, 21, 22-23, 75, 76-77, 104-5, 126, 132-33, 139-40, 146, 149-51, 154-55, 157, 190-91
—process, 136-41, 154
—rationale for, 49-50, 89, 182
—relation to competency, 22-23, 49-50, 51-53, 108, 132-34, 142-43, 146
—standards, 138, 182
competency
—determinations, 22-23, 24, 25, 27, 92, 108, 131-32, 145-46
—generally, 115-19, 131-34, 157
—relationship to commitment, 22-23, 28, 49-50, 52-53, 143-44, 146, 157, 187-88

—role of psychiatrist, 118-19, 145
—standards, 26, 117-18, 188
Curran, William 40, 150

decision-making, 26-28, 28, 36, 39, 53, 77, 131, 156
Delay, J., 9
Deniker, P., 9
due process, 27, 31, 40, 52-53, 76, 89, 139-40, 191

electroconvulsive therapy, 19, 26, 77
emergency exception. *See* Right to refuse treatment

family, role of, 13, 97, 98, 124

Gill, Michael, 189
guardians, 45, 52, 53, 57, 61, 62, 74, 77, 78, 85, 102, 131, 134, 138-41, 144-45, 145, 148-49, 150-51, 155-56, 157, 197-98

independent psychiatrist, 28, 36, 39, 44, 51. 127, 131
informed consent, 19, 21, 24, 36, 57, 67, 107-8, 143, 181, 187

Joint Commission on Accreditation of Hospitals, 19
Jones, Maxwell, 81

Kety, Seymour, 6

Laborit, H., 9
Lehman, Heinz, 10-11

Madness Network News, 163
Massachusetts Department of Mental Health, 86, 102, 136, 138
Massachusetts Psychiatric Society, 57
Mental Health Advocates Coalition, 173
Mental Health Association, 173
mental health programs (state), 92-94, 171
Mental Health Systems Act, 89, 169-71, 176
Mental Patients' Liberation Front, 42, 163, 164

National Alliance for the Mentally Ill, 173
National Commission for the Protection of Human Subjects, 169
National Institute of Mental Health, 176, 182
New England Journal of Medicine, 40
neuroleptic drugs. *See* psychotropic drug treatment

patients
—role of, 19-22, 23, 32-33, 96-97, 107, 116, 153, 163-68, 176-78, 198, 199-200, 202-3
—advocacy for, 172-76, 190
parens patriae, 25, 45, 50
Perkins, Clifton T., Hospital, 45
President's Commission on Mental Health, 170-71
psychiatry, generally, 3-6, 109-10, 122-23
psychotropic drug treatment
—efficacy of neuroleptics, 11, 13-16, 33-35, 43, 57-58, 59, 60, 123-27, 182-84
—experimental, 19, 62-63
—history, 3, 9-11, 165-66
—involuntarily administered antipsychotic medications, 59, 183-84, 185
—medications refusal, 84-85, 95-99, 104-5
—right to refuse. *See* right to refuse
—of schizophrenia, 9-17, 33-35, 42, 43, 60, 125-26, 183, 184-85
—side effects, 11-13, 33-35, 42, 89, 145, 181, 185-86

Redlich, Fritz, 203
right of privacy, 22, 31, 36, 52, 69, 88-89, 131
right to refuse treatment
—based on First Amendment, 22, 69-70, 187
—economic implications, 44-45, 91, 101, 144, 151, 152-53
—effects upon institution, 64, 65-66, 75, 76, 81-87, 90-91, 98-99, 152-53, 188-90, 197
—emergency exception, 23-24, 25, 53-54, 56, 156
—for competent patients, 20-22, 103, 130-31, 143
—for incompetent patients, 26-27, 31, 45, 88, 89-92, 101, 132, 155, 201
—generally, 49, 51-52, 56-57, 61, 74, 88-94, 100-5, 130-34, 164-65, 167-68, 180-81, 188-90, 191
—judicial perspective on, 32-41, 135-41
—psychiatric perspective on, 21, 38, 57, 67, 81-87, 95-97, 102-5, 110, 151-52, 158, 180-81
—role of federal government, 169-76
right to treatment, 19-20, 51, 121, 164
Rogers, Paul, 135
Roth, Loren, 92

schizophrenia
—causes, 5-7
—concept of, 4, 15-16
—effects of drug therapy on, 11-17, 43, 84-85
—patients view of, 42, 164-65
—treatment of, 139
seclusion, 85-86, 102
substituted judgment, 140

tardive dyskinesia, 13, 34, 35, 92, 125, 184, 185-87
Tauro, Justice Joseph, 23, 24, 26, 27, 82, 100, 102, 133, 149, 188
therapeutic alliance, 20, 57, 58-59, 63, 81, 97-98

Weinstein, H. C., 189, 190

Zoll, Samuel, 137

About the Editors

A. EDWARD DOUDERA is Executive Director of the American Society of Law & Medicine, Executive Editor of the *American Journal of Law & Medicine*, and Managing Editor of *Law, Medicine and Health Care*. He received his J.D. from Suffolk University Law School in 1978 and is a member of the Massachusetts bar. Before joining the American Society of Law & Medicine in 1977, Mr. Doudera was associate administrator for research at Tufts-New England Medical Center in Boston.

JUDITH P. SWAZEY is Executive Director of Medicine in the Public Interest, Inc., and Adjunct Professor of Socio-Medical Sciences at Boston University Schools of Medicine and Public Health. She received her Ph.D. in History of Science from Harvard University in 1966. Professor Swazey is a member of the National Academy of Sciences' Institute of Medicine, and a fellow of the Institute of Society, Ethics and the Life Sciences. Her publications include *Chlorpromazine in Psychiatry: A Study of Therapeutic Innovation, The Courage to Fail: A Social View of Organ Transplants and Dialysis*, and *In Sickness and in Health: Social Aspects of Medical Care*.